Paddling·Georgia

Help Us Keep This Guide Up to Date

Every effort has been made by the author and editors to make this guide as accurate and useful as possible. However, many things can change after a guide is published—trails are rerouted, regulations change, techniques evolve, facilities come under new management, etc.

We welcome your comments concerning your experiences with this guide and how you feel it could be improved and kept up to date. While we may not be able to respond to all comments and suggestions, we'll take them to heart, and we'll also make certain to share them with the author. Please send your comments and suggestions to the following address:

FalconGuides
Reader Response/Editorial Department
P.O. Box 480
Guilford, CT 06437

Or you may e-mail us at:

editorial@GlobePequot.com

Thanks for your input, and happy trails!

Paddling Georgia

A Guide to the State's Best Paddling Routes

Johnny Molloy

FALCONGUIDES ®

GUILFORD, CONNECTICUT
HELENA, MONTANA
AN IMPRINT OF THE GLOBE PEQUOT PRESS

FALCONGUIDES®

Copyright © 2009 by Morris Book Publishing, LLC

Project manager: David Legere
Interior designer: Nancy Freeborn
Layout: Joanna Beyer
Maps: Bruce Grubbs © Morris Book Publishing, LLC
Photo credits: All photos by Johnny Molloy unless indicated
otherwise

Library of Congress Cataloging-in-Publication Data

Molloy, Johnny, 1961-
  Paddling Georgia : a guide to the state's best paddling routes /
Johnny Molloy.
    p. cm.
  ISBN 978-0-7627-4638-5
  1. Canoes and canoeing—Georgia—Guidebooks. 2. Kayak
touring—Georgia—Guidebooks. 3. Georgia—Guidebooks. I. Title.
  GV776.G4M65 2009
  797.12209758—dc22

                                    2008036953

Printed in the United States of America

10 9 8 7 6 5 4 3 2

This book is for Jessica Taylor, a Georgian who loves her water.

Contents

◄ *Southwest Georgia streams are both brooding and alluring.*

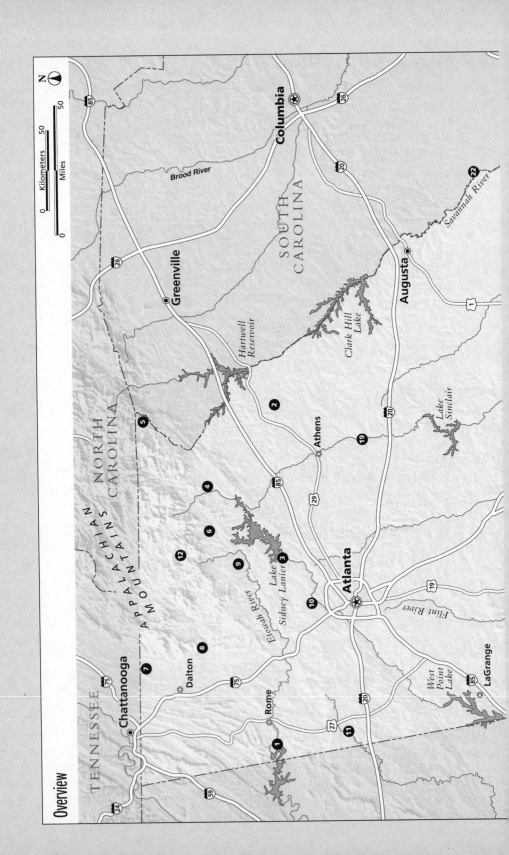

Overview

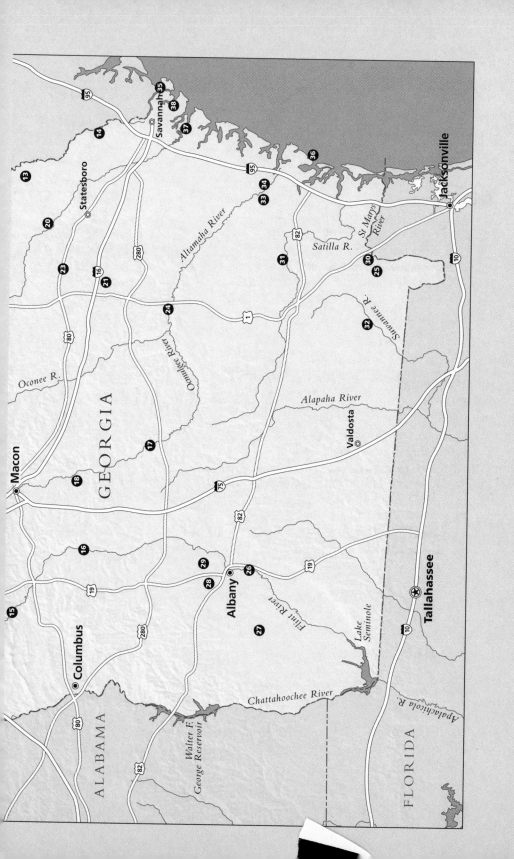

South Georgia

Coastal Georgia

Map Legend

Transportation

≡⟨80⟩≡ Freeway/Interstate Highway

≡⟨101⟩≡ U.S. Highway

≡⟨1⟩≡ State Highway

≡≡≡≡≡ Other Road

▪▪▪▪▪▪ Railroad

Trails

- - - - - Paddling Trail

⟶ Direction of Travel

Water Features

Body of Water

Major River

Minor River or Creek

Intermittent River or Creek

Rapids

Waterfalls

Marsh

Spring

Land Management

National Forest, State Parks & Wilderness Areas & Refuges

Symbols

Beach

Boat launch

Bridge

■ Building/Point of Interest

▲ Campground

∩ Cave

† Church

Dam

Fishing dock

Lighthouse

Marina

1 Mileage marker

P Parking

Power line

Put-in/Takeout

Ranger Station

Scenic View

Visitor Center/Information

N True North (Magnetic North is approximately 15.5° East)

Acknowledgments

First and foremost, thanks to Jessica Taylor for her help with this book. She paddled, camped, helped with shuttles, and took lots of great pictures. Thanks, Jessica! I would like to thank Joe and Carol Bishop as well for all their help in the greater Albany area, and for paddling the creeks and rivers with me, too—y'all made it more fun. Thanks to Jay-Mac for his help on the Ohoopee River; to Murray Lamb for all the information about the Chestatee River; to Thomas McDaniel, master fishermen on the Ocmulgee River; and to Taton Taylor for a ride on the Ogeechee River.

I would also like to thank all the people on the Satilla River, including Judy Moore, David Chesser, and Don Douglas, for making it a Fourth of July to remember. Thanks to Mills, Cheryl, and Alex Fitzner on Brier Creek and for Mills's help on Cedar Creek as well, and thanks to Ken Wettstein for his help on the Tallapoosa.

Thanks to Robby at Southeast Adventures on St. Simons Island for sharing his paddling expertise. Also thanks to Nigel at Savannah Canoe & Kayak for his help with Savannah paddling destinations. Thanks to Al Redmond for his sharing of a lifetime of exploring southwest Georgia; to Jerry Brimberry for sharing his knowledge about the lower Flint River; and to Daniel Brown, manager at Fort McAllister State Park. Thanks to Jess Alexander and Rett Downs of Southwest Georgia, and to John Stone of Pitts for their help on multiple occasions. And thanks also to paddler Kim Purvis for his quick action with some tools to fix the latch on my vehicle.

Thanks to Wenonah for providing me with a great canoe to paddle on many rivers—the Spirit II. The 17-footer handled wonderfully, and its light weight made for easy loading and unloading.

Introduction

Enjoying the natural aquatic abundance of Georgia was an extension of my camping, hiking, and paddling obsession that began in the Smoky Mountains of Tennessee more than two decades ago. Later I moved to Atlanta, and adventuring in Georgia became much easier. I explored the mountains from top to bottom and also began canoeing down many of the state's rivers, from the Etowah to the Chattahoochee and waterways beyond, all flowing off the Blue Ridge and Piedmont. More trips led south to Cumberland Island National Seashore and the one and only Okefenokee Swamp. I have since made repeated trips to these South Georgia treasures, paddling along dark water trails of the swamp that contrast mightily with the open, sandy Atlantic shoreline of Cumberland Island.

Time passed, and I began writing outdoor guidebooks for a living, or maybe as a lifestyle—I still haven't decided. When the opportunity arose to write this guidebook, I jumped on it excitedly and began systematically exploring Georgia's waterways landscape for great paddling destinations, including some of the most appealing coastline in America.

I sought to include paddling destinations that would not only be rewarding but also would be exemplary paddles of the varied landscapes Georgia has to offer. In the northeast, the Chattooga River forms the crown jewel of Blue Ridge paddling destinations. But these mountains offer other paddling places, such as the crystalline Chestatee River. And what good is a Georgia paddling guidebook without including Georgia's contribution to great rivers of the world—the Chattahoochee? Big Cedar Creek, in the state's northwest ridge-and-valley country, offers a limestone-lined paddling experience. The Ocmulgee and Oconee Rivers flow through the heart of Georgia in the botanically rich Piedmont. The Flint River has a little bit of everything, flowing from the upper Piedmont to and through the Coastal Plain. Expect a lot from the mighty Altamaha River. This wild river will deliver. The Satilla River flows, brooding and black, toward the ocean. There simply is no other Okefenokee Swamp. You must come here and experience it for yourself—with the help of this guidebook of course. Coastal paddles will lead you to lighthouses, barrier islands, and beaches and, just a little inland, past huge old-growth trees. When you cobble the paddling destinations together, they present a mosaic of Peach State beauty and biodiversity that's hard to beat!

As you may guess, the hardest part of writing this book may have been picking out the paddling destinations! With each of these waterways, I sought out a combination of scenery, paddling experiences, ease of access—including shuttling when necessary—and a reasonable length for day-tripping. Now it is your turn—get out there and paddle Georgia!

Georgia Weather

Each of the four distinct seasons lays its hands on North Georgia and its mountains. Elevation factors into weather patterns. Summer can get hot but is generally coolest up here. The north also receives the most precipitation, although it arrives with slow-moving frontal systems in winter, including snow, and with thunderstorms in summer. Fall offers warm days followed by cool, crisp evenings. Spring varies with elevation, too, and climbs its way up the mountains. Mountain paddlers must be prepared for cool to cold conditions on the water in winter and early spring, the time when the highland waters will be running at their fullest—and their coldest. However, most streams included in this guidebook can be paddled well into summer, most year-round.

Middle Georgia offers warm to hot summers and mostly moderate winters. Early spring is the most variable, with periodic warm-ups broken by cold fronts bringing rain then chilly temperatures. Later, temperatures stay warm, becoming hot by July. Typically mornings start clear, then clouds build and hit-or-miss thunderstorms occur by afternoon. The first cool fronts hit around mid-September. Fall sees warm, clear days and cool nights with the least amount of rain. Precipitation picks up in November, and temperatures generally stay cool to cold, broken by occasional mild spells. Most Middle Georgia streams can be paddled year-round, although, as with the mountains, they'll be running their boldest during winter and early spring. Summertime paddlers should consider beginning their trips in the morning to avoid the heat of the day and afternoon thunderstorms.

South Georgia offers the warmest climate, yet it has four distinct seasons. During the long summer, highs regularly reach the 90s, and a thunderstorm will come most any afternoon. Warm nights stay up in the 70s. Fall brings cooler nights and warm days with less precipitation than summer. Winter is variable. Highs push 60 degrees. Expect lows in the 40s, though subfreezing temperatures are the norm during cold snaps. There are usually several mild days during each winter month. Precipitation comes in strong continental fronts, with persistent rains followed by sunny, cold days. Snow is uncommon, though not unheard of. The longer days of spring begin the warm-up process, becoming even hot, but temperatures can vary wildly. South Georgia has the longest paddling season—year-round—but you must also be prepared for the variety of conditions on the water here. Mild winter days can offer some of the best paddling in this region, as the insects will be few and the sun will be at its weakest. But this can also be the windiest time, especially along the coast.

◀ *Sugar white sandbars can rise steeply from the Saint Marys.*

Flora and Fauna

The landscape of Georgia offers everything from mountain bears furtively roaming beneath trees more common in Pennsylvania than down South to dense swamp forests bordering remote waterways to sea oats swaying by the seashore. A wide variety of wildlife calls these dissimilar landscapes home.

Speaking of black bears, they can be found in most areas of the state. Though most commonly thought of as being in the mountain regions, they also thrive along the Ocmulgee River Valley in Middle Georgia and in the impenetrable regions of the Okefenokee Swamp, numbering over 2,200 in the state. Consider yourself lucky if you do see a bruin on the shoreline. Your only potential troubles may be while camped on a river, but even then bears want your food not your flank.

The alligator is another critter far up the food chain of interest to paddlers. More than 20,000 gators called Georgia home. They occur in the southern part of the state below Macon. Alligators are found not only along rivers but also in marshes, swamps, and the lakes. As their numbers continue to rise and Georgia becomes more populated, especially its coastal region, they are increasingly found in man-made watery areas such as ditches, canals, and even swimming pools! Many paddles in this book will take you places where these reptiles reside, but they are normally shy creatures. They will often be sunning on the shoreline and then slink under the water upon your passage.

Deer are the land animal you most likely will see as you paddle Georgia's waterways. They can be found throughout the state and number more than a million. A quiet paddler may also witness turkeys, raccoons, or even a coyote. Don't be surprised if you observe beavers, muskrats, or a playful otter in the water.

Overhead, many raptors will be plying the waterways for food, including eagles, falcons, and owls. Of special interest is the osprey. Watch for this bird flying overhead with a freshly caught fish in its talons! Depending on where you are, other birds you may spot range from kingfishers, woodpeckers, and herons to seagulls, pelicans, and more species along the coast. Under the water Georgia has ninety-eight species of mussels, fourth most among the states, and more than forty rare and endangered species of fish, from sturgeons to darters to sunfish.

Georgia's flora offers just as much variety. Along the riverways of the north, towering white pines and imperiled hemlocks reign over rhododendron and mountain laurel that bloom in late spring and early summer. Other shorelines will harbor river birch, sycamore, and willow. Massive cypress trees are a common sight along slower, warmer waterways in Middle and South Georgia. The unique Ogeechee lime occupies riverbanks of the state's south. Wildflowers will grace shorelines throughout the state well into fall. The coastal regions have spartina grass and an estuarine ecosystem as unique as the blends of salt and fresh water that come and go with the tides.

Georgia's River Regions

Georgia is drained by five primary river systems—the Coosa, Chattahoochee, Savannah, Altamaha, and Flint Rivers. Starting in the northwest, the Coosa drains the ridge-and-valley country bordering Tennessee and Alabama but also includes much of Georgia's mountain region. Paddling destinations in this guidebook include Big Cedar Creek and the Etowah, Coosawattee, and Conasauga Rivers, among others. More than eighty-seven species of fish ply the Coosa River drainage. The Chattahoochee starts in the Blue Ridge Mountains in northeast Georgia, yet flows southwest ultimately to turn southward, transforming from mountain river to Piedmont river and finally to Coastal Plain waterway. Along the way, Atlanta residents consume over 300,000,000 gallons of Chattahoochee River water per day! All the above rivers are separated from the rest of Georgia's waterways by a long southwest-to-northeast-running ridge upon which Atlanta sits.

The Savannah River captures the eastern edge of the state from its northernmost boundary with North Carolina all the way to the ocean. The streams of this waterway, from the Chattooga to Ebenezer Creek, also reflect the changes in topography that follow the elevational transition from mountain to sea. The town of Savannah was Georgia's first settlement, and thus the state's early history spread from this watershed.

The Altamaha River is Georgia's largest Atlantic watershed. Starting south and east of Atlanta, the Ocmulgee and Oconee Rivers drain the heart of the Peach State and come together in South Georgia to form the Altamaha River. The lower part of this waterway has all sorts of unique plant life, including giant old-growth hardwood forests and sandhill communities. Closer to the coast it is one of the most important tidal regions.

The Flint River starts southwest of Atlanta and flows mostly southerly through the Pine Mountains, then changes from Piedmont to coastal stream before meeting the Chattahoochee in Georgia's most southwesterly corner. Interestingly, the Flint has the densest concentration of amphibians and reptiles on any waterway in the continent north of Mexico. Smaller drainages in the state include Georgia's extreme northwest corner flowing into the Tennessee River. This includes the Toccoa River, which is detailed in this guidebook.

Your Rights on the River

Georgia laws generally do not favor paddlers. Under an 1863 code, a navigable stream is defined as "a stream which is capable of transporting boats loaded with freight in the regular course of trade either for the whole or a part of the year. The mere rafting of timber or the transporting of woods in small boats shall not make a stream navigable." Examples of two navigable rivers are the lower Chattahoochee and the lower Altamaha.

The rights of the owner of lands adjacent to navigable streams extend to the low-water mark in the bed of the stream. If a stream is deemed nonnavigable, then the owner of the land through which the stream flows has "the same exclusive possession of the stream as he has any other part of his land. The legislature has no power to compel or interfere with the owner's lawful use of the stream, for the benefit of those above him or below him on the stream, except to restrain nuisances."

If the landowner owns only one side of the nonnavigable stream, then he owns it to the midpoint of the stream. He could join forces with the owner across the stream, and together they could block passage of the entire stream.

So when a stream has been determined to be nonnavigable, even if it actually can be paddled in a canoe or kayak, the landowner or landowners can simply block passage. This has happened on portions of Brier, Armuchee, and Ichawaynochaway Creeks, among others.

In reality, what does this mean for the Georgia paddler? The vast majority of landowners do not mind passage through waters along their property. However, if you are stopped or asked to get off a river, then I suggest you adhere to the land-owner's request—and live to paddle another day. All the paddling destinations in this guidebook are open to passage as of this writing, including paddles on Brier and Ichawaynochaway Creeks.

How to Use This Guide

This guidebook offers trips covering every corner of Georgia. The paddles are divided into the three primary regions of the state—North Georgia, Middle Georgia, South Georgia—plus Coastal Georgia. Each paddle included in the book is chosen as a day trip, although overnight camping can be done where noted. The following is a sample of what you will find in the information box at the beginning of each paddling destination:

Ohoopee River

County: Toombs, Tattnall
Start: Highway 152 bridge N32° 17' 4.6", W82° 13' 45.8"
End: Jarrells Bridge Road N32° 13' 6.5", W82° 12' 23.0"
Length: 7.4 miles
Float time: 3.5 hours
Difficulty rating: Easy to moderate
Rapids: Class I
River type: Coastal Plain swiftwater creek
Current: Moderate to swift
River gradient: 2.8 feet per mile
River gauge: Ohoopee River near Reidsville; 120 cfs minimum runnable level

Season: Year-round
Land status: Private
Fees or permits: No fees or permits required
Nearest city/town: Cobbtown, Georgia
Maps: USGS: Cobbtown, Ohoopee; DeLorme: *Georgia Atlas and Gazetteer,* page 45
Boats used: Canoes, kayaks, occasional johnboat
Organizations: Altamaha Riverkeeper, Inc., P.O. Box 2642, Darien, GA 31305; (912) 437-8164; www.altamahariverkeeper.org
Contacts/outfitters: Georgia Department of Natural Resources, 2 Martin Luther King Jr. Drive SE, Suite 1252 East Tower, Atlanta, GA 30334; (404) 656-3500; www.gadnr.org

County: From the information box we can see that the paddle is in Toombs and Tattnall Counties. The **start** of the paddle is at the Highway 152 bridge. The GPS coordinates for the put-in are given using NAD 27 data, which you can plug into your GPS for direction finding. The paddle's **end** is at Jarrells Bridge Road. The trip is 7.4 miles in **length,** a distance I acquired from using a GPS during my research.

Float time: The paddle should last around 3.5 hours, but this is just an average. The time you will spend on the water depends on whether you fish, picnic, swim, paddle, or simply relax. Use the float time as a gauge to help you determine how long you need/want to spend on your particular trip.

Difficulty rating: This paddle is rated as easy to moderate. Here the difficulty arises from the swift waters passing around logs that you will have to avoid. The river has no **rapids** per se, but the swift water rates as Class I. This river difficulty rating system goes from Class I to Class VI. Class I has easy waves requiring little maneuvering and few obstructions. Class II rapids may have more obstructions and require more maneuvering, and the rapids may be flowing faster. Most paddles in this guidebook are Class I to Class II. Class III rapids can be difficult, with numerous waves and no clear defined passage, and require precise maneuvering. Classes IV to VI increase in difficulty, with Class VI being unrunnable, except by the best experts.

River type reflects the river's geographic placement within the state and what type of river it is. This paddle flows through the Coastal Plain in fast fashion. The **current** is moderate to swift, depending on the width of the water where you are paddling. The **river gradient** reflects the rate at which the river falls during the paddle.

The **river gauge** listed will be near the destination and will help you determine the paddleability of the river. Some rivers, such as this one, have minimum flow rates listed so that you know there will be sufficient water in the river when you get there. Waterways that don't have a minimum runnable level can be paddled year-round. Concerning water gauges, the key variable is the height of the river at a fixed point. Gauge houses, situated on most rivers, consist of a well at the river's edge with a float attached to a recording clock. The gauge reads in hundredths of feet. Rating tables are constructed for each gauge to get a cubic fee per second (cfs) reading for each level. Other gauges are measured in height, given in feet. This gauge information can be obtained quickly, often along with recent rainfall! U.S. Geological Survey (USGS)— Real-time Water Levels for the United States can be found on the Web at http://waterdata.usgs.gov/nwis/rt. This in-depth Web site has hundreds of gauges for the entire country, updated continually, and graphs showing recent flow trends along with historic trends for any given day of the year, available at the touch of a mouse. Consult these gauges before you start your trip!

Season gives the recommended time of year to execute the trip. **Land status** indicates that the lands bordering this section of the Ohoopee are private. Many paddling destinations included in this guidebook border public lands. (See Your Rights on the River.) **Fees or permits** tells whether or not your trip will require anything other than simply showing up.

Nearest city/town: Cobbtown is the nearest municipality to this paddle. This listing will help you get oriented to the paddle destination area while looking at a map or looking up map information on the Internet.

Maps lists maps you can use for your paddle in addition to those provided in this guide. The first listing is the pertinent USGS 7.5-minute quadrangle. These very detailed "quad maps" cover every parcel of land in this country. Each quad name is usually based on a physical feature located within the quad. In this case the paddle traverses two quad maps, Cobbtown and Ohoopee. Quad maps can be obtained online at www.usgs.gov. Also listed is the page for this paddle in the *Georgia Atlas and Gazetteer,* published by DeLorme. The gazetteer is an invaluable aid in making your way through the Peach State.

Boats used simply tells you what other river users will be floating in.

Organizations lists groups that charge themselves with taking care of the particular waterway included in the paddle. If you are interested in learning more about the river's health and other water-quality issues, or you simply want to get involved in preserving Georgia's waterways, consult these groups. Their contact information is listed.

The **Contacts/outfitters** listing will tell you if an outfitter operates on the particular segment of river. This can help with shuttles. In this case the Georgia Department of Natural Resources is listed, which can also provide helpful information about the waterway.

Additional information follows the at-a-glance listings. Next comes **Put-in/takeout information.** This gives you directions from the nearest interstate or largest community—first to the takeout, where you can leave a shuttle vehicle, then from the takeout to the put-in. By the way, look before you leap! Many of the put-ins and takeouts use dirt or sand roads just before reaching the waterways. After periods of extreme weather, such as heavy rains or long dry periods, the roads can become troublesome. If you are at all unsure about the road ahead of you, stop, get out, and examine it on foot before you drive into a deep mudhole or get stuck in the sand.

A **Paddle summary** follows the driving directions. It provides a short overview of the paddle trip, giving you an idea of what to expect that will help you determine whether or not you want to experience this waterway. The **River overview** that follows gives an overview of the entire river, not just the section paddled. This way you can determine whether you want to paddle other sections of the river being detailed. It also gives you a better understanding of the entire watershed rather than just a section of river in space and time. Next comes **The Paddling,** the meat-and-potatoes narrative, giving you detailed information about your river trip, including flora, fauna, and interesting, not-to-be-missed natural features. It also details important information needed to execute the paddle, including forthcoming rapids, portages, bridges and stops along the way, and the mileages at which you will encounter them.

Finally, each paddle has a sidebar. This is simply interesting information about the waterway that doesn't necessarily pertain to the specific paddle but gives you some human or natural tidbit that may pique your interest to explore beyond the simple mechanics of the paddle. In this case, the sidebar is about the Ohoopee Dunes, a fascinating ecosystem within the greater Ohoopee Valley.

Fixing to Paddle

Which Boat Do I Use?

This book covers waterways from crashing mountain rivers to massive watercourses a mile across to still and silent blackwater streams to narrow creeks barely wide enough for a boat. Faced with such variety, what boat do you use? The answer—just like the diversity of paddling destinations in Georgia—is multiple choices. Canoes and kayaks offer different venues for plying the waters of Georgia.

Canoes

When looking for a canoe, consider the type of water through which you will be paddling. Will it be through still bodies of water or moving rivers? Will you be on big lakes and maybe the ocean, or mild whitewater or sluggish streams? Canoes come in a wide array of oil-based materials and are molded for weight, performance, and durability. Don't waste your time or money on an aluminum canoe. They are extremely noisy and are more likely to get hung up on underwater obstacles rather than slide over them. Consider material and design. Canoe materials can range from wood to fiberglass to composites such as Polylink 3, Royalex, Kevlar, and even graphite. I prefer more-durable canoes and thus seek out the tougher composites, such as Royalex.

Canoe design comprises the following factors: length, width, depth, keel and bottom curve, as well as flare and tumblehome. The length of a canoe should be at least 16 feet, for carrying loads and better tracking. Shorter canoes are available, and are often used in ponds, small lakes, and smaller streams for shorter trips.

Wider canoes are more stable and can carry more loads but are slower. Go for somewhere in the middle. Deeper canoes can carry more weight and shed water, but they can get heavy. Again, go for the middle ground.

A keel helps for tracking in lakes but decreases maneuverability in moving water.

The more curved the canoe bottom, the less stable the boat. Seek a shallowly arched boat, which is more efficient than a flat bottom boat but not as tippy as a deeply curved boat. Flare, the outward curve of the sides of the boat, sheds water from the craft. How much flare you want depends upon how much whitewater you expect to encounter.

Tumblehome is the inward slope of the upper body of the canoe. A more curved tumblehome allows paddlers to get their paddle into the water easier. Rocker, the curve of the keel line from bow to stern, is important. More rocker increases maneuverability at the expense of stability. Again, go for the middle ground.

And then there are situation-specific canoes, such as whitewater or portaging canoes. Whitewater boats will have heavy rocker and deeper flare, but they will be zigzagging tubs on flatwater. Portaging canoes are built with extremely light materials and will have a padded portage yoke for toting the boat on your shoulders.

I recommend multipurpose touring/tripping tandem canoes, those with adequate maneuverability, so that you will be able to adjust and react while shooting rapids. You want a boat that can navigate moderate whitewater, can handle loads, and can track decently through flatwater. If you are solo paddling a tandem canoe, weight the front with gear to make it run true. But if you have a solo boat, you can't change it to a two-person boat.

Consider the Old Town Penobscot 17-footer, long a favorite of mine. It is a great all-around boat that I have used on varied trips, from day paddles on rivers to multinight adventures, over years and years. Ultra-lightweight canoes, such as those built by Wenonah, are designed to be carried from lake to lake via portages, but they have their place throughout Georgia's waterways. I highly recommend the Wenonah Spirit II 17-footer. At forty-two pounds, this ultralight Kevlar boat can perform well in the water and not break your back between your vehicle and the water. I used it often while writing this book. Other times you may be going down rivers with significant stretches of whitewater, where you will want a boat that can take bone-jarring hits from rocks in North Georgia. Finally, choose muted colors that blend with the land and water.

Kayaks

The first consideration in choosing a kayak is deciding between a sit-on-top model and a sit-in model, also known as a touring kayak. Sit-on-tops are what their name implies—paddlers sit on top of the boat—whereas a touring kayak requires you to put your body into the boat, leaving your upper half above an enclosed cockpit.

In making your decision, ask yourself: What type of waters are you going to paddle? Are you going to paddle near shore—on calm, flat waters—or are you going to paddle bigger waters, such as the islands off the Georgia coast? If paddling bigger water, you will need a cockpit. Sit-on-top kayaks are generally more comfortable and allow for more freedom of movement. They also take on water more readily and are used almost exclusively in warmer water destinations. Sit-in touring kayaks are inherently more stable, since the user sits on the bottom of the boat rather than on top of it. Sit-on-top kayaks make up for this stability shortcoming by being wider, which makes them slower.

Base your decision primarily on what types of waters you will be paddling and whether you will be going overnight in your kayak. Sit-on-top kayaks are a poor choice when it comes to overnight camping. However, sit-on-tops do have their place. Smaller waters such as tidal creeks and gentle, smaller streams are good for sit-on-top kayaks.

Sit-in kayaks are the traditional kayaks, based on models used by Arctic aboriginals. Some factors to consider when choosing a sit-in touring kayak are length, volume, and steering. These longer touring kayaks are built to cover water and track better. Look for a boat anywhere from 14 to 18 feet in length if overnighting. Sit-on-top kayaks will range generally from 8 to 15 feet. Narrow touring kayaks have less "initial stability." They feel tippier when you get into them, although their very narrowness prevents waves from flipping the boat as waves can tip wider sit-on-top kayaks, which have better initial stability.

Kayak materials vary from the traditional skin-and-wood of the Inuits to plastic and fiberglass composites like Kevlar and the waterproof cover of folding kayaks. (Folding kayaks have an assembled frame and skin method of becoming a kayak.) For touring kayaks I recommend a tough composite model, simply because they can withstand running up on sandbars, scratching over oyster bars, or being accidentally dropped at the boat launch. I look for durability in a boat and don't want something that needs babying.

For touring boats, consider storage capacity. Gear is usually stored in waterproof compartments with hatches. Look for watertight patches that close safely and securely. The larger the boat, the more room you will have. This is a matter of personal preference. Today there are not only single kayaks but also double and even triple kayaks. Most touring kayaks come with a foot pedal–based steering system using a rudder.

Overall, kayakers need to be fussier when choosing their boats than do canoeists, as kayaks are more situation specific. Surf the Internet and read reviews thoroughly to get an idea of what you want, then go to a store that sells kayaks and try them out. Look for "demo days" at these outdoors stores. Borrow a friend's kayak. A well-informed, careful choice will result in many positive kayaking experiences.

What about a whitewater kayaks? These are used for many of Georgia's whitewater streams. Most of these waterways are not included in this guidebook, which is designed for a larger audience of recreational paddlers.

Which Paddle Do I Use?

Wood is still holding on strong as a material for paddlers, although plastics dominate the market, especially lower end paddles, such as those used by outfitters, and ultralight high-end paddles. Some cheap varieties combine a plastic blade with an aluminum handle. Bent-shaft paddles are popular as well, although I don't recommend them myself. They are efficient as far as trying to get from point A to point B; but while floating you are often drifting and turning, making constant small adjustments, turning the boat around, and doing all sorts of maneuvers other than simply paddling in a straight line. Bent-shaft paddles are poor when it comes to precision steering moves.

How about a square versus a rounded blade? I prefer a rounded blade for precision strokes, whereas a power paddler—maybe the bow paddler—will desire a square blade. Paddles can vary in length as well, generally from 48 to 60 inches. I recommend a shorter paddle for the stern paddler, because that is the person who makes the small adjustments in boat direction. A shorter paddle is easier to maneuver when making all these small adjustments, not only in the water but also when shifting the paddle from one side of the boat to the other.

Kayak paddles are double bladed—they have a blade on both sides, resulting in more efficient stroking. Kayakers seem more willing to part with a lot of money to use an ultralight paddle. Almost all kayak paddles are two-piece, snapping in the middle. This makes them easier to haul around, but more importantly it allows paddlers to offset the blades for more efficient stroking. Four-piece blades are not unusual, though. Kayak blades are generally 6 inches by 18 inches, with paddles averaging between 7 and 8 feet in length. Weight wise, expensive paddles can go as low as twenty-four ounces or less, while average paddles are thirty to forty ounces. Like anything, you get what you pay for. A paddle leash is a wise investment to prevent losing your paddle.

Whether in a canoe or a sea kayak an extra paddle is a smart idea. It's easy to stow an extra paddle in a canoe, but a kayak can be more troublesome. A four-piece paddle is easier for a kayaker to stow.

Paddling Accessories

Personal Flotation Device

I admit to never wearing my life vest unless I feel threatened by the waters in which I ply. But I do always have a life vest with me. In the bad old days, I would use anything that would meet Coast Guard standards just to get by. But now I carry a quality life vest, not only for safety but also for comfort. The better kinds, especially those designed for sea kayaking, allow for freedom of arm movement. Speaking of sea kayaking, that is when I most often wear my life vest.

Chair Backs

These hook on to the canoe seat to provide support for your back. I recommend the plastic models that cover most of your back, especially giving lower-lumbar support. The more elaborate metal-and-canvas chair backs get in the way of paddling. However, having no chair back on multiday trips can lead to "Canoer's Back"!

Dry Bags

Waterproof dry bags are one of those inventions that give modern paddlers an advantage of leaps and bounds over those of yesteryear. Dry bags, primarily made of rubber and/or plastic, have various means of closing that result in a watertight seal, keeping your gear dry as you travel any waterway, whether oceanic or riverine. Today's choices of dry bags range from tiny, personal-size clear bags in which you might throw such things as sunscreen, keys, bug dope, and a hat to massive rubber "black holes" with built-in shoulder straps and waist belts designed not only to keep your stuff dry but to be carried on portages. Dry bags come not only in various sizes but also differing shapes, designed to fit in the tiny corners of a kayak or an open canoe. They can be long and thin to hold a tent or wide, which will fit most anything. Kayakers should consider deck bags, which are attached to the top of the kayak just in front of the paddler. Store your day-use items in there.

Plastic Boxes

Plastic storage boxes, available at any mega-retailer, come in a variety of sizes and shapes. They are cheap, easily sit in the bottom of the canoe, and can double as a table. Store items in here such as bread that you don't want smashed. Plastic boxes are not nearly as waterproof as a rubber dry bag, so consider using these if you are on flatwater.

Paddlers Checklist

- ❏ Canoe or kayak
- ❏ Paddles
- ❏ Spare paddle
- ❏ Personal floatation device
- ❏ Dry bags for gear storage
- ❏ Whistle
- ❏ Towline

- ❏ Bilge pump for kayak
- ❏ Spray skirt for kayak
- ❏ Paddle float/lanyard for kayak
- ❏ Maps, charts, and tide tables
- ❏ Throw lines
- ❏ Boat sponge

You may want to consider other items depending on your personal interests as a paddler, including fishing gear, sunglasses, trash bag, GPS, weather radio, camera, watch, sunscreen, lip balm, extra batteries, binoculars, and wildlife identification books.

Traveling with Your Boat

Boats, whether canoes or kayaks, need to be carried atop your vehicle en route to the water. How you load your boat depends not only on whether it is a canoe or kayak but also on the type of vehicle and whether you have an aftermarket roof rack. No matter how you carry your boat, be sure to tie it down securely, for the sake of not only your boat but also your fellow drivers, who will be endangered if your boat comes loose. I have seen a canoe fly off the car in front of me, and I have seen what a boat will do to a car after sliding off the side of said car while still tied on! After cinching your boat down, drive a short distance and then pull over and recheck your tie job. I recommend using the flat straps with buckles, which are sold at any outdoor retailer and also big-box stores.

A quality aftermarket roof rack installed atop your vehicle makes for a much safer way to transport boats. Invest in one of these if you paddle frequently. Roof racks can be customized to different types and numbers of boats as well. And don't skimp on tie-down straps either; they're what hold the boat to the rack.

Parking

In writing this book and other Georgia guidebooks, among more than thirty outdoor guidebooks, I have parked all over the country, often for days and weeks at a time. Use your intuition when leaving your vehicle anywhere. It is always best to arrange with someone to look after your car, and a small fee is worth the peace of mind.

National, state, and county parks with on-site rangers are a good choice for leaving your vehicle overnight. Also check with fish camps and liveries—many of these provide shuttle service and a safe place to park. Private businesses sometimes allow overnighters to park in their lots. Be sure to ask permission and offer to pay. When parking for day trips, it is better to leave your vehicle near the road rather than back in the woods out of sight.

Shuttles

River trips require a shuttle. Setting up these shuttles is a pain, but the payoff is getting to continually explore new waters in an ever-changing outdoor panorama. The closer you are to home, the more likely you are to be self-shuttling. Always remember to go to the takeout point first, leaving a car there, with the put-in point car following. Leave no valuables in your car. Take your keys with you, and store them securely while you are floating!

Outfitters can save you the hassle of shuttling and allow you to leave your car in a safe, secure setting. Of course you will pay for this service. This especially helps on river trips that are far away from home. Don't be afraid to ask about prices, distances, and reservations. Also ask about camping and potential crowds, especially during weekends. If outfitters are available, they are listed with each paddle.

Camping

Overnight camping can add to the paddling experience. Where camping is a possibility, I have noted it in the paddling narratives. Other places may have strict private property situations or other elements that prohibit camping. However, you may want to consider camping either before or after your paddle. Check out the plethora of Georgia state parks, and national forests and other public lands.

Paddler Safety

A safe paddler is a smart paddler. Be prepared before you get on the water and you will minimize the possibility of accidents on the water. And if they do happen, you will be better prepared to deal with them.

Lightning

Lightning can strike a paddler. Play it smart. When you sense a storm coming, have a plan as to what you will do when it hits. Most plans will involve getting the hell off the water. Seek shelter in a low area or in a grove of trees, not against a single tree, and then wait it out.

Poisonous Plants

Yep, poisonous plants are growing out there. You know the adages: Leaves of three let it be, etc. If you are highly allergic to poisonous plants, check ahead for their presence in the area in which you will be paddling, then take the appropriate action, such as having Benadryl-based creams.

Bugs

Sometimes when paddling, we consider the possibility of death by blood loss from mosquitoes, but actually your chances of dying from a bug bite in the wilds are less than your chances of dying on the car ride to the river. Watch out for black widow spiders and deer ticks, which can carry Lyme disease. A real danger is from bee stings to those who are allergic to them.

Snakes

Paddlers will see snakes in freshwater areas, especially rivers. Some snakes prefer being near the water, and you may have to watch out for them, especially on sunny stream-side rocks. This is a preferred area for copperheads. I have seen other snakes swimming while I floated by in a boat. Give them a wide berth and they'll do the same for you.

Sun

When paddling, the sun can be your enemy and your friend. You welcome its light and warmth. Then it tries to burn your skin, penetrate your eyes, and kick up gusty winds. Finally you lament its departure every night as darkness falls.

Sun can be a real threat no matter where you are. While boating, you will be on the water and thus open to the prowess of old Sol. Be prepared for sun. Use sunscreen, and wear a hat, a bandanna, and long pants and long-sleeve shirt. Clothes are your best defense. Put on the sunscreen before you get in the sun. Consider covering your hands. I have personally seen several cases of sun poisoning on paddlers' hands.

Heat

Heat is normally associated with the sun. Heat problems are likely to occur while paddling on really hot days. While paddling in the heat of summer, take shade breaks and swim to cool off.

Cold

In our eagerness to hit the river, especially after a string of nice March days, we take off for the nearest stream, disregarding the fact that twenty-one days of March are classified as winter, and the waterways can be really cold then. The possibility of hypothermia is very real if you take a tumble into the water. Try to stay dry if at all possible—it is easier to stay dry and warm, or even dry and not so warm, than to get wet and cold and then warm up.

Medical Kit

Medical kits have come a long way. Now you can find activity-specific medical kits that also come in different sizes for each activity, including paddling. Medical kits designed for water sports come in waterproof pouches. I recommend Adventure Medical Kits. They not only have a good variety of kits but also divide their kits into group size units as well. Whether you are a solo paddler or on a multiple-boat multiple-day river trip, you will have not only the right kit but also the right size one.

A Final Note

Paddling Georgia is about having a good time, whether you are sea kayaking on the coast, winding along a remote Piedmont stream, or stroking a translucent mountain waterway. Now get out there and make some memories!

North Georgia

1 | Big Cedar Creek

This is a classic creek float down an attractive valley waterway.

County: Floyd
Start: Big Cedar Creek Campground N34° 8' 3.5", W85° 18' 29.2"
End: Highway 100 bridge N34° 9' 56.4", W85° 20' 36.1"
Length: 5.1 miles
Float time: 3 hours
Difficulty rating: Easy to moderate
Rapids: Class I–I+
River type: Rock-bottomed valley river
Current: Moderate
River gradient: 8.0 feet per mile
River gauge: Big Cedar Creek near Cedartown; minimum runnable level 80 cfs

Season: March to November
Land status: Private
Fees or permits: Parking fees at the put-in
Nearest city/town: Cedartown, Georgia
Maps: USGS: Livingston; DeLorme *Georgia Atlas and Gazetteer,* page 18
Boats used: Canoes, kayaks, johnboats, tubes
Organizations: Georgia River Network, 126 South Milledge Avenue, Suite E3, Athens, GA 30605; (706) 549-4508; www.garivers.org
Contacts/outfitters: Big Cedar Creek Park, 6770 Cave Spring Road SW; Cave Spring, GA 30124; (706) 777-3030; www.bigcedarcreek .com

Put-in/takeout information:

Takeout: From Rome take U.S. Highway 27 south for 9 miles, then bear right onto U.S. Highway 411 south/Highway 53. Go for 7.3 miles, crossing a bridge over Big Cedar Creek and passing the put-in at Cedar Creek Park. Continue beyond Cedar Creek Park on US 411 south for 1.1 miles, then turn right onto Spout Springs Road. Follow Spout Springs Road for 3.7 miles to dead-end at Blacks Bluff Road. (Along the way the road crosses Big Cedar Creek, but do not stop here.) Turn left onto Blacks Bluff Road and follow it just a short distance to Highway 100. Turn left onto Highway 100 and follow it just a short distance to the takeout on the right before the bridge over Big Cedar Creek.

To put-in from takeout: Backtrack on Highway 100, then turn right onto Blacks Bluff Road. Follow Blacks Bluff Road for 0.1 mile, then turn right onto Spout Springs Road. Follow Spout Springs Road for 3.7 miles to reach US 411. Turn left and take US 411 north for 1.1 miles; turn left into Cedar Creek Park. There is a launching fee. Big Cedar Creek Park also offers canoe rentals and shuttles.

Paddle Summary

Big Cedar Creek flows placidly through wooded hills and open valley country in the rural Coosa River watershed of northwest Georgia. The many cedar trees of this area thrive because of the limestone base of the valley here. Not only do these limestone rocks promote the growth of cedar trees, they also form the rocky bed of this stream. And this rocky bed partly accounts for the clarity of this attractive watercourse. Leave

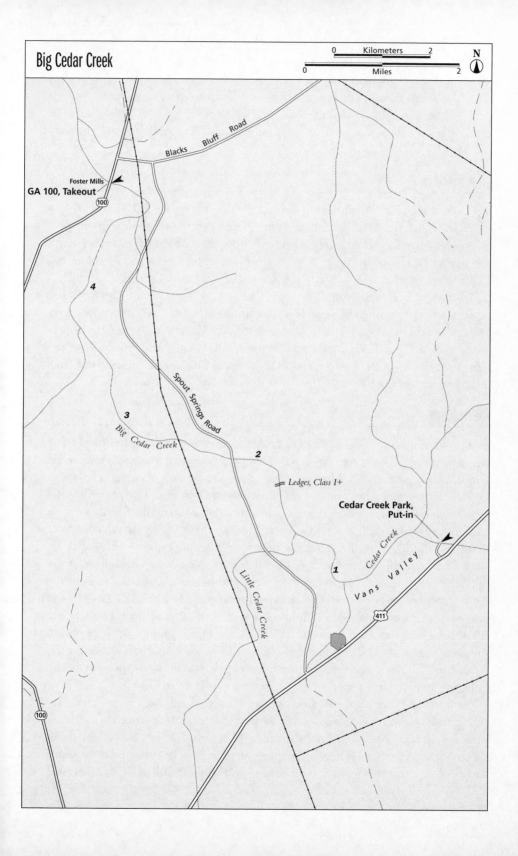

Big Cedar Creek

Blacks Bluff Road

Foster Mills
GA 100, Takeout
100

4

Spout Springs Road

3

Big Cedar Creek

2

Ledges, Class I+

**Cedar Creek Park,
Put-in**

Cedar Creek

1

Vans Valley

411

Little Cedar Creek

100

0 ___ Kilometers ___ 2
0 ___ Miles ___ 2

N

Big Cedar Creek Park, and flow northwest. The river falls in easy shoals before culminating in a set of Class I+ rapids where the stream is pinched in by hills on both sides. The creek then opens into a larger, more-level valley and becomes a more-relaxed float. Then, just toward the end, the stream breaks apart into many channels coursing amid islands and becomes swift once again before ending at the Highway 100 bridge.

River Overview

Big Cedar Creek is a partially spring-fed watercourse that is part of the greater Coosa River watershed. It starts in southern Polk County, flowing off the north slopes of Hightower Mountain, then into Cedartown. It becomes paddleable at higher water just north of Cedartown. Lake Creek, a major feeder branch, comes in before Big Cedar Creek reaches US 411 and Vanns Valley, where this paddle begins.

Little Big Cedar Creek joins Big Cedar Creek at the lower end of Vans Valley. Big Cedar Creek cuts through hills before passing through the small community of Foster Mills, where this paddle exits, then continues to reach Weiss Lake. Weiss Lake Dam is in Alabama, but it backs up the Coosa River well into Georgia and thus backs up the lowermost section of Big Cedar Creek, which offers a little over 20 miles of paddling, including parts of the lake.

The Paddling

The put-in is just north of the US 411 bridge, next to an island that ends just a few feet downstream. The creek varies in width here, averaging about 40 feet in the slower sections and usually narrower where there are rapids and curves. The waters are clear with a rocky bottom and are heavily forested on both sides. Stay near the Cedar Creek Park campground on river-left for a distance. The first shoals are soon encountered—rock gardens with fairly straightforward chutes. Be careful around the shoals and if walking in the creek; the limestone rocks are quite sharp. Houses are scattered around this upper stretch of creek but don't provide any imposition, as the banks are wooded. At 0.9 mile the creek splits around an island and curves to the right, now heading northwest. The creek had been roughly paralleling US 411 and now begins to turn away from it. Ironwood, sycamore, ash, and nonnative Chinese tallow hang over the water. Pine and cedar hold the higher ground along with oaks. An old iron railroad bridge is just ahead. Come to a nice ledge drop just below the railroad bridge. The creek splits around more islands, where shoals rush past before gathering again in slack water.

At 1.4 miles Little Big Cedar Creek comes in on your left. Big Cedar Creek widens, and a long pool stretches out until you reach the next shoal, which is a series of ledge rapids. A hillside constricts the stream, which forces the fall. Not all the shoals are limestone ledges. Often Big Cedar Creek drops in gravelly riffles. Float through a long pool, reaching the Spout Springs Bridge at 2.2 miles. Small gravel bars, revealed

Shoal below abandoned bridge

at low water, can be found along the creek and will be covered with grass later in summer.

Pass under a power line at 2.5 miles. Big Cedar Creek becomes wide and shallow. Small creeklets occasionally flow forth from the brushy banks. Occasional hills rise forth and steepen the shoreline. Fallen trees are somewhat common, but they are not problematic and actually provide cover for the many fish species found here, including bream, bass, catfish, and stripers that swim upstream from Lake Weiss. Civilization is never far away; small scattered creek camps are located on the bank here and there, but they don't intrude on the stream's natural beauty.

Big Cedar Creek turns north and becomes a very placid, very gentle float. Big Cedar Creek begins to run roughly parallel to Highway 100, and you can hear it. The current slackens down here as it comes ever nearer Lake Weiss. At 4.4 miles the creek divides into islands then narrows and becomes swift again. Pass under a second power line twice in succession in the swift area. Interesting outcrops emerge from the stream. Houses are perched upon them. Some last-minute riffles speed you onward, and you reach the Highway 100 bridge at 5.1 miles. Takeout is on your right, just past the bridge.

CAVE SPRING

The town of Cave Spring is located just a few miles southwest of this paddle, on the southwest end of Vann's Valley. The town was named for the mineral spring flowing from a hillside cave in what is now Rolator Park. The spring emits several million gallons a day. Cave Spring feeds Little Cedar Creek, which actually begins farther south in the community of Prior. Little Cedar Creek flows through the park and the town of Cave Spring before meeting Big Cedar Creek. Rolator Park is an alluring attraction of this historic town, founded in the 1820s. Today the park has covered pavilions and picnic tables under shady trees. Cave Spring flows into a large wading pool, shaped like the state of Georgia, where visitors frolic in the summertime. This pool was built by the Civilian Conservation Corps (CCC) in the 1930s. During the Civil War, Cave Spring was used as a respite by both the Confederates and the Yankees.

To this day you can not only visit the spring but also explore the cave from which the spring flows. Tours are open to the public during summer, when it is 56 degrees in the cave all the time. You can see some interesting formations, especially stalagmites, which, if you remember from your school days, form from the bottom of the cave upward. (Stalactites form from the top down.) The most famous of these stalagmites is the Devil's Stool. In addition to the cave and spring, the town of Cave Spring also has historic buildings worth visiting.

2 Broad River

With its rocky rapids strewn bank to bank between high, wooded hills, this is the most popular section of the Broad River.

County: Madison, Elbert
Start: Highway 281/Broad River Outpost N34 10' 50.1", W83 8' 46.5"
End: Near Highway 172 at the Sandbar N34° 9' 18.7", W83° 4' 19.9"
Length: 7.2 miles
Float time: 4 hours
Difficulty rating: Moderate to difficult at higher water levels
Rapids: Class I-II; Class III at higher water levels
River type: Float, shoals, ledges
Current: Moderate
River gradient: 8 feet per mile
River gauge: Broad River near Carlton; minimum runnable level 300 cfs. The river gets pushy above 2,000 cfs.
Season: March to November
Land status: Private
Fees or permits: Fees at put-in and takeout points

Nearest city/town: Danielsville, Georgia
Maps: USGS: Danielsville North, Bowman; DeLorme: *Georgia Atlas and Gazetteer,* pages 22-23
Boats used: Whitewater kayaks, funyaks, canoes
Organizations: Broad River Watershed Association, P.O. Box 661, Danielsville, GA 30633; www.brwa.org
Contacts/outfitters: Broad River Outpost, 112 Witcher Road, Carlton, GA 30627; (706) 795-3242; www.broadriveroutpost.com. Offers boat rentals and shuttles; used boats for sale; campground.
The Sandbar, 3435 King Hall Mill Road, Bowman, GA 30624; (706) 245-4163; www.thesandbarbroadriver.com. Offers boat rentals and shuttles; used equipment for sale; cabin rental.

Put-in/takeout information:

To takeout: From Athens take Highway 72 east to Highway 172, just beyond Colbert. Veer left onto Highway 172 east and travel 13 miles to the bridge over the Broad River. Continue 0.5 mile past the bridge to turn right onto Kings Hall Mill Road. Go for 0.6 mile and then turn right into the Sandbar. The takeout is by the outfitter office. There is a fee.

To put-in from takeout: From the Sandbar return to Highway 172, then turn right onto 172 east and follow it just a few hundred yards to Parham Town Road. Turn left and follow Parham Town Road for 4.2 miles to dead-end into Highway 281. Turn left onto Highway 281 and follow it for 3.1 miles, bridging the Broad River before turning left into Broad River Outpost. There is a launching fee.

Paddle Summary

Expect flat water broken by longer shoals that exhibit different characteristics with different water levels. Lower water makes the run rocky, whereas higher water creates

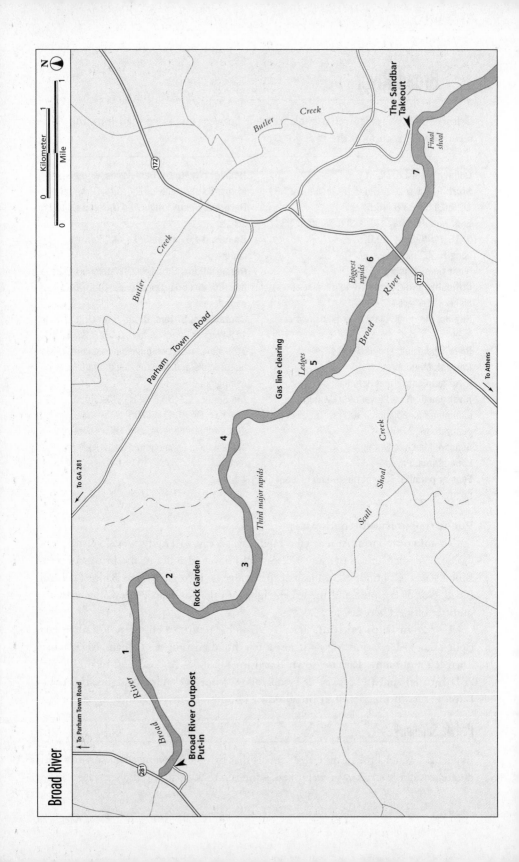

Taking a loaded canoe down the Broad
COURTESY OF JESSICA TAYLOR

big waves. Not to worry, though—most rapids have easier routes versus some of the taller ledges sought by helmeted kayakers. Before passing this section by, consider that throngs of completely inexperienced paddlers hop in rubber funyaks and bounce down the river on nice weekends. During these times, if you're unsure about the best route, someone will be ahead of you showing the way to go—or not to go. If in doubt during high water, consult outfitters regarding whether to run the river. Outfitters on either end of the run make shuttles and parking a breeze.

River Overview

The forks of the Broad River, along with the Hudson River, gather north of this paddle, flowing off the foothills of the North Georgia mountains. All provide paddling opportunities. The main Broad River, after its feeder branches have joined it, then travels southeast approximately 50 miles from rocky, hilly country into increasingly gentle terrain to reach the Savannah River. This confluence is stilled under the waters of Strom Thurmond Lake, but the river is entirely free flowing until this confluence. The Broad River drains 944,000 acres in parts of thirteen Georgia counties.

The Paddling

The river veers left beyond the put-in, revealing its broad nature and high hills beyond. Sycamore, river birch, ash, and beard cane line the banks. Mountain laurel and sparkleberry stretch higher up the hills. Occasional flats border the stream, which has a tan coloration and will run mud brown at higher flows.

The Broad River then makes a big bend to the right, splitting around an island at 1.7 miles. Here is the first major rapid, which travels through a rock garden for a couple hundred yards. A very small island with trees is in the middle. Paddling routes multiply at higher water levels. Pass through another rock garden in 0.5 mile, and reach the third rapid at 3.2 miles. Beyond here, the Broad calms down for a while. The hills recede somewhat, and a few houses appear. Pass a gas line clearing at 4.7 miles. This is your warning for a forthcoming drop, a series of ledges. The biggest ledges occur on river-right, around an island. Average paddlers will pick their way through the middle. A gravel bar forms below the ledges.

The biggest and best rapid is yet to come. Get on your toes when the Highway 172 bridge comes within sight. Here, at 5.9 miles, watch for a rocky island with a deck atop it. The steepest ledges are on the right. However, paddlers can work left through a rock garden with less-steep drops. Paddlers gather here and in the areas below to watch others make their way through this whitewater area.

Continue working through milder rapids under and below the Highway 172 bridge. The river flattens below the bridge. Swimmers, anglers, and sunbathers will be found here during warmer times. Reach one last shoal just before reaching the takeout at the Sandbar on river-left.

THE SPIDER LILY
The Broad River is home to one of the most interesting riverside flowers to be found not only in Georgia but also in the entire United States. The rocky shoals spider lily (*Hymenocallis coroniaria*) grows along shoals of this river in Elbert, Wilkes, and Lincoln Counties, blooming in May. Officially listed as endangered in Georgia, it also grows along shoals of the Savannah River near Augusta in the Peach State and along the lower Chattahoochee and Flint Rivers at the Fall Line. It is also found on the Catawba River in South Carolina, which claims to have the most spider lilies in the country, and in Alabama along the Cahaba River south of Birmingham, where they are known as Cahaba lilies. With a limited number of plant colonies in the Southeast, the spider lily is susceptible to water pollution, especially siltation and sediment runoff.

Spider lilies are found in open, well-lit rocky shoals of streams and rivers, such as can be found on the Broad River. The waters must be clean, swift moving, and well oxygenated. Early American naturalist William Bartram is credited with first describing the rocky shoals spider lily in 1773, along the Savannah River: "Nothing in vegetable nature is more pleasing than the odoriferous *Pancratium fluitans* (spider lily), which alone possesses the little rocky islets which just appear above the water." Bartram's scientific name was changed, partly due to the sphinx moth, which pollinates the lily on nocturnal flights across the shoals.

3 Chattahoochee River below Buford Dam

A distinctly different river trip on Georgia's master river. Be sure to check Buford Dam generation schedules before getting on the water.

County: Gwinnett, Forsyth
Start: Buford Dam N34° 9' 30.5", W84° 4' 36.1"
End: Settles Bridge N34° 5' 53.4", W84° 6' 33.8"
Length: 5.1 miles
Float time: 2.5 hours
Difficulty rating: Moderate
Rapids: Class I–II
River type: Dam-controlled coldwater river
Current: Moderate at normal levels
River gradient: 2.1 feet per mile
River gauge: Chattahoochee River at Buford Dam; no minimum runnable level; Buford Dam release schedule: (770) 945-1466
Season: March to November
Land status: Chattahoochee National River parkland; private

Fees or permits: No fees or permits required
Nearest city/town: Buford, Georgia
Maps: USGS: Buford Dam, Suwanee; DeLorme: *Georgia Atlas and Gazetteer*, page 21; USDA Forest Service: Chattahoochee National River Recreation Area
Boats used: Rafts, canoes, kayaks, float tubes, dories
Organizations: Upper Chattahoochee River-keeper, 3 Puritan Mill, 916 Joseph Lowery Boulevard, Atlanta, GA 30318; (404) 352-9828; www.ucriverkeeper.org
Contacts/outfitters: Up the River Outfitters, 6144 Highway 20; (770) 614-3322; www.uptheriveroutfitters.com

Put-in/takeout information:

To takeout: From exit 4 on Interstate 985, take Highway 20 west for 5.7 miles to Suwannee Dam Road. Turn left onto Suwannee Dam Road; follow it for 1.3 miles, and then turn right onto Johnson Road. Go 1 mile on Johnson Road, then turn right onto Settles Bridge Road. Travel on Settles Bridge Road, entering the Chattahoochee National Recreation Area. A short trail leads to the river takeout.

To put-in from takeout: From Settles Bridge, backtrack to Suwannee Dam Road and turn left (northbound), this time crossing Highway 20. Go north for 2.3 miles beyond Highway 20 to dead-end into Buford Dam Road. Turn left onto Buford Dam Road and follow it for 1.6 miles; turn left just after crossing the dam toward Lower Pool Park to dead-end at the boat ramp.

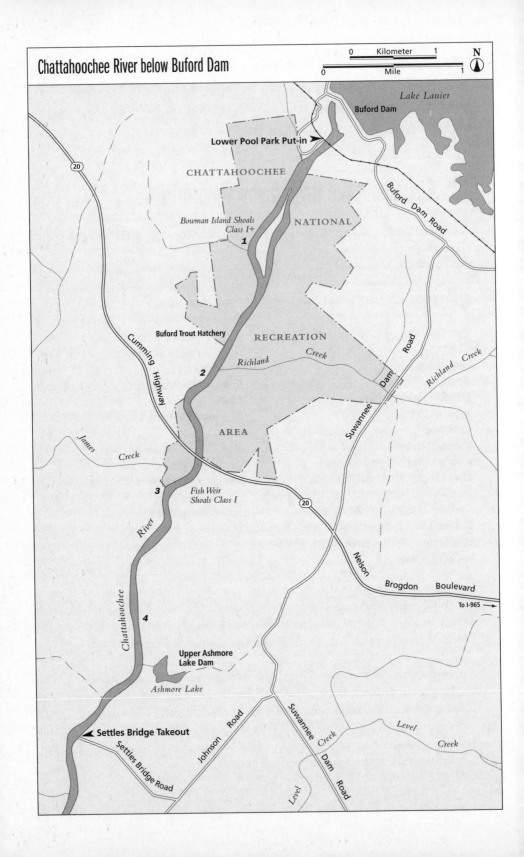

Chattahoochee River below Buford Dam

Paddle Summary

Frigid water releases from Buford Dam flow through the Chattahoochee National River corridor and provide a cool escape for hot summer days. Class I+ rapids keep your attention as you travel through gin-clear waters harboring trout. Much of the river flows through a park-protected corridor.

River Overview

The Chattahoochee starts as a mere spring in the mountains, but by the time it is released from Lake Lanier—and the beginning of this paddle—it is a significant waterway. By the time it passes through Atlanta, it is a bona fide big river and is changing from mountain stream to a flatland waterway that forms the border between Georgia and Alabama. It is the most important waterway in the Peach State, providing not only recreation but also drinking water and transportation.

The Paddling

Massive Buford Dam looms above the put-in. You will likely see fishermen in waders braving the cold water while vying for the trout that thrive here. The waters, emerging from the chilly depths of Lake Lanier, are normally superlatively clear, and you can see moss growing on larger rocks, exposed at lower flows.

Depending on whether they are generating or not, this is two completely different rivers. It is not recommended that you float the river while the dam is generating. Generation is usually done in the later afternoon or evening, and it takes the raised river a few hours to make it to Settles Bridge, where you are taking out. Plan your departure for morning or early afternoon and you will be fine, but always call ahead at the number listed above for generation schedules. Loud horns sound along the river prior to generation, allowing recreationalists to get off the water.

The Chattahoochee is a couple of hundred feet wide below the dam, but the river soon divides around Bowman Island. Most paddlers stick to the right side of the island while traveling through Class I–I+ Bowman Island Shoals. The first 2.0 miles are protected and forested river corridor. River birch, ironwood, tulip trees, ash, and sumac grow along the mud or brush banks, which extend anywhere from 8 to 30 feet high. Many fallen trees are exposed along the banks when the dam's not generating, as are gravel bars. Don't be surprised to see wildlife such as deer along the river corridor in the midst of fast-growing North Georgia.

The gin-clear water reveals trout swimming throughout the river. Beyond the island the Chattahoochee widens again. Look for the horns on river-right that sound when the dam releases its water. If you hear what you think may be a large upcoming rapid, it is actually the outflow from the Buford Trout Hatchery at 1.7 miles. The outflow drops 15 or so feet over rocks from the right bank of the river. Just a little ways downstream on river-left, Richland Creek merges with the Chattahoochee. Pass a small shoal 0.3 mile before reaching the Highway 20 bridge at 2.7 miles. This rapid may be washed out at higher water levels.

Note the old bridge abutment on river-left and the piling in the center of the river just below the Highway 20 bridge. The waters are superlatively clear here, and you can plainly see trout moving about, especially as they swim above the sandy bottom. On weekends you will see anglers in boats and float tubes vying for the wary fish. James Creek comes in below Fish Weir Shoals on river-right. The Hooch moves at a moderate downriver pace and shifts to a pleasant float where your mind can drift and relax. Eventually the metal span of the now-defunct Settles Bridge will come into view. Pass through a small riffle and take out on river-left at the base of the bridge. Steps lead away from the river and to the parking area.

A WATERY VEIN CONNECTING THE MOUNTAINS TO THE SEA The Chattahoochee River is the Peach State's contribution to the great rivers of the world. The 542-mile waterway starts at Chattahoochee Spring, just below Jacks Knob in the North Georgia mountains and a short stroll off the Appalachian Trail, which also starts here in Georgia. From this mountainside it flows south into the splendid trout waters of the Chattahoochee Wildlife Management Area of the Chattahoochee National Forest; down through the tourist town of Helen, where tubers float its cool riffles; and down to Lake Lanier, where boaters pull water-skiers over its impounded waters and lake homes overlook the still waters. From this point the river is freed of its reins at Buford Dam. On it goes to Atlanta and becomes the centerpiece of the Chattahoochee River National Recreation Area, where rafters, canoeists, and kayakers enjoy a slice of nature amidst Georgia's most urban locale—and where this paddle takes place. From Atlanta the Chattahoochee turns southwest, flowing to the Alabama state line, where it is dammed again as West Point Lake. And from here on it has a job to do: delineating the Alabama-Georgia state line. The river heads south into a series of dams before reaching the river town of Columbus, Georgia, and then flows through Fort Benning military base. Now in southwest Georgia, the Hooch is dammed again, as massive Lake Walter F. George. After leaving this lake and passing Fort Gaines, the river runs ever southward and at one point flows past the exact spot where Alabama, Georgia, and Florida all meet—way down yonder on the Chattahoochee. Its final penning occurs at Lake Seminole, where another great Georgia river, the Flint, meets the Chattahoochee. Together they form the Apalachicola River, which flows through Florida to the Gulf.

4 Chattahoochee River near Lula

A scenic run just below a busier section of the Chattahoochee.

County: White, Hall, Habersham
Start: Duncan Bridge Road/Wildwood Outfitters N34° 32' 27.5", W83° 37' 19.6"
End: Belton Bridge Road at Lake Lanier N34° 26' 42.1", W83° 41' 3.9"
Length: 10.7 miles
Float time: 5 hours
Difficulty rating: Moderate
Rapids: Class I–II
River type: Mountainesque river valley with nice houses along upper half; lower half, wooded valley; sandbars near lake
Current: Moderate
River gradient: 5.1 feet per mile
River gauge: Chattahoochee River near Cornelia; minimum runnable level 250 cfs

Season: March to November
Land status: Private; some public
Fees or permits: No fees or permits required
Nearest city/town: Lula, Georgia
Maps: USGS: Clarkesville, Leaf, Lula; DeLorme: *Georgia Atlas and Gazetteer,* pages 15, 16, 21
Boats used: Kayaks, canoes, johnboats
Organizations: Upper Chattahoochee Riverkeeper, 3 Puritan Mill, 916 Joseph Lowery Boulevard, Atlanta, GA 30318; (404) 352-9828; www.ucriverkeeper.org
Contacts/outfitters: Wildwood Outfitters, 140 Mossy Creek Point, Cleveland, GA 30528; (800) 553-2715; www.wildwoodoutfitters.com. Offers trips upriver on the Chattahoochee and sells paddling equipment; parking available.

Put-in/takeout information:

To shuttle point/takeout: From the intersection of Highway 52 and Lanier Parkway (Highways 365/5000, the extension of Interstate 985), take Lanier Parkway 1.6 miles north to Belton Bridge Road. Turn left on Belton Bridge Road and follow it 2.3 miles. At the intersection with Pea Ridge Road, stay left and follow Belton Bridge Road 1 mile farther to cross a bridge over the Chattahoochee River. Parking is available on both sides the bridge.

To put-in from takeout: From Belton Bridge, backtrack 1 mile to Pea Ridge Road. Turn left (northbound) onto Pea Ridge Road, and follow it for 8 miles to Duncan Bridge Road. Turn left onto Duncan Bridge Road and follow it 1.4 miles to Wildwood Outfitters, on your right.

Paddle Summary

The high wooded banks and clear waters of this section of the Chattahoochee mimic the more mountainous river sections without all the rougher rapids, although several shoals are Class II. There are houses along the upper half of the run, but the lower offers seclusion.

River Overview

The Chattahoochee starts as a mere spring in the mountains, but by the time it is released from Lake Lanier—and the beginning of this paddle—it is a significant

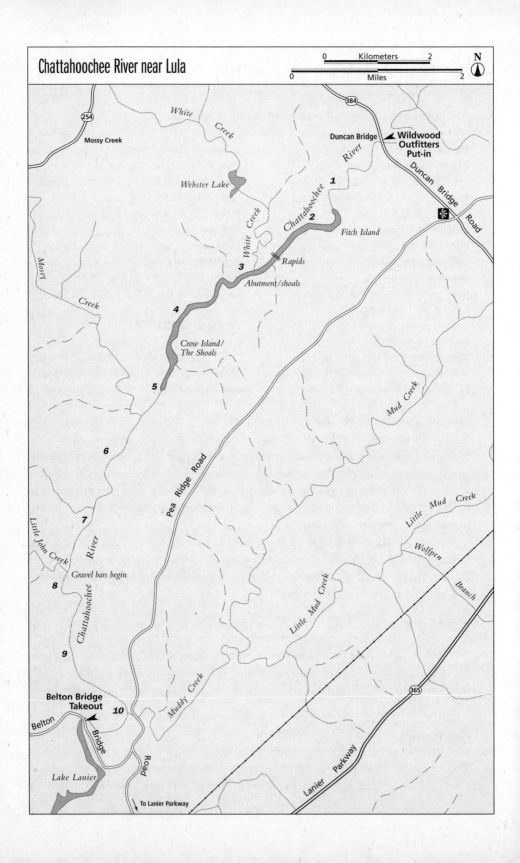

Chattahoochee River near Lula

Kilometers
Miles

N

White Creek

254
Mossy Creek

Webster Lake

Duncan Bridge

384

Wildwood Outfitters Put-in

Chattahoochee River

1

2

Fitch Island

White Creek

3

Rapids

Abutment/shoals

Duncan Bridge Road

Mossy Creek

4

Crow Island/ The Shoals

5

Mud Creek

6

Pea Ridge Road

7

Little Mud Creek

Little John Creek

Chattahoochee River

Gravel bars begin

Wolfpen Branch

8

9

Little Mud Creek

365

Belton Bridge Takeout

10

Belton

Muddy Creek

Bridge Road

Lake Lanier

Lanier Parkway

To Lanier Parkway

waterway. By the time it passes through Atlanta, it is a bona fide big river and changes from mountain stream to a flatland waterway that forms the border between Georgia and Alabama. It is the most important river in the Peach State, providing not only recreation but also drinking water and transportation.

The Paddling

Wildwood Outfitters has a good put-in. A 5.0-mile classic Chattahoochee white-water run ends here at Duncan Bridge, coming from the Highway 115 bridge, and includes Buck Shoals and Horseshoe Rapids. Contact Wildwood if you are interested in that trip.

The shoals immediately below Duncan Bridge begin the action for this run. Continue downriver, bordered by houses. The wooded parts of bluffs will have mountain laurel, which blooms in spring, as well as white pine. Sycamores, tulip trees, and ironwood trees line the banks. Gray rock outcrops add a scenic touch to the river. Occasional flats break up the high banks. The clear, greenish river is 80 to 100 feet wide in most places. Small creeklets cut deep minigorges as they slice to the banks to reach the Chattahoochee.

Reach Fitch Island, which is actually three islands, at 1.5 miles. Your initial view is a pair of islands. Your best bet is to go on the far left at the end of the rapid, which falls in stages. At the bottom of this rapid, you will find a third piney island. A smaller rapid comes at 2.5 miles, before White Creek enters on your right.

At 3.1 miles pass an old bridge abutment in the middle of the river, once part of Heads Ferry Road. Just ahead, the Hooch drops in three ledges then curves back to the left. The river keeps its southwesterly course until 4.7 miles, reaching Crow Island and The Shoals. At lower water, the shoals look to be impassable; stay far left around Crow Island. This far-left channel isn't immediately visible. The roar becomes audible. Make a multitiered drop, hugging the island shore, before reaching the lower end of Crow Island.

The water calms below Crow Island and The Shoals, moving swiftly but without whitewater to reach the confluence with Mossy Creek at 5.5 miles. The state of Georgia purchased acreage here at the confluence with the Chattahoochee, making canoe camping practicable. From here down, the river is currently free of houses and displays an everywhere-you-look beauty. Gravel bars appear on the inside of sharp bends with increasing frequency on the lower river, especially below Little John Creek, which is passed at 6.6 miles. Occasional riffles keep the action lively.

Fallen tree snags lie along the banks closer to the lake, especially in a storm-damaged area before Muddy Creek, on your left at 10.0 miles. The river slackens as it enters Lake Lanier. Shoreline anglers and other river visitors appear with frequency from here down before you reach Belton Bridge at 10.8 miles.

GEORGIA'S "FRESHWATER OCEAN"
This paddle ends at the point where the Chattahoochee River becomes slowed by the backwaters of Lake Lanier. This impoundment has sometimes been called Georgia's "freshwater ocean." Back in 1946 the U.S. Congress authorized a development program for a series of dams on the Chattahoochee River, among other waterways in the United States. These dams were to provide hydroelectric power, ensure water quality and supply, and benefit boat navigation and flood control protection. Buford Dam, which backs up the Chattahoochee and forms Lake Lanier, is the highest dam on the Chattahoochee River. In what was then rural Georgia, the 58,000 acres that would be inundated and form the shoreline of Lake Lanier were purchased at roughly $40 per acre. As with other dam and lake projects, the people were uprooted from their land and their cemeteries relocated, then the forestlands were cut over.

By 1956 Buford Dam was completed, the Chattahoochee River backed up, and what was to become Lake Lanier spread over five counties—Forsyth, Dawson, Lumpkin, Hall, and Gwinnett. It took over three years for the lake to reach its full pool, at 1,070 feet. At full pool the lake covers more than 38,000 surface acres of water. Its shoreline winds for 692 miles. Electricity was first produced from Buford Dam on June 17, 1957.

Today more than 7.5 million people use Lake Lanier each year. The lake is named for the poet Sidney Lanier, who was born and raised in Macon, Georgia. He fought for his Georgia homeland in the Civil War and later produced a body of writing and music for which he is known today. Lanier succumbed to tuberculosis in 1881.

◀ *Mountain laurel graces the shoreline of the Chattahoochee River.*
Courtesy of Jessica Taylor

5 Chattooga River

This float traverses the most doable section of the Wild and Scenic Chattooga River, which forms the boundary between Georgia and South Carolina.

County: Rabun
Start: South Carolina Highway 28 River Access N34° 54' 11.9", W83° 10' 54.0"
End: Earls Ford N34° 52' 32.9", W83° 13' 43.7"
Length: 7.0 miles
Float time: 4 hours
Difficulty rating: Moderate to difficult
Rapids: Class I-II, III (Big Shoals)
River type: Mountain whitewater river worthy of its Wild and Scenic designation
Current: Moderate to swift
Gradient: 11.2 feet per mile
River gauge: Chattooga River near Clayton; minimum runnable level 1.2 feet; maximum runnable level 3.0 feet

Season: April to November
Land status: Public—Chattahoochee National Forest; Sumter National Forest
Fees or permits: A free river float plan must be filed.
Nearest city/town: Clayton, Georgia
Maps: USGS: Satolah; DeLorme: *Georgia Atlas and Gazetteer,* page 16; USDA Forest Service: Chattooga Wild and Scenic River
Boats used: Decked kayaks, canoes, rafts
Organizations: Chattooga Conservancy, 2368 Pinnacle Drive, Clayton, GA 30525; (706) 782-6097; www.chattoogariver.org
Contacts/outfitters: Wildwater Rafting, Ltd., P.O. Box 309, Long Creek, SC 29658; (800) 451-9972; www.wildwaterrafting.net

Put-in/takeout information:

To takeout: From Clayton, just north of the intersection between U.S. Highways 76 and 441, take Warwoman Road for 14 miles east to Georgia Highway 28. Turn right onto GA 28 south. Cross the bridge over the Chattooga River at 2.1 miles. Continue on into South Carolina, now on SC 28, 1.5 miles further to the SC 28 river access. This is the put-in, so continue for 4.4 miles and turn right onto Chattooga Ridge Road. Follow Chattooga Ridge Road for 3.5 miles and turn right onto Earls Ford Road (South Carolina County Road 493). Follow Earls Ford Road for 3.9 miles to dead-end at the parking area.

To put-in from takeout: Backtrack on Earls Ford Road, then take a left onto Chattooga Ridge Road. Turn left onto SC 28 west and follow it to the SC 28 river access.

Paddle Summary

The protected corridor of the Wild and Scenic Chattooga River offers unspoiled mountain scenery at its finest. The trip is challenging for the novice paddler, although it is much tamer than sections of river downstream. That being said, this section does have several solid Class II rapids and one Class III rapid, Big Shoals. Be apprised that the takeout from the river at Earls Ford requires a 0.25-mile uphill carry up to the parking area.

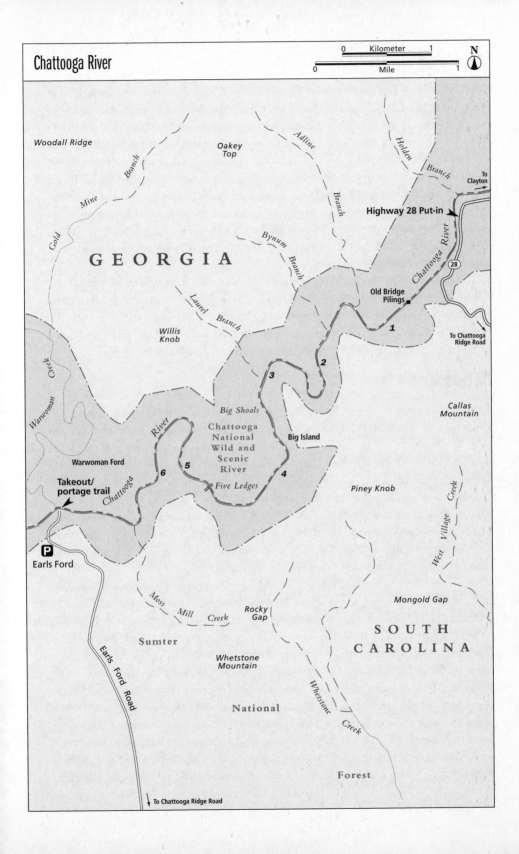

Kilometer

Mile

N

Woodall Ridge

Gold Mine Branch

Oakey Top

Adline Branch

Holden Branch

To Clayton

Highway 28 Put-in

Chattooga River

28

GEORGIA

Bynum Branch

Old Bridge Pilings

To Chattooga Ridge Road

Laurel Branch

1

Willis Knob

2

3

Warwoman Creek

Big Shoals

Chattooga National Wild and Scenic River

Callas Mountain

River

Big Island

Warwoman Ford

6

5

4

Takeout/ portage trail

Chattooga

Five Ledges

Piney Knob

West Village Creek

P

Earls Ford

Mongold Gap

Moss Mill Creek

Rocky Gap

SOUTH CAROLINA

Sumter

Whetstone Mountain

Earls Ford Road

Whetstone Creek

National

Forest

To Chattooga Ridge Road

River Overview

The Chattooga River deserves its Wild and Scenic designation, and then some. Culled from Georgia's Chattahoochee National Forest, the Nantahala National Forest of North Carolina, and the Sumter National Forest of South Carolina, this river corridor protects one of the most significant free-flowing streams in the Southeast. The river itself is 50 miles long. It starts in North Carolina then heads southwest for 40 miles, forming the Georgia–South Carolina border before meeting the Tallulah River and forming the Tugaloo River. The Chattooga is perhaps best known for being the backdrop of the Burt Reynolds's movie *Deliverance*. It was around this time, in 1974, that the Chattooga was designated a Wild and Scenic River—a place where rafters, canoers, kayakers, and anglers enjoy this valley of massive boulders, clear trout- and bass-filled waters, and deep forests.

The following section of river is the mildest in terms of rapids. Downstream, the following 20 miles of waterway—known as Sections 3 and 4—have rapids up to Class V and are known for both their challenging nature and extraordinary scenery. Additionally, the Wild and Scenic River corridor offers 36 miles of river hiking and more in adjacent national forestlands, which include the Ellicott Rock Wilderness.

The Paddling

You can lengthen your trip by putting in at the SC 28 bridge, which crosses the Chattooga at the South Carolina–Georgia state line. This adds a little less than 2.0 miles to your paddle. The put-in is on the southwest side of the bridge. A trail leads down to the river. Be apprised that many anglers will be in the river around the bridge on nice days.

Make sure to file a float plan before you get on the river. You can file your float plan at either the put-in or the takeout. The SC 28 put-in has a steep concrete ramp that leads down to the rocky river. Here the Chattooga is about 50 to 60 feet wide, completely wooded with species such as mountain laurel, maple, and hemlock, the last unfortunately dying from hemlock woolly adelgid infestation.

A few houses line the South Carolina side for a bit. The clear water has a brownish tint, and in the shallows, pyrite—fool's gold—shimmers in the sandy shallows. The Bartram Trail, a footpath, runs along the Georgia bank, which is to your right as you travel downstream. The paddling is easy at first, with just a few minor shoals. At 0.8 mile pass the remnants of an old wooden bridge in a long, slack pool. As you make a curve to the right, you can look downstream directly at Oakey Top Mountain.

Islands border the river, which widens to more than 100 feet in places. Occasional logjams and sandbars accumulate on the river's edge. White and shortleaf pines tower high on the forested hills. The rapids remain Class I as you cruise downriver amid large boulders, especially at low water. At 2.4 miles the Chattooga goes over a small shoal then makes a nearly 180-degree turn to the right before reaching the first named shoal—Turn Hole Rapid. A nice high beach, suitable for camping, collects at the base of the rapid on river-right. It will also collect unwary paddlers. This rapid has several routes that change as the waters rise and fall, so stop and scout it before continuing downriver.

The river narrows, and several small smaller rapids lie between Turn Hole Rapid and Big Shoals, which you reach at 3.3 miles. Look for a pine island in the middle of the river, combined with a roar suitable for a Class III rapid. Large boulders line the river. You can paddle up to the boulders then scout your route over the fairly short rapid. Most paddlers go far right or far left and, at higher water, down the middle. Novices shouldn't be afraid to portage.

Once beyond Big Shoals, don't forget to look upstream for another view of Oakey Top. Below Big Shoals the river continues to divide into islands and the scenery remains magnificent. The longest island is appropriately called Big Island. Just below Big Island, look for the old Big Island ford that crosses the shallows here with roadbeds extending away from the Chattooga. A long pool ensues. Doghobble and mountain laurel grow in thickets along the river; white pines tower above the rest of the forest.

At 4.5 miles reach the Five Ledges Rapid. This Class II rapid has multiple ledges—and multiple routes. Two islands split the river amid the Five Ledges. Most paddlers stay to the right of the islands. Moderate shoals and superlative scenery continue. The Chattooga makes a hard curve to the right (west) at 6.4 miles, as Moss Mill Creek flows in from your left. Pass a few more islands downstream. You will recognize Earls Ford, as Warwoman Creek comes in on the right, just downstream of a large gravel bar on river-left. Now the real fun begins; a portage trail leads 0.25 mile to the takeout.

THE RUSSELL FARMSTEAD
Near the site of the GA Highway 28 bridge was once the Cherokee village of Chatuga Old Town. This settlement took advantage of the flats among the steep mountains that rise from the Chattooga. This small Cherokee village consisted of no more than ten to fifteen homes with fewer than one hundred people living here. By the 1750s this Cherokee town had been abandoned, likely due to smallpox. The same flats beside the Chattooga proved alluring to the European settlers that came behind them. Today you can visit the Russell farmstead, located on the South Carolina side of the Chattooga between the GA 28 bridge and the put-in for this paddle. The farmstead is signed.

The Russell farmstead was a hub of activity—farm, stagecoach stop, and inn—in the late nineteenth and early twentieth centuries. The historic site contains the foundations and remains of the Russell house and nine outbuildings, including barns, corncrib, springhouse, and pig farrow. The Russell farmsite was first settled in the 1820s by Ira Nicholson, but Union troops destroyed his house in 1864.

William Russell purchased the property in 1867 and built most of the buildings, including the main house, dating from the 1880s. The large two-story frame house was gradually expanded, with a projecting rear two-story ell added around 1890, and provided rooms for travelers. A two-story front porch was added later. William Russell performed the function of a local doctor and dentist. A blacksmith shop was located at the farm.

William Russell died in 1921, and his wife died in 1935, but the family continued to operate the establishment into the 1950s. In 1970 the federal government purchased the property. A fire destroyed the main house in 1988.

6 Chestatee River

This section of the Chestatee retains its mountain characteristics—cool, clear, and rocky—yet doesn't dish out the tough mountain rapids.

County: Lumpkin
Start: Highway 60, Appalachian Outfitters N34° 30' 23.5", W83° 58' 19.9"
End: Highway 400 N34° 27' 59.3", W83° 58' 10.0"
Length: 6.1 miles
Float time: 3 hours
Difficulty rating: Moderate
Rapids: Class I
River type: Mild section of mountain river
Current: Moderate to swift
River gradient: 6.6 feet per mile
River gauge: Chestatee River near Dahlonega; minimum runnable level 0.3 gauge height

Season: April to October
Land status: Private
Fees or permits: No fees or permits required
Nearest city/town: Dahlonega, Georgia
Maps: USGS: Dahlonega, Murrayville; DeLorme: *Georgia Atlas and Gazetteer,* page 15
Boats used: Canoes, kayaks, tubes
Organizations: Georgia River Network, 126 South Milledge Avenue, Suite E3, Athens, GA 30605; (706) 549-4508; www.garivers.org
Contacts/outfitters: Appalachian Outfitters, 2084 South Chestatee/Highway 60, Dahlonega, GA 30533; (706) 864-7117; www.canoegeorgia.com

Put-in/takeout information:

To takeout: From Atlanta take Highway 400 north to its end, meeting Highway 60 just after crossing the Chestatee River. From here backtrack south on Highway 400 back over the Chestatee River, then veer right (west) to the first road to the takeout under the bridge. Future takeout here will be off Highway 60 just west of the Highway 400 bridge.

To put-in from takeout: Cross back north over the Highway 400 bridge, then head west on Highway 60/U.S. Highway 19 north. Follow it 3.5 miles; the outfitter is on your left.

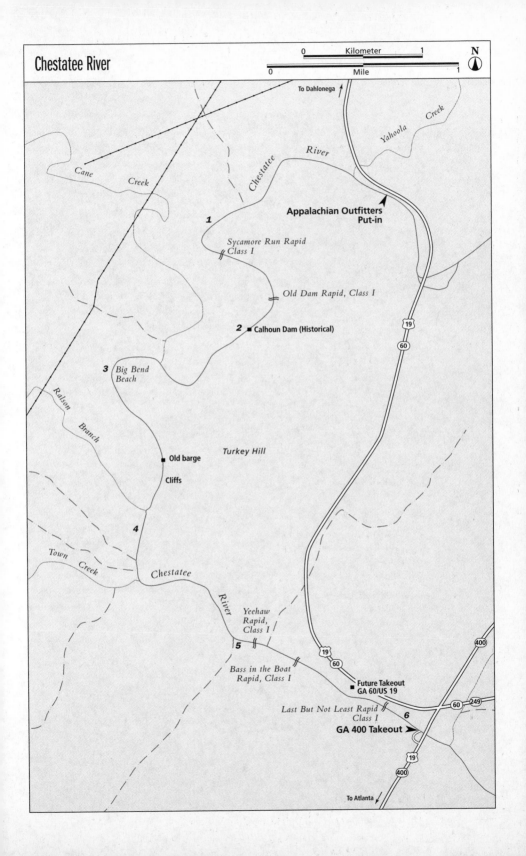

Chestatee River

To Dahlonega

Yahoola Creek

Chestatee River

Cane Creek

1

Sycamore Run Rapid
Class I

Appalachian Outfitters
Put-in

Old Dam Rapid, Class I

2 Calhoun Dam (Historical)

3 Big Bend Beach

Ralson Branch

Old barge

Cliffs

Turkey Hill

4

Town Creek

Chestatee

River

Yeehaw Rapid, Class I

5

Bass in the Boat Rapid, Class I

Future Takeout
GA 60/US 19

Last But Not Least Rapid
Class I

6

GA 400 Takeout

To Atlanta

Paddle Summary

Begin the relaxing yet scenic paddle at a long-established outfitter, which also rents boats and provides shuttles. Then enjoy the ride down a watercourse bordered by high hills alternating with lower flats, all fed by clear streams. The rapids—all Class I—will keep you awake and move you on but won't loom over the trip like a black rain cloud.

River Overview

The Chestatee River is a tributary of the Chattahoochee. Springing forth from the south side of George's famed Blood Mountain, its tributaries such as Waters Creek offer excellent trout fishing destinations inside the boundaries of the Chattahoochee National Forest. The waterway becomes paddleable at the confluence of Dick's and Boggs Creeks, where it officially becomes the Chestatee. From here it makes a 33.0-mile journey to reach the slack waters of Lake Lanier, where its confluence with the Chattahoochee is now stilled. The section above this paddle has rapids ranging from Class I to Class IV, including Grindle Falls, dropping more than 50 feet in stages.

The Paddling

Leave the outfitters along high wooded banks. Highway 60 is audible in the distance at this point. A few houses are sprinkled along the beginning of the trip. The river is about 40 feet wide, moving in small riffles, and runs clear green over a rocky bed bordered with occasional fallen trees. The river is partly canopied nearly the entire distance. Yahoola Creek comes in on your right just 100 yards down and adds significant water to the flow. River birch, sycamore, and ironwood overhang the Chestatee, which widens to 60 feet in places. Mountain laurel, doghobble, and ferns grow along the steeply sloped forest floor. The north-facing hillsides rise high and display North Georgia mountain vegetation such as rhododendron and imperiled hemlock.

Massive boulders rise from the waters edge. At 1.3 miles reach Sycamore Run just after a left curve. It shoots over a little rock ledge. At 1.8 miles pass over the Old Dam Rapid. This refers to the long-gone Calhoun Dam, named for South Carolina Senator John C. Calhoun, who was a strong proponent of states rights in the first half of the nineteenth century and also had stakes in the North Georgia gold rush boom. The northwest Georgia town of Calhoun was also named for him.

Below the Old Dam Rapid, the hills recede and beard cane thrives along the shore. Small gravel and rock bars are exposed at lower water levels. At 2.7 miles clear

Paddler at Yeehaw Rapid

Cane Creek and the Chestatee River quietly merge. Beyond Cane Creek the river begins a 180-degree curve, passing Big Bend Beach at 3.0 miles. This property is owned by Appalachian Outfitters, and you are welcome to stop and relax or picnic on the large, long gravel bar on the inside of the sharp left curve. A nice little section of mild shoals extend around the bend.

At 3.6 miles the wood remnants of an old barge lie against the right bank. It is about 50 to 60 feet long and is embedded into the bank here, its story lost to time. Soon pass high rock cliffs topped with pine and mountain laurel. Beyond the cliffs, the Chestatee flows wide, mild, and shallow over small riffles, passing near fields. Ralston Branch flows in on river-right as mild as the Chestatee is at this point.

At 4.3 miles Town Creek comes in on river-right as the Chestatee curves left and passes a large sand-and-gravel bar. White pines grow along this lower section. The river widens here and becomes a series of wide, shallow riffles before reaching the most significant rapid of the run, Yeehaw Rapid, with straightforward chutes. The next shoal, Bass in the Boat Rapid, is a series of small ledges that make for a fun ride. By this point road sounds from Highway 60/US 19 are drifting in from your left and a few houses appear. In the not-too-distant future, a boat ramp and canoe takeout will be on river-left just below this point. This will be your takeout. But for now, pass Last But Not Least Rapid as the Highway 400 bridge comes into sight. Last But Not Least is a series of big rocks with small channels between them. Reach the bridge and takeout on river-right.

A FALSE PROCLAMATION? Dahlonega, located just west of this paddle, proclaims itself to be the site of the nation's first gold rush—but that's a bit of a stretch. True, Georgia was the state where this first gold rush happened, but the gold was actually discovered in adjacent White County, along the drainages of Dukes Creek. Dahlonega had no gold. Why Dahlonega's claim then? Dahlonega was the nearest town to the gold rush and, perhaps most important, had the newspaper to get out the word.

Martin's Mine was one of the most productive gold mines during this 1820s boom that saw gold fever spread over a 60-square-mile area. But the Englund Mine was the first operating mine in these parts. Most mining was done by placer—panning for gold on a bigger scale—and hydraulic mining using gravity-driven water cannons to blast soil loose for later gold extraction. Martin's Mine, named for Scottish transplant John Martin, used a third method, known as hard rock mining. He dug shafts and tunnels to get out the ore, then went through a process using mercury and heat to extract the pure gold from the ore. Tailings left over from the process are quite visible during the winter months. Today you can visit Martin's Mine, located within the confines of Georgia's second-largest state park: Smithgall Woods Dukes Creek Conservation Area.

You can not only enjoy a slice of mining history, and see an amazing recovery of nature, but also enjoy the clear waters of Dukes Creek on trails that course through the park. It is here that the largest gold nugget east of the Mississippi was found, not in Dahlonega—but keep it to yourself while paddling the Chestatee, since the river is in Lumpkin County, right by Dahlonega.

7 Conasauga River

This parcel of the Conasauga makes a relaxing pastoral float through northwest Georgia farm country.

County: Whitfield, Murray
Start: Beaverdale N34° 55' 13.9", W84° 50' 33.0"
End: Norton Bridge Road N34° 51' 11.1", W84° 50' 39.9"
Length: 8.7 miles
Float time: 5 hours
Difficulty rating: Easy
Rapids: Class I
River type: Meandering valley river
Current: Moderate
River gradient: 3.4 feet per mile
River gauge: Conasauga River at Highway 286 near Eton; minimum runnable level 75 cfs
Season: March to November

Land status: Private
Fees or permits: Offer to pay the storekeepers for parking/launch privileges.
Nearest city/town: Chatsworth, Georgia
Maps: USGS: Beaverdale, Chatsworth; DeLorme: *Georgia Atlas and Gazetteer*, page 13
Boats used: Canoes, kayaks, johnboats
Organizations: Georgia River Network, 126 South Milledge Avenue, Suite E3, Athens, GA 30605; (706) 549-4508; www.garivers.org
Contacts/outfitters: Georgia Department of Natural Resources, 2 Martin Luther King Jr. Drive SE, Suite 1252 East Tower, Atlanta, GA 30334; (404) 656-3500; www.gadnr.org

Put-in/takeout information:

To takeout: From the Murray County Courthouse in Chatsworth, drive north on U.S. Highway 411 for 4.1 miles to Highway 286. Turn left onto Highway 286 west. Go for 2.8 miles to Highway 225; turn right onto Highway 225 north and follow it for 1.6 miles to a left turn onto Norton Bridge Road. Follow Norton Bridge Road for 2.6 miles to the takeout, just over the bridge on the left (southwest) side.

To put-in from takeout: From Norton Bridge continue forward (west) on Norton Bridge Road for 0.3 mile and turn right onto River Road. Stay on River Road for 5.2 miles, and turn right onto Beaverdale Road. Follow Beaverdale Road for 0.2 mile, then turn right onto Highway 2 east. Follow Highway 2 for 0.4 mile to the Beaverdale store, on the right just before crossing the Conasauga. The put-in is behind the store. Before launching, notify the storekeepers and offer to pay for parking/launch.

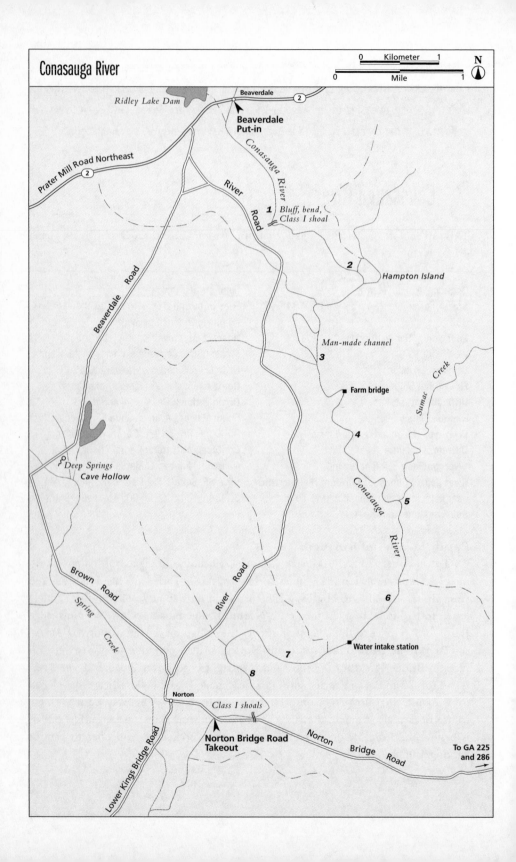

Conasauga River

Ridley Lake Dam

Beaverdale

Beaverdale
Put-in

Prater Mill Road Northeast

Conasauga River

River Road

1 *Bluff, bend,
Class I shoal*

2 Hampton Island

Beaverdale Road

Man-made channel

3

■ Farm bridge

4

Sumac Creek

Deep Springs
Cave Hollow

5

Conasauga River

Brown Road

6

Spring Creek

7 ■ Water intake station

River Road

8

Norton

Class I shoals

Norton Bridge Road
Takeout

Lower Kings Bridge Road

Norton Bridge Road

To GA 225
and 286

Paddle Summary

The narrow, mostly shaded watercourse runs slow to moderate, with long sections broken by a few Class I riffles. Most of the riverside land is held in large farms, so development is virtually nonexistent. Allow plenty of time to make your trip so that you can become as laid back as the setting deserves.

River Overview

The Conasauga starts as a crashing mountain river, leaving the North Georgia mountains before entering the state of Tennessee. It then turns south and reenters the Peach State just upstream from the beginning of this paddle. At this point the Conasauga becomes a pastoral waterway, winding its way south to meet the Coosawattee River, which together form the Oostanaula River. The uppermost part of the river is for highly skilled whitewater experts, but after it reenters Georgia, the Conasauga offers 80 more miles of paddling in northwest Georgia that is doable by most.

The Paddling

The Conasauga averages between 15 and 40 feet in width, narrowing where gravel bars force it along a bank or divide it around islands. The river is normally clear except for after rains. Banks range from 10 to 20 feet high and are mud, brush, rock, and roots. A canopy of sycamore, ash, and river birch borders the Conasauga. Ironwood also abounds. Tulip trees grow on the higher banks. Grasses grow atop the frequent gravel bars in summer.

After a few initial riffles, the river straightens out, slows down, and travels southeast. Fallen stumps and logs provide harborages for smallmouth bass and bream. Locals often float a johnboat on this stretch, fishing. While fields may come near the river, a corridor of trees nearly always provides a screen.

At 1.2 miles a bluff rises high to your right. The Conasauga makes a sharp bend to the left that culminates in a Class I rocky shoal. Watch for small creeks continually feeding the river. At 2.1 miles a channel leaves left, circling around ten-acre Hampton Island. The left channel rarely flows, save for times of flood. Below Hampton Island the river widens considerably. At 2.6 miles the river joins an obviously man-made channel, bypassing a large bend to the right.

Here is the story as it was told to me: In 1941, with the river flowing high, two men drowned in a swimming hole on the part of the river now bypassed. This swimming hole, popular with locals, had a "swirl" when the water was up. Not wanting to wait for the water to drop, some local men dynamited a channel bisecting the bend in order to lower the waters so that they could find the victim's bodies. The blast altered the river course, but they ended up finding the bodies downstream after the water dropped. Over time the Conasauga abandoned the old meandering channel for the straight dynamited one, leaving the meander to dry up. The slough of the old river comes in on your right at the lower end of the channel.

At 3.5 miles the river passes under a farm bridge and ford. The waterway continues southward down the valley in a mostly wooded corridor, with fields just off in the distance. Occasional riffles keep the river moving, and the frequent bends keep it interesting. Don't be surprised if you run into a few submerged logs stretching across the flowage. At 5.0 miles Sumac Creek, a clear stream also born in the mountains, comes in on your left. The Conasauga meanders less below Sumac Creek. At 6.0 miles a second farm road fords the river. Just below, you may see the remnants of an old wooden bridge that once spanned the Conasauga. At 6.4 miles you pass a water intake building on river-right. Not too far beyond the intake valve, the river resumes curving, with occasional shoals. The Conasauga, despite making a few bends, has widened to 80 feet or more and is running slow. As you come alongside Norton Bridge, one last set of Class I shoals speed you toward the takeout just beyond the bridge on river-right.

WILDERNESS BEGINNINGS The Conasauga River is born east of this paddle, in the nearby Cohutta Mountains. Much of this mountain range is part of Georgia's largest federally designated mountain wilderness, the Cohutta Wilderness, with more than 35,000 acres in the Peach State. (The Okefenokee Wilderness is the Peach State's largest, at 353,000 acres.) It is here in this wilderness where small springs above 4,000 feet gather to form the Conasauga and its bigger wilderness tributary, Jacks River, emerges from the wilderness at the Georgia-Tennessee state line. Even though the Jacks is bigger, the watercourse retains the name of Conasauga River.

The Cohutta Wilderness was established in 1984 and expanded in 1991. It offers more than 40 miles of hiking trails, including the 13.0-mile Conasauga River Trail, which follows the uppermost reaches of this river to its headwaters flowing off the north slope of the Cohutta Wilderness and Cowpen Mountain. While hiking this trail you will become well acquainted with the mountain stretch of Conasauga River—the trail fords it thirty-eight times. Consider complementing your paddle with a visit to the Cohutta Wilderness. A hike here will allow a firsthand view of the Conasauga's wilderness beginnings.

8 Coosawattee River

Because it's dam controlled, this part of the Coosawattee River is runnable year-round.

County: Gordon
Start: Carters Lake Dam N34° 36' 14.1", W84° 41' 37.3"
End: Montgomery Bridge N34° 36' 1.1", W84° 46' 46.0"
Length: 8.6 miles
Float time: 4 hours
Difficulty rating: Easy
Rapids: Class I
River type: Dam-controlled valley river
Current: Moderate to swift
River gradient: 2.2 feet per mile
River gauge: Coosawattee River at Carters; no minimum runnable level; 240 cfs guaranteed

Season: March to November
Land status: Private
Fees or permits: No fees or permits required
Nearest city/town: Calhoun, Georgia
Maps: USGS: Oakman, Redbud; DeLorme: *Georgia Atlas and Gazetteer,* page 13
Boats used: Canoes, kayaks, some johnboats
Organizations: Georgia River Network, 126 South Milledge Avenue, Suite E3, Athens, GA 30605; (706) 549-4508; www.garivers.org
Contacts/outfitters: Georgia Department of Natural Resources, 2 Martin Luther King Jr. Drive SE, Suite 1252 East Tower, Atlanta, GA 30334; (404) 656-3500; www.gadnr.org

Put-in/takeout information:

To takeout: From exit 320 on Interstate 75, take Highway 136 east for 11.6 miles to Montgomery Bridge over the Coosawattee River. The takeout is located on the right-hand (southwest) side of the bridge, coming from I-75, and is before you cross the river.

To put-in from takeout: From the takeout continue east on Highway 136 for 4.8 miles to U.S. Highway 411. Stay on Highway 136 east 0.5 mile farther, for a total of 5.3 miles from the takeout, then turn left onto Old US 411. Go for 0.7 mile north on Old US 411, then turn right into the Carters Dam Recreation Area to reach the parking area below the dam.

Paddle Summary

The Coosawattee below Carters Lake is dam controlled, and the Army Corps of Engineers has a standing agreement to provide at least 240 cfs of flow at all times, making this part of the river runnable year-round. When generating beyond the normal flows, the flow rates generally don't increase much, but call ahead (706-334-2248) for the generation schedule. (*NOTE:* Schedules are usually given for that day only.)

Leaving the dam at Carters Lake, the river flows steadily between high wooded banks and past fallen trees aplenty. The shores are little developed, and the current is joined by numerous named tributaries as it makes its way to Montgomery Bridge. A few Class I shoals provide a little action on a pleasant float.

Coosawattee River

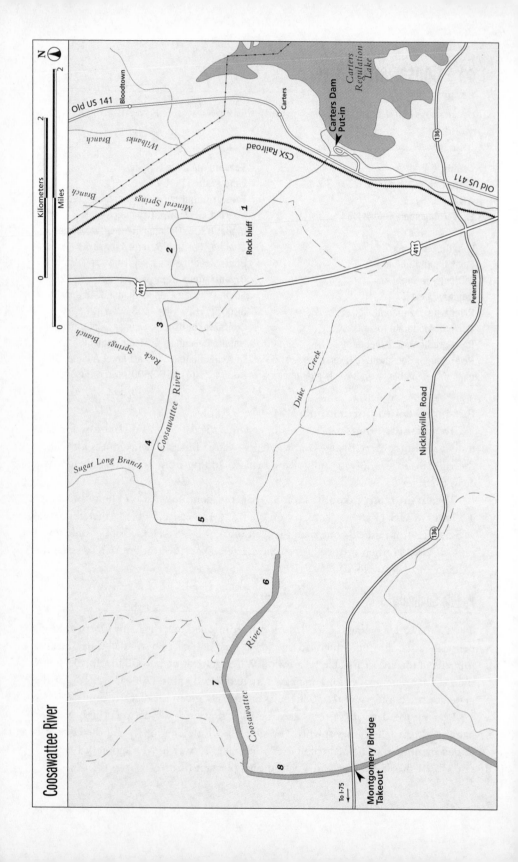

River Overview

The Coosawattee is formed near Ellijay. This upper section of river then flows westerly 9.0 miles through Class I–II rapids to enter Carters Lake. Beneath these waters lies the Coosawattee River Gorge, which had some superlative whitewater rapids. However, because the river had a tendency to flood the towns of Rome and Calhoun after it left the gorge, it was damned in 1974. This paddle begins below the regulation reservoir of Carters Lake, where the Coosawattee offers 25.0 miles of pastoral floating before meeting the Conasauga River to form the Oostanaula River.

The Paddling

Unfortunately there is no ramp at the dam; however, it is but a short carry down riprap to the water's edge. Leave the dam recreation area. The dam is right behind you in a pool area where anglers line the shore to fish. Just ahead, a pair of bridges and a pair of shoals immediately greet paddlers. The river narrows to 30 feet at the second shoal, just below the railroad bridge. The clear, greenish Coosawattee settles down and is about 80 feet wide. The banks are relatively steep, rising 30 to 40 feet above the river. Ash, sycamore, walnut, and river birch grow along the banks and overhang the watercourse. Brush and vines spread to the water's edge into and atop some trees.

Downed trees below the dam don't stay in midriver for long, as occasional higher dam releases force them toward the shoreline. At 1.0 mile the river alters its northwesterly course, veering north past a stark rock bluff. Shortly pass under a power line at 1.3 miles, just after Wilbur Branch comes in on the right. Mineral Springs Branch flows in on river-right as the Coosawattee curves west, its primary direction on this river stretch.

Occasional rocks line the shore but pose little obstacle. Downed trees are much more frequent. An occasional picnic shelter or house borders the river, but the steep mud-and-brush banks do not lend themselves to accessing the stream, discouraging riverside use of the Coosawattee. However, there are enough rock and gravel bars to avail a paddler stop. At 2.5 miles pass under the US 411 bridge on a curve. Here the river is making a nearly 180-degree turn before resuming a westerly direction. Make a relatively long western straightaway as Rock Springs Branch shyly flows into the Coosawattee. Fields extend beyond a corridor of trees in places.

At 4.3 miles Sugar Long Branch streams in clear just above a small shoal. Submerged logs border the river and are easily visible just beneath the water line. The Coosawattee makes a turn to the south at 4.7 miles. The banks rise and the river constricts. Tree snags become more frequent, too. Duke Creek enters on river-left at 5.5 miles, before the river resumes its westerly course. Bluffs rise on the left bank beyond Duke Creek. This steep north-facing hillside displays interesting ferns, rhododendron, and mosses.

At 7.7 miles the Coosawattee makes a sharp turn to the south and flows swiftly from there. Just as the Highway 136 bridge comes into view, look for the abutments

of an old bridge on the right bank, one of which is still standing. Pass a few houses before reaching the takeout just beyond the bridge on river-right at 8.6 miles.

RESTORING THE LAKE STURGEON Historically present in the Coosa River basin, of which the Coosawattee River is a part, the lake sturgeon disappeared in the late 1960s. Once ranging from Canada south throughout the Midwest and Mississippi Valley to the Coosa Basin, the present lake sturgeon population is less than 1 percent of its pre-1900 size. Habitat loss, pollution, and overfishing were its demise in the Coosawattee. But today the lake sturgeon is on the way back.

In 2002 the Georgia Department of Natural Resources (DNR) made its first release of sturgeon fingerlings into the Oostanula River, another Coosa River tributary. The twenty-year restoration effort began with eggs from Wisconsin (so don't be surprised if the lake sturgeon talk funny; they may learn to talk Southern eventually). In 2003 lake sturgeon were released into the Coosawattee River. The Georgia DNR hopes to establish a self-reproducing population of lake sturgeon to not only rebalance the ecosystem but also provide a sport fishery. To this end, more than 41,000 fingerlings have been released.

Lake sturgeons are bottom feeders and use their mouths to suck up food such as insect larvae, worms, leeches, snails, and small clams. They can live more than 200 years and grow to 6 feet in length. Anglers have reported seeing or catching lake sturgeons, so the prospects are good. Anglers catching a sturgeon should release it immediately and report their catch to the DNR to help them evaluate the restoration effort.

◀ *A paddler floats past a large rock outcrop.*

9 Etowah River

The intimate Etowah courses through Dawson State Forest, availing a protected corridor with mountain scenery and vegetation along banks 10 to 15 feet high.

County: Dawson
Start: Highway 9 N34° 21' 27.5", W84° 6' 48.1"
End: Kelly Bridge Road N34° 21' 9.6", W84° 12' 21.4"
Length: 9.5 miles
Float time: 5 hours
Difficulty rating: Easy
Rapids: Class I–I+
River type: Creek float on intimate, clear-green waterway in state forest
Current: Moderate
River gradient: 4.7 feet per mile
River gauges: Etowah River at Highway 9 near Dawsonville; minimum runnable level 110 cfs
Season: March to November

Land status: Public–Dawson State Forest
Fees or permits: No fees or permits required
Nearest city/town: Dawsonville, Georgia
Maps: USGS: Coal Mountain, Matt; DeLorme: *Georgia Atlas and Gazetteer,* page 20; Dawson State Forest map
Boats used: Canoes, a few kayaks, occasional johnboats
Organizations: Upper Etowah River Alliance, Route 2, Box 104, Eastanollee, GA 30538; www.etowahriver.org; e-mail: info@etowahriver.org
Contacts/outfitters: Georgia Department of Natural Resources, Dawson State Forest, 2150 Dawsonville Highway, Gainesville, GA 30501; (770) 535-5700; www.gatrees.org

Put-in/takeout information:

To takeout: From the junction of Highways 400 and 369 north of Cumming, take Highway 369 west toward Coal Mountain for 1 mile to Highway 9. Turn right and follow Highway 9 north for 5.4 miles, then turn left onto A. T. Moore Road, just after crossing into the Dawson County line. After 0.7 mile A. T. Moore Road becomes Kelly Bridge Road. Continue on Kelly Bridge Road. Go for a total of 6.4 miles to reach the put-in on your right past the bridge over the Etowah. It is a private fee launch with gate.

To put-in from takeout: Backtrack on Kelly Bridge Road/A. T. Moore Road to Highway 9. Turn left and take Highway 9 north for 1.7 miles to the bridge over the Etowah. Park on the right-hand side before the bridge crossing, and take the trail right and downhill to a gravel bar launch. (*NOTE:* Stay tuned—another launch will be built at the park about 0.5 mile north of the river on your left.) If you cross the bridge and go to the left, a sometimes-muddy dirt path leads down to another gravel bar and put-in.

Paddle Summary

This is one of the best paddles in North Georgia. The tree-canopied, clear-green waters drop gently over rocks, riffles, and logs, with no rough rapids. Since this is state land, canoe camping is a possibility.

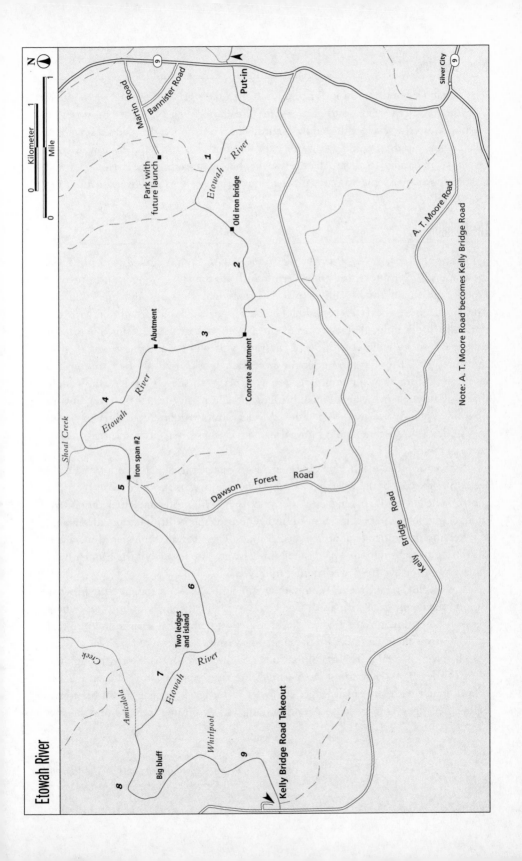

Etowah River

N

0 1 Kilometer

0 1 Mile

Martin Road

Bannister Road

9

Put-in

Park with future launch

1

Etowah River

Old iron bridge

2

Silver City

9

A. T. Moore Road

Note: A. T. Moore Road becomes Kelly Bridge Road

Abutment

3

Etowah River

Concrete abutment

4

Shoal Creek

Iron span #2

5

Dawson Forest Road

Kelly Bridge Road

6

Two ledges and island

Etowah River

7

Amicalola Creek

Whirlpool

Big bluff

8

9

Kelly Bridge Road Takeout

River Overview

The tributaries of the Etowah River drain North Georgia near Springer Mountain. The Etowah then heads south, leaving the Chattahoochee National Forest before turning westerly, where this paddle begins. The river above this paddle has some challenging rapids, including Etowah Falls. Beyond this paddle, the Etowah travels almost 50 miles to meet Allatoona Lake, before breaking free once again and continuing westerly for 50 more miles to meet the Oostanaula River, forming the Coosa River.

The Paddling

The Etowah is narrow—30 or 40 feet wide—with high, wooded banks of sand, rock, and soil. Sycamore, ash, and river birch shade the river, along with ironwood. Beard cane forms thick walls in places. Occasional clearings and breaks in the canopy brighten the river corridor. The few upstream sandbars glitter with the pyrite, or fool's gold, characteristic of the North Georgia mountains. This upper stretch has rocky riffles, but most of the time you will be dodging trees fallen in the water. At 1.8 miles pass under the iron framework of an old one-lane bridge over a long-forgotten logging road. You will begin to see why this is the paddle that time forgot—many abandoned bridges and abutments border the river, now in disuse and grown over with vegetation. Modern infrastructure does intrude as you pass under a power line and a railroad bridge. Despite their presence, the scenery remains remote.

Pass yet another old bridge abutment. These are large concrete ones, about 40 feet, on both sides of the river. Just beyond here, the river makes a curve to the right (north). The left bank rises high and rocky, adorned with mountain laurel, rhododendron, doghobble, and beech trees—all indigenous to the North Georgia mountains. Pass yet another concrete abutment at 3.3 miles. The Etowah curves northwest, and the setting remains remote. The deadfalls in the water are fewer, but the paddler must remain wary for live trees overhanging the river.

At 4.4 miles Shoal Creek, a mountain stream, flows clear and cool into the Etowah. Beyond the confluence with Shoal Creek, the river shortly passes an iron span where Dawson Forest Road once crossed the Etowah. Just below that span, a multiuse trail fords the river then continues on the right-hand bank.

The river maintains its gorgeous setting, now heading southwesterly through the heart of the 10,000-acre forest. At 6.4 miles the river turns northwest then reaches a small island with two small ledges. At lower water levels, a small gravel bar forms below the ledges. This could be a good sunning and swimming spot. Beyond the two

Paddling shallows on the Etowah ▶
Courtesy of Jessica Taylor

ledges the river narrows somewhat. Attractive boulders protrude from the water and along the banks.

At 7.3 miles Amicalola Creek comes in on your right, about 25 feet wide. The confluence of Amicalola Creek, which has Georgia's highest falls (more than 700 feet), and the Etowah is as calm and undramatic as the descent of Amicalola Falls is loud and remarkable. Here the Etowah widens to 80 feet before narrowing again. At 8.2 miles you pass a massive bluff on your right, bursting skyward from the stream. At 8.8 miles a pair of large boulders stretches across the river, creating a riffle, whirlpool, and large gravel bar. Large gray outcroppings continue, but the sounds of Kelly Bridge Road soon echo across the river, ending the float at 9.5 miles.

ETOWAH MOUNDS West of this paddle, near the confluence of the Etowah River and Pumpkinvine Creek, are the Etowah Mounds. This area was home to Georgia aboriginals from A.D. 1000 to A.D. 1550. Now preserved as Etowah Mounds State Park, this fifty-four-acre preserve is said to be the most intact Mississippian culture site in the Southeast. Just a small portion of the site has been excavated, but much has been learned.

The Etowah Mounds symbolize a society rich in ritual. Towering over the community, the 63-foot flat-topped earthen knoll was used as a platform for the home of the priest-chief. In another mound, nobility were buried in elaborate costumes accompanied by items they would need in their afterlives. Today you can visit the six earthen mounds, a plaza, village area, borrow pits, and a defensive ditch. Many artifacts at the park museum show how the natives of this political and religious center decorated themselves with shell beads, tattoos, paint, complicated hairdos, feathers, and copper ear ornaments. Well-preserved stone effigies and objects made of wood, seashells, and stone are also displayed.

10 Metro Hooch

This urban section of the Chattahoochee River flows through the heart of greater Atlanta.

County: Cobb, Fulton
Start: Johnson Ferry N33° 56' 45.1", W84° 24' 16.3"
End: Paces Mill N33° 52' 13.4", W84° 27' 12.1"
Length: 6.5 miles
Float time: 3 hours
Difficulty rating: Moderate
Rapids: Class I–I+
River type: Cool, fast-moving urban river
Current: Mostly swift
River gradient: 5.6 feet per mile
River gauge: Chattahoochee River above Roswell; no minimum runnable level; maximum runnable level, flood stage
Season: March to October
Land status: Public—Chattahoochee National River; private

Fees or permits: Parking fee at put-in and takeout
Nearest city/town: Sandy Springs, Georgia
Maps: USGS: Sandy Springs, Northwest Atlanta; DeLorme: *Georgia Atlas and Gazetteer*, page 20
Boats used: Canoes, kayaks, rafts, tubes
Organizations: Upper Chattahoochee Riverkeeper, 3 Puritan Mill, 916 Joseph Lowery Boulevard, Atlanta, GA 30318; (404) 352-9828; www.ucriverkeeper.org
Contacts/outfitters: High Country Outfitters, 3906-B Roswell Road, Atlanta, GA 30342; (404) 814-0999; www.highcountryoutfitters.com

Put-in/takeout information:

To takeout: From Atlanta take Interstate 75 north to Interstate 285 west. Once on I-285 west, take exit 259 for Cobb Parkway, Dobbins Air Force Base. Turn left and head south on Cobb Parkway (U.S. Highway 41) for 1.5 miles and then turn right into the Chattahoochee River National Recreation Area—Palisades West, Paces Mill. Follow the road under Cobb Parkway to reach the parking area. You'll see a nice launch here. A parking fee is required.

To put-in from takeout: Return to US 41 and follow it north. Backtrack to I-285, and take I-285 east for 4.4 miles to exit 24, Riverside Drive. Turn left onto Riverside Drive, and travel 2.3 miles to Johnson Ferry Road. Turn left onto Johnson Ferry Road and follow it 0.2 mile, bridging the Chattahoochee, then turn right into the recreation area. A parking fee is required. When pulling in you'll enter a parking area; turn right into a gravel turnaround and unloading area. There is a picnic pavilion at the put-in.

Paddle Summary

Before imagining all the negativity that could go with the name "Metro Hooch," understand that much of the river corridor here is protected as part of the Chattahoochee

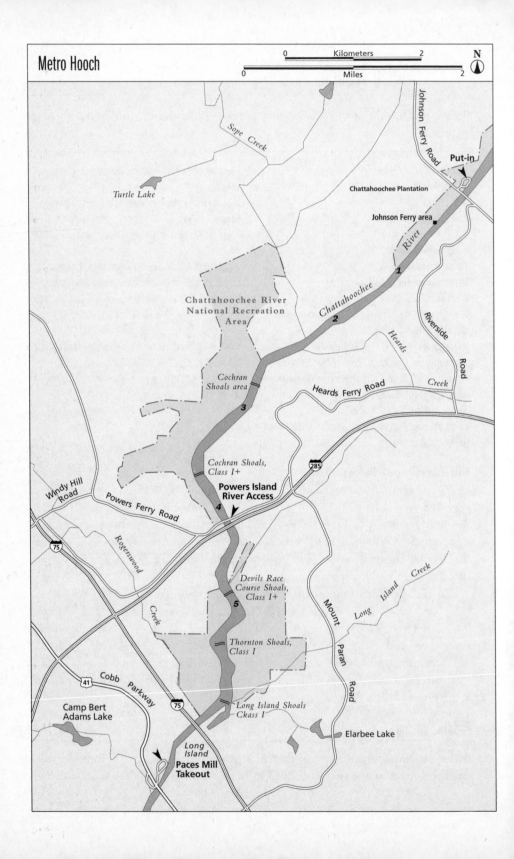

Metro Hooch

Kilometers
0   2
0   2
Miles

N

Sope Creek

Turtle Lake

Johnson Ferry Road

Put-in

Chattahoochee Plantation

Johnson Ferry area

Chattahoochee River

1

Chattahoochee River National Recreation Area

Chattahoochee

2

Heards

Riverside Road

Creek

Heards Ferry Road

Cochran Shoals area

3

285

Windy Hill Road

Powers Ferry Road

Cochran Shoals, Class I+

Powers Island River Access

4

75

Rogerswood

Devils Race Course Shoals, Class I+

5

Long Island Creek

Mount Paran Road

Thornton Shoals, Class I

Creek

Cobb Parkway

41

75

Camp Bert Adams Lake

Long Island Shoals Ckass I

Elarbee Lake

Long Island

Paces Mill Takeout

National River—a federal recreation area that not only provides launching facilities and protected corridor but also hiking trails and picnic areas that provide a wonderful outdoor recreation haven for greater Atlanta. This float leaves Johnson Ferry Road as the Chattahoochee heads south, traveling quickly before entering a large tract of protected land and passing Cochran Shoals. The cool river then passes under I-285 and comes to the second tract, a large public parcel that has the largest collection of rapids, adding some spice to the surprisingly fast paddle.

River Overview

The Chattahoochee starts as a mere spring in the mountains, but by the time it is released from Lake Lanier, and the beginning of this paddle, it is a significant waterway. After passing through Atlanta, it is a bona fide big river and is changing from mountain stream to a flatland waterway that forms the border between Georgia and Alabama. It is the most important waterway in the Peach State, providing not only recreation but also drinking water and transportation.

The Paddling

This used to be a much more popular paddle, but an unfair rap of poor water quality has kept people off it in recent years. Yes, the water quality may suffer after a big rain with excessive urban runoff, but under normal conditions it is just fine. Trout live here, and for me that is sufficient ground for paddling.

Leave the put-in. Notice how cool the water is here—the discharge from Buford Dam still keeps the water chilly, even 37 miles downstream. Immediately pass under the Johnson Ferry Road bridge. The river is more than 100 feet wide at this point. It is well forested, clear, and attractive, with public land on river-right. River birch, ash, and sycamore overhang the river, which is mostly open to the sun. Oaks cover the higher ground. Since this is an urban area, you may see some litter, but it is surprisingly clean overall. Waterweeds grow in the mostly swift current, which tends to boil in places but poses no hazard.

If looking on the left bank you can see rock bluffs beyond the wooded shoreline. Paddling is an option here, as the river keeps you moving without stroking. Cool breezes drift off the chilly water, moderating a hot summer day and sometimes producing fog as well. You'll pass some fine riverfront homes where the land is private. At 2.2 miles Sope Creek comes in on river-right and Heards Creek comes in on the left. The river has been keeping an almost due southwest course. Sope Creek flows over a little concrete dam, making a splashy sound.

The Chattahoochee briefly slackens as it curves to the left, then back to the right, and then widens, availing views of office buildings beyond the heavily wooded river corridor. Small streams continue to feed the Hooch and warm its waters. Bluffs once again rise from the river on the left. You will likely see hikers on the riverside trails in this large tract of the Chattahoochee River National

Geese and anglers share the river with paddlers near Cochran Shoals.

Recreation Area. This is known as the Cochran Shoals area. At 4.2 miles the river travels over Cochran Shoals, a Class I+ rapid. The wide river offers multiple routes. Ahead, more-modern elements reveal themselves as cell towers rise from the greenery. As you pass the Powers Island river access on the left, steps rise from the river and are easily visible.

At 4.6 miles pass under the I-285 bridge and two other parallel bridges. Signs urge you to stay in the middle channel of these three bridges. Despite the noise of the bridge, the Chattahoochee River stays beautiful and sports more rock bluffs on river-left below the bridge. Pass a few small islands on river-right before reaching the Class I+ Devils Race Course Shoals. The best chute is on the far right. A nice sand beach on river-right beckons a stop. The rest of the paddle is entirely within a protected corridor. Beautiful wooded hills rise from the watercourse. Class I Thornton Shoals flows ahead. The rapid is a straight shot down the middle. You will see a second beach here below Thornton Shoals.

Long Island Shoals, also Class I, comes on a curve at the head of Long Island. Most paddlers go around the left side of the island, where Long Island Creek is coming in. Long Island has a tall rock bluff in the middle. Attractive sheer bluffs, sometimes used as a river-jumping platform, continue below the shoals. This may be the most scenic part of the paddle.

Pass under the I-75 bridge, navigating mild shoals. Stay right here—the takeout is forthcoming. The Paces Mill area has been rehabilitated and offers a fine takeout as well as hiking trails, picnic areas, and restrooms. The takeout is on river-right.

URBAN RECREATION In the early 1970s Georgians realized that the city of Atlanta was lucky to have a river as beautiful as the Chattahoochee running within its confines. They understood the importance of the river as a source of drinking water for the growing metropolis. They also saw the early signs of pollution in the river and had the foresight to seek public protection for its preservation.

In 1978 Congress responded, and President Jimmy Carter signed a bill creating the Chattahoochee River National Recreation Area. The combination of its scenic vistas, urban location, geologic features, and biodiversity fit the standards for establishment of a federal recreation area. Having a Georgian as president certainly helped the process along.

The Chattahoochee River National Recreation Area stretches along 48 river miles, with fourteen land units along the riverbanks. It begins at Lake Lanier's Buford Dam near Buford, Georgia, and continues downstream through four counties to Peachtree Creek near downtown Atlanta, where this paddle ends. More than three million visitors a year utilize the recreation area, not only for paddling but also for fishing, hiking, picnicking, and simply enjoying nature in the city. The recreation area is an important resource for greater Atlanta and becomes even more valuable as the city continues to expand.

11 Tallapoosa River

This river, paddled almost exclusively by locals, winds through hills near the Alabama state line.

County: Haralson
Start: Steadman Road N33° 46' 39.1", W85° 18' 34.0"
End: Liner Road Bridge N33° 44' 13.5", W85° 20' 21.4"
Length: 7.6 miles
Float time: 4 hours
Difficulty rating: Easy
Rapids: Class I
River type: Wooded valley river
Current: Slow to moderate
River gradient: 3 feet per mile
River gauge: Tallapoosa River Below Tallapoosa; minimum runnable level 100 cfs
Season: March to October

Land status: Private
Fees or permits: No fees or permits required
Nearest city/town: Tallapoosa, Georgia
Maps: USGS: Tallapoosa North, Tallapoosa South; DeLorme: *Georgia Atlas and Gazetteer*, page 24
Boats used: Canoes, kayaks, johnboats
Organizations: Georgia River Network, 126 South Milledge Avenue, Suite E3, Athens, GA 30605; (706) 549-4508; www.garivers.org
Contacts/outfitters: Georgia Department of Natural Resources, 2 Martin Luther King Jr. Drive SE, Suite 1252 East Tower, Atlanta, GA 30334; (404) 656-3500; www.gadnr.org

Put-in/takeout information:

To takeout: From exit 5 on Interstate 20 take Highway 100 north for 5 miles to the town of Tallapoosa. From the town square in Tallapoosa, take U.S. Highway 78 west for 3 miles, going over the bridge on the Tallapoosa River. Turn left at Liner Road, and follow it over the railroad tracks to the takeout, beyond the tracks on your right just over the bridge over the Tallapoosa River.

To put-in from takeout: Backtrack on Liner Road, then take US 78 east to the town of Tallapoosa to reach Highway 100 north. Turn left onto Highway 100 north toward Cedartown; travel 1.5 miles, then veer left onto Steadman Road. Follow Steadman Road for 1.2 miles. The put-in is on your left just after the river bridge.

Paddle Summary

After paddling the Tallapoosa it's hard to decide whether it is a mountain river with Piedmont characteristics or a Piedmont river trying to act like a mountain waterway. The Tallapoosa flows over gravel and past rock outcrops aplenty through a wooded corridor. Gentle riffles and occasional shoals keep the river moving, but overall it is quite easy to paddle. There is very little development along the banks. Starting at Steadman Road near the town of Tallapoosa, the river begins its winding journey south and west, picking up a few feeder branches before reaching US 78. Here the river nearly doubles back upon itself before the paddle ends at the Liner Road bridge.

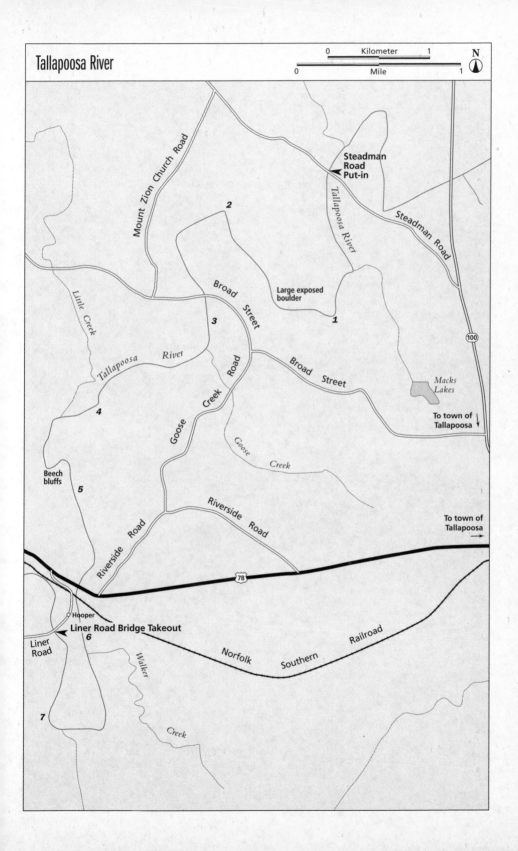

Tallapoosa River

0   Kilometer   1

0   Mile   1

N

Mount Zion Church Road

Steadman Road Put-in

Steadman Road

Tallapoosa River

2

Broad Street

Large exposed boulder

1

Little Creek

3

Tallapoosa River

Broad Street

100

Macks Lakes

Goose Creek Road

4

Goose Creek

To town of Tallapoosa

Beech bluffs

5

Riverside Road

Riverside Road

To town of Tallapoosa

78

Hooper

Liner Road Bridge Takeout

Walker

Norfolk Southern Railroad

Liner Road

6

7

Creek

River Overview

The Tallapoosa River starts not too far east of this paddle, coming out of the hills of Paulding County. It then flows westerly into Haralson County, becoming paddleable near Draketown. The waterway then keeps westerly, coming near the town of Tallapoosa, where this paddle begins.

Just before leaving the state of Georgia, the Tallapoosa enters extremely hilly terrain, torturously winding its way toward Alabama as it offers more than 30 miles of paddling pleasure in the Peach State. It leaves Georgia, where it flows west then south into Harris Reservoir. Below this dam the waterway continues south and west, passing Horseshoe Bend National Military Park. Beyond the battlefield site the river is dammed again as Lake Martin. The river leaves the lake to meet the Coosa River, which also starts in Georgia. Here the Coosa and the Tallapoosa form the Alabama River in Montgomery.

The Paddling

The put-in can be tough. I suggest going from the far left downstream side as you drive in and carrying your boat to the bridge to work it down the steep bank and under the bridge. The river has a brownish tint and a rock-and-gravel bottom. It is clear more often than not but will easily mud up after a rain. White mussel shells are scattered in the bottom of the river and contrast with the darker rocks. A rich thicket of trees overhang the river and form a shady cathedral. Fallen trees will be obstacles in places, but you can usually get around them. Unfortunately, the Tallapoosa seems to have a little bit more litter than your average river. Despite the visual trash, the river's health seems to be very good, as evidenced by the plethora of mussel shells.

Sycamore, oak, and river birch rise from the steeply sloped brushy banks about 15 feet above the river. The waterway is about 30 to 40 feet wide at this point, and the current is slow to moderate. Gravel bars are plentiful at lower water. The river makes its first big bend at 1.0 mile, exposing rock bluffs. The rapids are Class I riffles that break up long shady pools. Pass a large house on river-left as the Tallapoosa makes a hard right. Habitations along this part of the river are very infrequent. Mountain laurel grows on these bends. Notice on the river's edge where the rock is undercut by the flowing water. Vines and brush grow thick along the banks where trees allow sunlight.

The banks often rise higher, and rock rises with the banks. At 1.4 miles a notable outcrop rises on river-left 30 or 40 feet above the stream surface. Reach the Broad Street Bridge at 2.8 miles. This bridge is likely to have trees piled up against its supports, so be careful upon approach. When high water hits the Tallapoosa River, fallen

◄ Upstream view of the Tallapoosa

trees flow downstream to rest against these bridges. There is a small shoal below the bridge.

Pass more rock outcrops on river-left. Within these outcrops, crevices, and overhangs are microhabitats of ferns and mosses. Goose Creek comes in on your left just beyond these outcrops. More riffles are scattered between longer pools. Rocks and rock shelves continue to line the Tallapoosa in many places. A quiet and alert paddler will see deer and birdlife in this valley. Beech trees rise in the shadiest narrows. The beauty of the waterway seems incongruous with the trash, such as old cars. However, it simply reflects a bygone era, when rivers were seen as dumps.

Little Creek comes in on river-right at 4.3 miles. Where rock bluffs rise, the Tallapoosa often narrows to 20 feet or less. At 4.7 miles the waterway is particularly attractive. Beech trees grow on a mossy bluff with many rock outcrops as the river makes a hard curve to the left then to the right.

The river finally straightens out and slows down after its meanderings before heading almost due south for the US 78 bridge. Big boulders continue to expose themselves, culminating in a large boulder garden just above the US 78 bridge, which you'll pass under at 5.7 miles. Just ahead you will see the Norfolk Southern Railroad trestle. This is where many locals put in to paddle the river for 1.8 miles, as the Tallapoosa almost doubles back on itself and eliminates the need for a shuttle, taking out on the Liner Road bridge, where this paddle ends. Look for the pilings of abandoned bridges in the area as well. If you really dislike the paddle, take out here—Liner Road is just beyond the trestle—and walk down to your vehicle. A small shoal flows under the railroad trestle.

The Tallapoosa continues south before making its convoluted course back to the north and the Liner Road bridge. Just ahead, Walker Creek comes in on your left. By now the Tallapoosa has widened but is still mostly canopied by a primeval forest. Come alongside a steep bluff before making a loping curve to the right. The bluffs soon peter out. A small branch comes in on your left just before the river makes its final turn, this time to the north, aiming for Liner Road bridge.

Float through a pair of small, noisy ledges where the stream narrows. The Tallapoosa widens and moderates on its final stretch. Reach the Liner Road bridge at 7.6 miles. The takeout is on your left beyond the bridge. Be careful when approaching this bridge; like the other bridges on the Tallapoosa, it has been logjammed in the past. This takeout is steep as well, but it is easier than Steadman Road.

RARE RIVER SPECIES When floating this river, you are in rare company. And I'm not talking about other paddlers. Five fish species, two crayfish species, and one aquatic snail species are endangered, occurring here and nowhere else on Earth. The Tallapoosa River and its sister stream, the Little Tallapoosa River, drain the extreme western portion of the state near Interstate 20. These two streams meet in the state of Alabama. The total river basin of the Tal-

lapoosa River is 4,680 square miles. Only 15 percent of this drainage is in Georgia. However, these waterways on the uppermost Tallapoosa basin are biologically very important. For starters, these two streams are free flowing while in the Peach State, which is important to the health of the rare river species.

During your paddle, you doubtless saw the many mussels on this river. One of these, *Lampsilis altilis*, is federally listed as threatened. The fish native only to the upper Tallapoosa basin are the lipstick darter, Muscadine darter, Tallapoosa shiner, Tallapoosa sculpin, and Tallapoosa darter. Since they are nongame species, these fish often are overlooked, and their very existence is virtually unknown to the public. Thus it is usually up to biologists and researchers to get the word out about these species, which compose about 8 percent of the native fish in the Tallapoosa. But now you know a little bit about the unique species that inhabit this Georgia waterway.

12 Toccoa River Canoe Trail

The Toccoa River Canoe Trail is designated by the Chattahoochee National Forest—much of the river here flows within the national forest's boundaries.

County: Fannin
Start: Deep Hole Campground N34° 44' 21.2", W84° 8' 29.1"
End: Sandy Bottoms N34° 47' 10.0", W84° 14' 23.9"
Length: 13.7 miles
Float time: 6 hours
Difficulty rating: Moderate
Rapids: Class I–II
River type: Forest-lined mountain river
Current: Moderate to swift
River gradient: 13 feet per mile
River gauge: Toccoa River at Dial; minimum runnable level 210 cfs; water-level information: www.tva.com or (800) 238-2264, press 3
Season: March to October
Land status: Public—Chattahoochee National Forest; private

Fees or permits: Parking fees at put-in and takeout
Nearest city/town: Blue Ridge, Georgia
Maps: USGS Noontoola, Wilscot; DeLorme: *Georgia Atlas and Gazetteer*, page14; USDA Forest Service: Chattahoochee National Forest; Toccoa River Canoe Trail (www.fs.fed.us/conf)
Boats used: Canoes, kayaks, tubes
Organizations: Chattahoochee National Forest, 1755 Cleveland Highway, Gainesville, GA 30501; (770) 297-3000; www.fs.fed.us/conf/
Contacts/outfitters: Jon Ron Toccoa River Outfitters, 7222 Aska Road, Blue Ridge, GA 30513-5509; (866) 857-8758; www.jonrontro.com

Put-in/takeout information:

To takeout: At the intersection of Highways 515 and 5, near the McDonalds in Blue Ridge, take Highway 515 east for 0.7 mile to Windy Ridge Road. Turn right

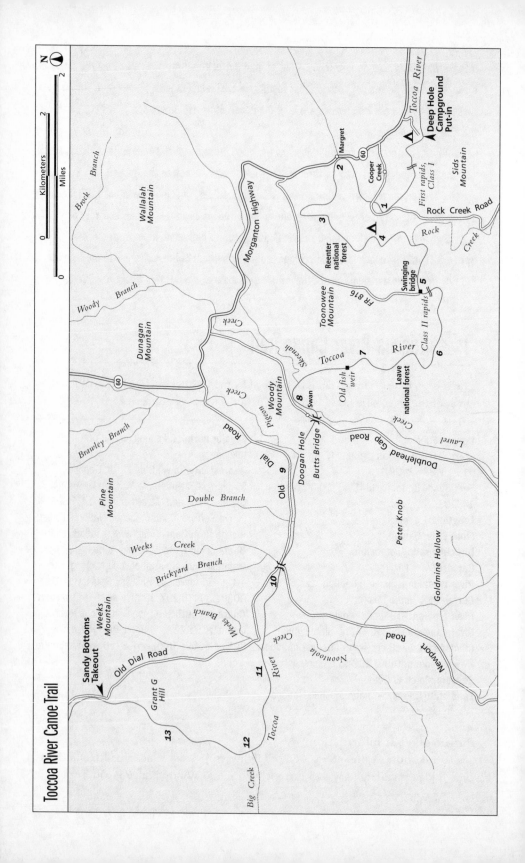

Toccoa River Canoe Trail

onto Windy Ridge Road and follow it for 0.1 mile, then turn left on the Old U.S. Highway 76. Follow Old US 76 for 0.2 mile, then turn right onto Aska Road. Follow Aska Road for 8.6 miles, turning left onto Shallowford Bridge Road. Cross the Toccoa River; stay right on Shallowford Bridge Road, following it for 1.3 miles, then turn right onto Old Dial Road. Follow Old Dial Road for 0.7 mile to the takeout on your right. There is currently a parking fee. The parking area has a boat launch, garbage cans, a restroom, and some fee campsites

To put-in from takeout: Continue on Old Dial Road, reaching Highway 60 after 5.2 miles. Turn right onto Highway 60 and follow it for 4.5 miles. Turn right into Deep Hole Campground. The boat ramp is on the back side of the campground.

Paddle Summary

Starting at Deep Hole Campground, the Toccoa makes its run through the mountains—flowing clear past boulders, through long pools, and beside towering forests. Part of the float travels through private land, much of which is mountain cabin developments that make it clear that you must pass through their section without stopping. However, since most of the land is public, fishing, hiking, and camping are favorite options. Despite the seemingly steep gradient of 13 feet per mile, the river rapids can be handled by most paddlers. If 13.0 miles seems a bit long for you, the Forest Service has a public takeout 8.3 miles downstream from Deep Hole Campground.

River Overview

The Toccoa River begins in the North Georgia mountains, flowing off the Blue Ridge and gathering volume in the many springs and creeks below the Appalachian Trail. Here much of the river flows through the Chattahoochee National Forest before being damned near the town of Blue Ridge. The river is then freed again, continuing northwest. It enters the state of Tennessee, where it goes under another name—the Ocoee River. In the Volunteer State the Ocoee River is one of the Southeast's famed whitewater destinations. Here the river is also dammed in places, but finally it is unleashed to meekly flow into the Tennessee River.

The Paddling

Leave the launch and immediately flow over a small shoal. The forest is gorgeous here; rhododendron and mountain laurel line the banks, while oaks, maples, and imperiled hemlocks overhang the trout stream. White pines tower above all. The water is translucent under normal conditions, and the rock bottom is visible. You shortly leave national forestlands on a left curve. Private land along the Toccoa River is being developed at a rapid rate.

At this point the river is 30 to 40 feet wide. Fine cabins are situated overlooking the river in places. Large rock outcrops line the Toccoa. At low-water times, small sandbars form. At 1.2 miles a rock-lined rapid flows above the Rock Creek Bridge.

Several smaller shoals follow the bridge. Enter a development, which allows passage of your craft but not fishing. At 1.9 miles come along Highway 60 at some shoals. This area is known as Margret and is a wide, flat valley where you can gain mountain views.

Occasional small islands reveal themselves. The rapids are formed where narrow upright rocks seemingly block the passage of the Toccoa. Leaving Margret, the waterway makes a 180-degree turn from north to south, reentering national forest property at 3.4 miles. The boundary is posted with signs. The completely wooded corridor resumes. At 3.8 miles pass a campsite on river-right as the Toccoa River curves to the right. The campsite is an alluring flat under dark, imperiled hemlock woods. A pair of small ledges follows the camping flat.

At 4.4 miles Rock Creek comes in on your left. A large, heavily used camping area stands at the confluence. Beyond here the Toccoa has many lively but easy shoals. At 5.0 miles the Benton McKaye Trail bridge comes into sight. The Benton McKaye Trail starts at Springer Mountain and heads north for more than 250 miles to reach the east end of Smoky Mountains National Park. The trail crosses the Toccoa River here.

The most strenuous rapids of the entire paddle begin at the bridge. You may want to pull over and walk atop the swinging bridge to scout the rapids below. Either way, it is fun to pull over and walk up to the bridge here. Forest Road 816 has come in and ends at the bridge, so you may see anglers and campers here accessing the river by car. These Class II bridge-area rapids require a little maneuvering between a lot of rock and some downed trees and last for approximately 100 yards.

Shoals continue, but at a much more moderate rate. The national forest scenery continues to be stunningly beautiful. Take your time through this section, which offers the best camping. At 6.2 miles the Toccoa turns north to leave national forest-land at 6.6 miles. The riverbanks open up and flatten out somewhat. At 7.2 miles the river passes over an old fish weir.

Scattered cabins occupy the banks. The river keeps its northbound ways and evolves into a pastoral float through level land inside a wooded corridor. Sycamores become more prevalent. Skeenah Creek comes in on river-right at 7.8 miles. Laurel Creek merges on river-left, just before reaching the Butts Bridge and Doublehead Gap Road at 8.3 miles. This is a good takeout if you want to make a shorter day trip.

National forestland resumes on river-left. Pass several small shoals. Pigeon Creek comes in on river-right before the Doogan Hole, a slow deep stretch. The land is national forest on both sides when it comes alongside Dial Road. However, there's no camping between the road and bridge, which is on river-right in this section. Cabins resume after a bit.

At 10.0 miles you'll see the stone pilings of the old Dial Bridge and the newer Dial Bridge just ahead. Notice the old bridge abutments, which were built with stones from the Toccoa. Fields stretch beyond the wooded corridor. At 10.7 miles

Noontoola Creek comes in on river-left. The river widens to 60 to 70 feet, and the Cohutta Mountains are visible ahead. The waterway becomes deep, slow, and open to the sun. At 12.0 miles the Toccoa curves back to the north, passing Big Creek and the Toccoa Valley Campground. From here join national forestland on both sides of the river, which avails your final camping opportunities if you want to stretch your paddle into a two-night trip. This next section is popular with tubers. National forestland is continuous from here to the paddle's end on the right-hand bank. Easy, rocky shoals continue on this final stretch and keep the river moving. One last rapid leads you directly to the takeout on river-right at 13.7 miles.

NAME CHANGES
In the border town of McCaysville, Georgia, the Toccoa River quietly flows from the Peach State into the Volunteer State—and takes on a new name. In Tennessee the river becomes the Ocoee, and thus begins one of the Southeast's prime whitewater destinations. For eons the Ocoee flowed through a rugged gorge, until it was diverted into a wooden flume as part of a power project run by the Tennessee Valley Authority (TVA). In September 1976 the wooden flume had become flimsy and leaky, so the TVA decided to close the flume for reconstruction. Once again the Ocoee River ran free, creating a heart-pounding 5.0-mile stretch of rapids that paddlers began to use.

Initially the river was run by rafters, then kayakers. Word of the exciting whitewater spread, luring river enthusiasts from all over. The flume was reconstructed, and the TVA wanted to continue to divert all the water through the flume all the time. However, paddlers banded together and pressured the TVA into agreeing to schedule water releases on the river. Commercial rafting companies located nearby, and the Ocoee as we know it today was born.

When Atlanta hosted the Centennial Olympic Games in 1996, the Ocoee River was selected as the site for the whitewater Olympic competitions. Today more than 300,000 people per year travel this stretch of river that is born in Georgia's mountains under the name of Toccoa.

Middle Georgia

13 Brier Creek

Brier Creek is a beautiful, often-swift stream that travels through a forest primeval.

County: Screven
Start: U.S. Highway 301 N32° 51' 37.0", W81° 36' 44.9"
End: Brannons Bridge N32° 48' 38.4", W81° 29' 3.2"
Length: 13.4 miles
Float time: 7 hours
Difficulty rating: Moderate to difficult
Rapids: Class I
River type: Canopied creek
Current: Moderate to swift
River gradient: 2.3 feet per mile
River gauge: Brier Creek at Millhaven; minimum runnable level 220 cfs; maximum runnable level, flood stage

Season: March to October
Land status: Private; some public
Fees or permits: No fees or permits required
Nearest city/town: Sylvania, Georgia
Maps: USGS: Jacksonboro Bridge, Brier Creek Landing; DeLorme: *Georgia Atlas and Gazetteer*, page 39
Boats used: Canoes, kayaks, johnboats
Organizations: Savannah Riverkeepers; www.savannahriverkeepers.org
Contacts/outfitters: Georgia Department of Natural Resources, 2 Martin Luther King Jr. Drive SE, Suite 1252 East Tower, Atlanta, GA 30334; (404) 656-3500; www.gadnr.org

Put-in/takeout information:

To takeout: From Sylvania take US 301/Highway 73 north to Highway 24, just outside town. Turn right and take Highway 24 east for 5.2 miles to Brannons Bridge Road. Turn left onto Brannons Bridge Road and follow it for 4.8 miles to the takeout on your left, after the bridge.

To put-in from takeout: Return to US 301. Turn right, away from Sylvania, and proceed on US 301 for 2.7 miles to a right turn toward what seems to be a driveway. Cut left immediately before the gates onto a sand road, and follow it about 200 yards parallel to US 301 to end up at a Georgia DNR boat ramp. This boat ramp is on the west side of the bridge over Brier Creek.

Paddle Summary

Overflow swamps border Brier Creek, which often branches out into multiple channels. Occasional bluffs rise, changing the scenery. Despite the rugged terrain, some cabins are stretched along the stream, but overall they are infrequent and don't rob the atmosphere. Pass many old bridge pilings, remnants of the logging days in this watershed. These will not be the only things sticking out of the water. Falling logs will obstruct the way in places, but do not let this deter you from enjoying this gorgeous canopied creek where silent sloughs, disappearing alligators, screaming woodpeckers, and Spanish moss dripping from the trees add to the primordial effect.

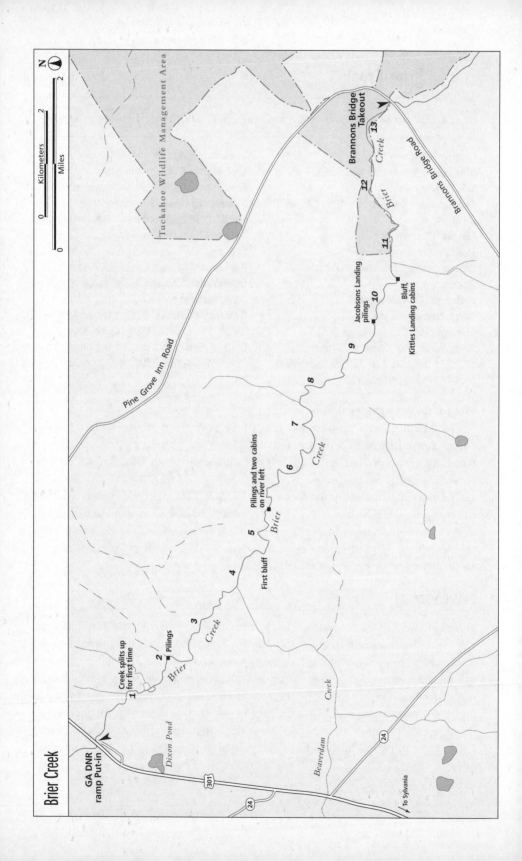

Brier Creek

The author pulls over a blowdown in Brier Creek.

River Overview

Brier Creek is a major tributary stream of the Savannah River. Born west of Augusta, this swampy watercourse heads south and east for a very long distance. It becomes paddleable at high water near Waynesboro. The swampy shores provide a layer of protection that keeps it remote for most of its 55 miles of paddling distance. *NOTE:* An unbending landowner does not allow passage near the community of Millhaven.

The Paddling

Brier Creek is very clear, despite its tannin coloration. The creek is often completely canopied and narrows to as little as 20 feet between big cypress trees from a maximum width of 40 to 50 feet, when it stretches into sandy shallows. Lush vegetation thrives everywhere except for the sandbars and the water itself. Paddling here is a trip through the forest primeval.

Logs obstruct stream in places, but regular use by paddlers and anglers keeps it cut open. The forest is lush with water oaks, cypress, gum, and river birch. Herons and other wading birds are seemingly stationed around every bend. Small tan sandbars gather where they can.

At 0.9 mile Brier Creek divides into numerous islands and channels. When picking the correct channel, look for previously sawn marks on fallen trees. Swift channels and sluggish sloughs continue breaking off the river with regularity. The pilings of an old bridge cross the stream at 2.0 miles. Look for the vestiges of Lambert Road, which once led to the bridge coming in on your left, forming a little grassy landing just beyond these first pilings.

At 3.8 miles spring-fed Beaverdam Creek comes in on your right, and the stream widens to about 40 feet before constricting again. At 4.6 miles Brier Creek comes alongside a wooded bluff on your right then quickly curves away, continuing its numerous twists and turns within a swamp corridor, often traveling over swift, sandy shallows. At 5.3 miles pass two old wooden bridge pilings in succession, along with two cabins on river-left. Watch for more pilings downstream.

Continue a twisting course that keeps mainly east, aiming for the Savannah River. At 6.3 miles come alongside another wooded bluff. Here Brier Creek widens and slows a bit. Note the rock at the waters edge on this bluff, which is topped with a few cabins. The stream continues to break into innumerable channels and then come together again.

Pass another bridge piling near the site of Jacobsons Landing at 9.8 miles. At 10.6 miles come alongside another bluff and some river cabins at Kittles Landing. At 11.0 miles Tuckahoe Wildlife Management Area begins to occupy the left bank. Small metal signs mark the boundary.

At the end of this cabin cluster, the watercourse makes a big bend to the left, passing a wall of riprap and a pine plantation. Continue easterly, passing some open areas on river-right parallel to the wooded river corridor. Reach Brannons Bridge; the takeout is on your left.

BATTLE OF BRIER CREEK
The swamps of Brier Creek and the nearby Savannah River played a role in this March 3, 1779, encounter. American patriots suffered a terrible defeat at the site of this takeout in the Battle of Brier Creek. At this time the Americans controlled Georgia and the British controlled South Carolina, with the Savannah River lying between them. The Americans were attempting to drive the British from Augusta into the swamps of the Georgia coast. But it was the Americans who ended up being caught in the swamps between Brier Creek and the Savannah River as the British outflanked the Americans, first routing them upstream on Brier Creek at Paris Mill.

Most American soldiers fled across into South Carolina at Burtons Ferry on the Savannah River, leaving General Samuel Elbert, for whom Elbert County is named, backed against Brier Creek. Here stood the Freeman-Miller Bridge on the Old Augusta Road.

Elbert was acting as a rear guard for the retreating Americans and was surrounded by British forces. He decided that the only hope for survival was to fight his way through the British lines.

Elbert and the 150 Georgia militiamen then began their fateful charge. All hope was lost when more British reserves came up as the first shots volleyed. Nearly all the Americans were killed, but Elbert was spared just before being bayoneted by giving the sign that he was a Mason.

The American loss at Brier Creek gave the British renewed confidence, but that confidence was due to be shattered at ensuing battles in South Carolina—especially Kings Mountain, which turned the tide of the Revolutionary War for good. It was but six years later that Elbert was elected governor of Georgia.

14 Ebenezer Creek

Ebenezer Creek is an ultrascenic blackwater stream bordered with giant cypress trees.

County: Effingham
Start: Long Bridge boat ramp N32° 22' 44.5", W81° 10' 58.1"
End: Ebenezer Landing N32° 21' 50.1", W81° 13' 50.8"
Length: 6.3 miles
Float time: 3.5 hours
Difficulty rating: Easy
Rapids: None
River type: Blackwater swamp creek
Current: Sluggish, slight tidal influence
River gradient: 0.2 foot per mile
River gauge: Ebenezer Creek at Springfield; no minimum runnable level; runnable year-round

Season: Year-round
Land status: Private
Fees or permits: Fee boat ramp at takeout
Nearest city/town: Springfield, Georgia
Maps: USGS: Rincon, Hardeeville; DeLorme: *Georgia Atlas and Gazetteer,* page 47
Boats used: Kayaks, canoes, fishing skiffs, johnboats
Organizations: Savannah Riverkeepers; www .savannahriverkeepers.org
Contacts/outfitters: Savannah Canoe and Kayak, P.O. Box 5405, Savannah, GA 31414; (912) 341-9502; www.savannahcanoeand kayak.com. Guides trips on Ebenezer Creek.

Put-in/takeout information:

To takeout: From Springfield take Highway 21 south for 4 miles to Highway 275. Turn left onto Highway 275 and follow it for 5.6 miles to dead-end at a private, fee boat ramp on the Savannah River.

To put-in from takeout: Backtrack from the ramp for 3.2 miles on Highway 275 to Long Bridge Road and turn right. Follow Long Bridge Road for 1.1 miles; turn left into the boat ramp before the bridge.

Paddle Summary

Formerly a designated state scenic river, Ebenezer Creek's beauty hasn't changed, just its designation. Normally the tidally influenced current is slack enough to make

Ebenezer Creek

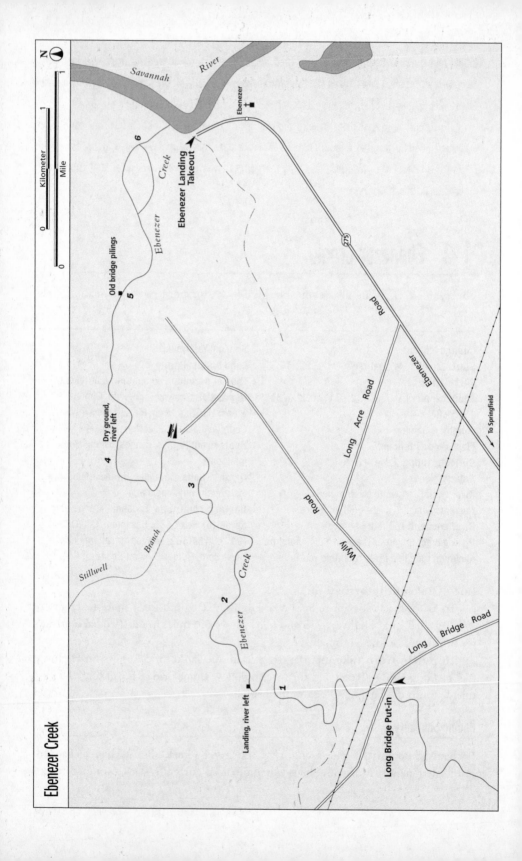

a fairly easy out-and-back paddle, eliminating the need for a shuttle. However, there is no saltwater intrusion. Ebenezer Creek widens and narrows seemingly on whim, sometimes passing under dark, wooded tunnels and other times opening into small lakes. Cabins and houses are scattered along the paddle. The takeout is on the Savannah River, which provides a contrast to the smaller Ebenezer Creek.

River Overview

Ebenezer Creek is a tributary of the lower Savannah River. Born at the confluence of Runs and Turkey Branches north of Springfield, this stream becomes paddleable below the town and offers nearly 20 miles of navigable—at higher water—stream for Peach State paddlers to enjoy.

The Paddling

Leave the boat ramp to paddle under the Long Bridge, joining Ebenezer Creek. The current is slack to nonexistent while passing under a power line. Immediately you can see the gigantic trunks of cypress trees, along with its brethren gum trees. The magnificent cypress trees have accompanying huge cypress knees that protrude from the dark water. Some of cypress trunks are upwards of 10 feet in diameter.

The coffee-colored water stretches about 40 feet from bank to bank but widens often in sloughs. Pine, palmetto, and regal oaks occupy the higher ground. Water grasses such as alligator weed grow on the edges of the channel in places where the water is most still. Duck moss grows in the slower margins atop the water. Wading birds find Ebenezer Creek a fine place to be. At higher waters, Ebenezer Creek will have a completely different character, as the overflow swamps on either side will be inundated. However, the main channel will have flow at these higher waters, making the primary route distinguishable. A GPS loaded with a topo map is not a bad idea here.

At 1.2 miles Ebenezer Creek emerges from a wooded tunnel into a small circular bay before leaving left. Ahead, pass a nice dry landing on river-left. The first houses appear on river-right. The creek opens a bit here then soon narrows again. Pass a couple more houses on river-left and Ebenezer Creek opens again. Cabins are located in some of the higher bluffs—and here were talking 15 feet.

At 2.8 miles Ebenezer Creek opens into a small lake then resumes its channel. Stillwell Branch has come in on the left at this small lake. "Still" is the operative word here, since there is little to no flow in this lake. Depending on the tides that push from the Atlantic Ocean up the Savannah River and into Ebenezer Creek, you may have the stream going against you, with you, or basically neutral. At 3.4 miles pass a public boat ramp on your right. This is off Wylly Road.

Beyond the boat ramp, Ebenezer Creek Lake makes a nearly 180-degree turn to the left and once again narrows. At 4.1 miles pass some dry ground on your left across from a deep tupelo swamp. This makes for a good stopping spot, as unoccupied high ground becomes scarce below here. Just ahead are some cabins on your right.

Ebenezer Creek becomes just a channel with overflow swamps on either side. At 5.0 miles pass the upright pilings of an old bridge in a narrow stretch of river. Beyond here the creek widens again. You know you're getting close when you pass a very high, wooded bluff, in excess of 80 feet, on river-right with houses up top. Another set of bridge pilings stands ahead. Look in the woods on either side of the bridge for the elevated roadbed. Willow trees join the shoreline here. Reach the wide and strong current of the Savannah River as it is making a big turn to the left. You, however, stay on the right shore, reaching Ebenezer Landing at 6.3 miles.

EBENEZER CHURCH
Located near the takeout point for this paddle, Ebenezer Church is the only remaining building from a community of German Salzburgers who settled in Georgia at the suggestion of James Oglethorpe, an early Georgia colonist. Officially known as Jerusalem Evangelical Lutheran Church, this brick structure is purportedly the oldest public building in the state. Built between 1767 and 1769, the church is still actively used. The bricks are made by hand, and you can look up close at them to see the fingerprints left from the brick makers.

Originally from Augsburg, Germany, the congregants who formed the Ebenezer Church were members of St. Ann's Church, which was formed in 1733. The congregation sailed from Holland as religious exiles seeking freedom and landed in Savannah in 1734. This move to a new land was the result of Prince and Archbishop Leopold von Firmian issuing the Edict of Expulsion on October 31, 1731, ordering all Lutherans and Calvinists to leave what is now Germany. They attempted their first colonization upstream on Ebenezer Creek, but the location was too swampy. They moved downstream to higher ground at the confluence of the creek and the Savannah River.

Ebenezer Creek was of strategic importance to Savannah's defense, and the community changed hands several times during the Revolutionary War. After the war it was left in ruins to all but disappear, leaving Ebenezer Church as the only remaining building from the era. You can view the church on your drive to the takeout.

◀ *Slow, swamp-like section of Ebenezer Creek*

15 Flint River near Thomaston

The Flint River is a large, majestic waterway at this point as it flows through the Pine Mountains, a relic Appalachian mountain range.

County: Upson, Talbot
Start: Goat Mountain (outfitter access only) N32° 51' 13.3", W84° 28' 48.7" (Sprewell Bluff State Park put-in)
End: Flint River Outdoor Center N32° 50' 16.8", W84° 25' 23.9"
Length: 11.6 miles
Float time: 6 hours
Difficulty rating: Easy to moderate
Rapids: Class I–II
River type: Wide, rocky river bordered by high ridges
Current: Moderate
River gradient: 10.6 feet per mile
River gauge: Flint River at U.S. Highway19 near Carsonville; minimum runnable level 200 cfs; maximum runnable level, flood stage

Season: March to October
Land status: Public—Sprewell Bluff State Park; private
Fees or permits: Entrance fee if starting at Sprewell Bluff State Park
Nearest city/town: Thomaston, Georgia
Maps: USGS: Woodbury, Sunset Village, Roland; DeLorme: *Georgia Atlas and Gazetteer*, page 33
Boats used: Canoes, kayaks, tubes, johnboats
Organizations: Georgia River Network, 126 South Milledge Avenue, Suite E3, Athens, GA 30605; (706) 549-4508; www.garivers.org
Contacts/outfitters: Flint River Outdoor Center; 4429 Woodland Road, Highway 36 at Flint River, Thomaston, GA 30286; (706) 647-2633

Put-in/takeout information:

To takeout: From the Upson County Courthouse in Thomaston, take Highway 36 west for 8.3 miles to the outfitter on your left, beyond the bridge over the Flint River.

To put-in from takeout: The put-in for this paddle is on private land owned by the outfitter. However, to reach the Sprewell Bluff State Park put-in from the outfitter, backtrack east on Highway 36 for 2 miles, turning left onto Roland Road. Follow Roland Road 2.2 miles to Sprewell Bluff Road. Turn left onto Sprewell Bluff Road and follow it to dead-end at the state park put-in. There is a park entrance fee. *NOTE:* The state park is open Wednesday through Sunday only.

Paddle Summary

The mostly clear waterway flows over a rocky bed, creating shoals and riffles for much of its distance that extend from riverbank to riverbank. River birch and syca-more grow on the banks, with oaks and pine predominant on the hillsides. Attractive rock formations border the river when trees aren't present.

River Overview

The Flint River rivals the Chattahoochee as Georgia's most important big river. From beginning to end, many argue that the Flint is the better for paddlers between the two. Born in a culvert beneath the Atlanta airport, the Flint flows south beyond this inauspicious start, forming county-line boundaries. By the time the Flint reaches the Pine Mountains, it is already a big river.

The river is at its most scenic as it cuts through these mountains. This is also where the most challenging rapids are located, especially if you include the area just below where this paddle ends, namely Class III Yellow Jackets Shoals. At this point the river drops off the fall line before settling down and continuing its southbound journey.

The Flint continues to widen and becomes more convoluted before being backed up at Lake Blackshear. Beyond the impoundment, the river flows to Albany, where it is stalled again, then flows through the town. By this point the Flint is a full-blown, massive waterway as it makes its way to and through Bainbridge before reaching Lake Seminole, near the Georgia, Florida, Alabama borders.

The Paddling

Long Branch, a clear tributary, flows into the Flint River at the put-in. Piney ridges rise from the river, creating quite a scenic area. The waterway is about 200 feet wide at this point and is heavily wooded on both sides. With such a wide river, be prepared to be totally open to the sun and subject to winds. Grassy islands and rocks are exposed above the normally clear water.

The first shoals occur shortly below the put-in. Shoals will often extend for long distances. Rocks are strewn all across the river, and you have to route-find your way through these minor rapids, which are generally easy and have multiple routes. The banks, if not rising to a mountaintop, generally go up just a few feet from the water and then level out in flats. You're looking dead ahead at Rockhouse Mountain while floating downstream. A segment of Sprewell Bluff State Park is on river-right; occasional houses are on the left bank. The Flint continues moving at a steady pace amid the rocks. Sandbars form where small creeks come in and meet the river.

The river makes a long curve to the left at 1.5 miles and makes a pretty fair ledge drop, passed by an open rock slab rising from the river up Rockhouse Mountain. These open rock slabs and sandy shoreline locales beckon you to stop. The river slices between wooded ridges in one continuous, 300-foot-wide rocky shoal bordered by trees. At 3.2 miles reach Pasley Island, which is actually a pair of islands—more at higher water—with the bigger ones on river-left. Multiple channels lead you through Class II Pasley Shoals. Occasional houses dot the river here.

The Flint soon narrows then curves back southwest to make a long straightaway. Mountains continue to rise, creating quite a spectacular scene, since the wide-open waterway allows views of this rising land. At 5.0 miles reach Natural Dam Rapid. Here the Flint River flows across a river-wide rock shelf that forms a natural dam.

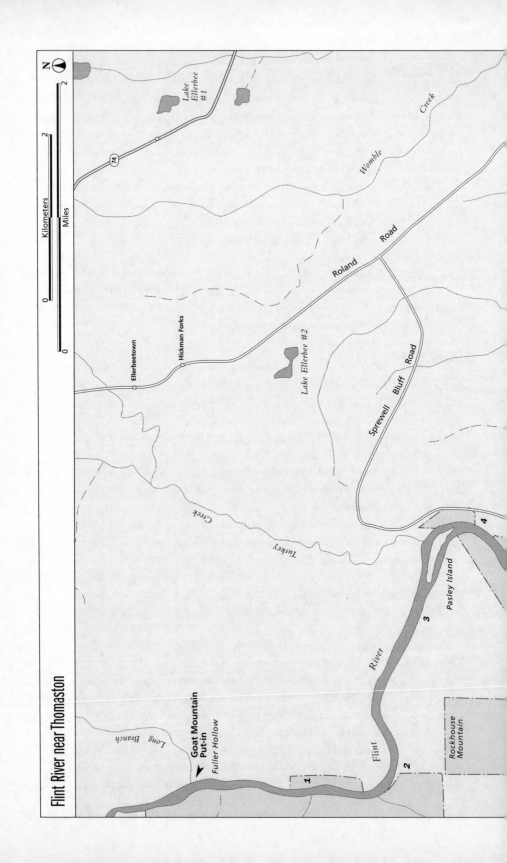

Flint River near Thomaston

N

Kilometers
0   2
Miles
0   2

Long Branch

Goat Mountain Put-in
Fuller Hollow

74

Ellerbeetown

Hickman Forks

Lake Ellerbee #1

Lake Ellerbee #2

Womble Creek

Roland Road

Sprewell Bluff Road

Turkey Creek

Flint River

Flint River

1

2

3

4

Pasley Island

Rockhouse Mountain

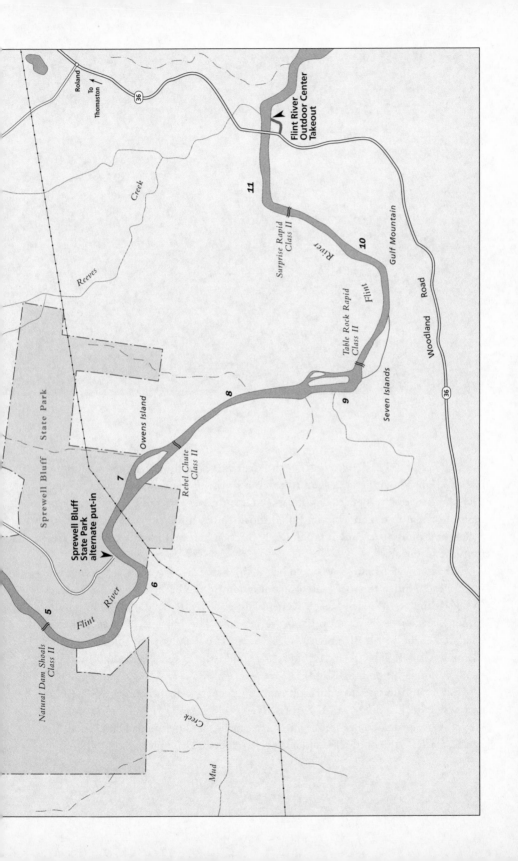

This part of the Flint flows through the Pine Mountains.

A pretty fair gravel bar builds up after the river curves to the left, leaving the greater Natural Dam Shoals behind, soon to reach a warm-up bluff before Sprewell Bluff. The bluff is easily recognizable with its reddish rock covered in pines and a viewing platform atop it. Curve around mild shoals to reach the river access/picnic area at Sprewell Bluff State Park at 6.2 miles. The actual Sprewell Bluff is across the river from the picnic area.

The Flint widens and slows down below the state park. Owens Island comes into view ahead. Notice the rock outcrop continuing on the left bank before you reach Owens Island at 7.0 miles. Reach Rebel Chute, a Class II rapid, just below Owens Island. The most exciting drop is on the left side. The Flint narrows again before widening at the Seven Islands area, at 8.7 miles. The islands are plentiful, so are the channels. Class II Table Rock Rapid swirls amidst the Seven Islands, and moderate rapids continue beyond the islands.

Gulf Mountain rises to your right, and the scenery remains gorgeous. The Flint narrows before reaching Class II Surprise Rapid at 10.9 miles. Houses pick up as the Highway 36 bridge comes into sight. Pass a small island before paddling under the bridge, reaching the outfitter takeout on river-right at 11.6 miles.

SHOAL BASS

SHOAL BASS The Flint River is renowned for its outstanding shoal bass fishery. This bass subspecies is native only to a few rivers in Georgia, Alabama, and Florida—generally those that are part of the greater Apalachicola River system. The section through which this paddle travels goes through the heart of the best shoal bass fishing on the Flint River. The current Georgia- and world-record shoal bass (8 pounds, 3 ounces) was caught on the Flint River in 1977. Most shoal bass weigh a pound or less. Recently one fortunate angler landed an amazing 8-pound, 2.5-ounce shoal bass on the Flint between Albany and Lake Blackshear, which is below this paddle.

The rocky, free-flowing reaches of the Flint, pocked with small deeper holes, are ideal habitat for the shoal bass, and this is where they reach their greatest numbers. Fortunately the upper Flint River remains undammed, protecting the fish's habitat. The shoal bass resembles a smallmouth bass but is a unique species, although shoal bass fight as hard as smallmouth do. Anyone moderately interested in fishing should bring a rod and reel on this paddle. To quote the Georgia Department of Natural Resources:

"Shoal bass can be caught on a wide variety of lures, and some of the favorites are small swimming minnows, spinner baits, top water poppers, and Texas-rigged worms and lizards. Wading the shoals is particularly suited to fly-fishing. Just bring your six to eight weight bass or trout rod and plenty of wooly buggers and poppers. A bronze flash will often follow a cast into the clear runs and pools as a shoal bass strikes your lure or fly. All serious Georgia anglers should experience this truly unique fishery."

16 Flint River at Montezuma Bluffs

This section of the Flint River is quite scenic as it winds its way south through the Piedmont, alternating between sheer bluffs and tan sandbars.

County: Macon
Start: East Leroy Ferry N32° 26' 11.6", W84° 1' 15.0"
End: Montezuma Bluffs Natural Area N32° 20' 12.1", W84° 1' 48.0"
Length: 11.7 miles
Float time: 5 hours
Difficulty rating: Easy
Rapids: None
River type: Winding Piedmont waterway
Current: Moderate
River gradient: 2.1 feet per mile
River gauge: Flint River at Highway 26 near Montezuma; no minimum runnable level; maximum runnable level, flood stage

Season: Year-round
Land status: Private; public
Fees or permits: No fees or permits required
Nearest city/town: Montezuma, Georgia
Maps: USGS: Garden Valley, Montezuma; DeLorme: *Georgia Atlas and Gazetteer,* page 42
Boats used: Canoes, kayaks, johnboats
Organizations: Georgia River Network, 126 South Milledge Avenue, Suite E3, Athens, GA 30605; (706) 549-4508; www.garivers.org
Contacts/outfitters: Georgia Department of Natural Resources, 2 Martin Luther King Jr. Drive SE, Suite 1252 East Tower, Atlanta, GA 30334; (404) 656-3500; www.gadnr.org

Put-in/takeout information:

To takeout: From exit 127 (Montezuma, Hawkinsville) on Interstate 75, take Highway 26 west for 17.3 miles. Turn right onto Highway 49 north on the east side of Montezuma. Head north on Highway 49 for 2.7 miles and turn left at Crooks Landing Road (County Road 267). Follow CR 267 for 0.6 mile to dead-end at a boat ramp.

To put-in from takeout: Backtrack to Highway 49. Turn left and head north for 6.9 miles. Turn left onto Highway 127 west, and travel for 0.5 mile. Veer right onto East Ferry Road, and follow it to dead-end at the Flint River.

Paddle Summary

There is next to no development along this section of the Flint River, although in a few places on one bank or another, a line of trees is the only divider between the river and fields. The shallow water and numerous tree snags on this river discourage boaters other than self-propelled craft, though johnboats occasionally float this section.

Wildlife is abundant. Shorebirds may be working the exposed shallows. The lowermost part of the paddle passes through the Montezuma Bluffs Natural Area, a protected area of about 500 acres that envelops some high bluffs and old-growth trees.

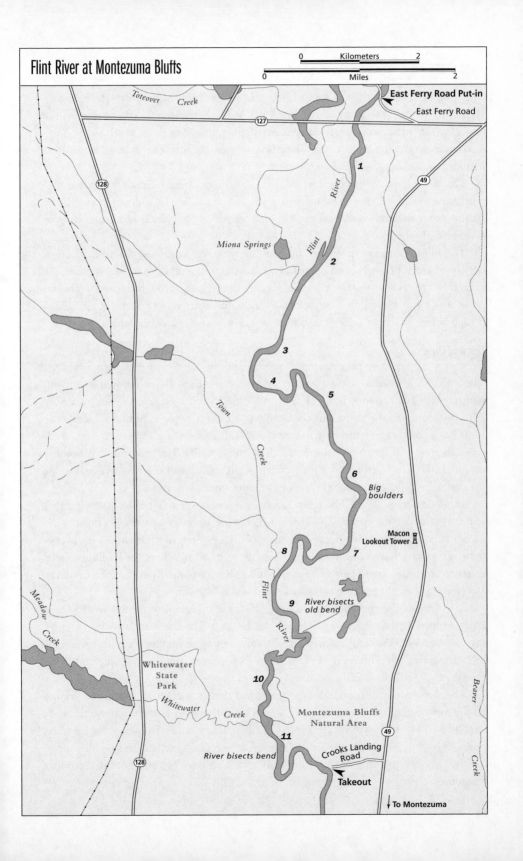

Flint River at Montezuma Bluffs

East Ferry Road Put-in

East Ferry Road

Toteover Creek

127

128

49

Flint River

1

Miona Springs

2

3

4

5

Town Creek

6

Big boulders

Macon Lookout Tower

8

7

Flint River

9

River bisects old bend

Meadow Creek

Whitewater State Park

10

Whitewater Creek

Montezuma Bluffs Natural Area

Beaver Creek

49

11

River bisects bend

Crooks Landing Road

Takeout

128

↓ **To Montezuma**

0 — Kilometers — 2

0 — Miles — 2

River Overview

The Flint River rivals the Chattahoochee as Georgia's most important big river. From beginning to end, many argue that the Flint is the better for paddlers between the two. Born in a culvert beneath the Atlanta airport, the Flint flows south beyond this inauspicious start, forming county-line boundaries. By the time it reaches the Pine Mountains, the Flint is already a big river.

The river is at its most scenic as it cuts through these mountains. This is also where the most challenging rapids are located, namely Class III Yellow Jackets Shoals. At this point the river drops off the fall line before settling down and continuing its southbound journey.

The Flint continues to widen and become more convoluted—where this paddle occurs—before being backed up at Lake Blackshear. Beyond the impoundment, the river flows to Albany, where it is stalled again, then flows through the town. By this point it is a full-blown, massive waterway as it makes its way to and through Bainbridge before reaching Lake Seminole, near the Georgia, Florida, Alabama borders.

The Paddling

The put-in is located at the last ferry operated on the Flint River. Known by various names, it ran twenty-four hours a day until 1988, when a bridge was built over the Flint just downstream of the put-in. Concrete landings, vestiges of the old ferry, rise from both banks. Here the Flint River is just 120 feet wide and bordered by bluffs running about 15 feet high on one side. The opposite bank is lower and commonly graced with river birch and willows, which often grow to the river's edge and drape the water. Sycamores and tupelo trees have a presence as well.

Shortly pass under the Highway 127 bridge. The river will be shallow where it's wide, and the current speeds up in small riffles. Pine, sweet gum, and oaks occupy the higher ground, along with occasional magnolia trees. Spanish moss hangs on everything. The water has a tannish tint but normally runs clear. Where the bluffs are sheer, they are often the lower part of a greater hill rising surprisingly high from the river. Water seeps down limestone walls and shimmers in the sun.

At 1.1 miles the river hits a long straightaway and widens to more than 150 feet. Dip your paddle into the water and easily hit bottom. The riverbed provides a changing mix of rock, sand, and sediment. At 2.0 miles a slough merges with the river. This interesting area has a little bit of everything—a tupelo swamp on one side and bluffs on the other with rock and sand bars, all mixed in one spot.

At 3.1 miles the long straightaway ends and the Flint resumes its curves. A large sandbar on your right beckons you to stop. This is the river at its finest—with sandbars backed by thick willow beds looking up at sheer bluffs. Between the bars and bluffs, the Flint flows swiftly around exposed tree snags, which the paddler must dodge. This curving section offers not only much scenery but also potential sandbar camping.

Fallen trees on bend create a ragged appearance in places

The riverside bluffs range in color from dark gray to light tan to an almost whitish tint and the red of Georgia clay. As the bluffs continue to change color and give varying looks, river snags remain constant. Keep on the lookout for rock outcrops that show themselves at the river's edge or in small riffles. Pass through such a rocky riffle at 5.1 miles. Below here, the river briefly straightens out, although sandbars are still frequent.

At 6.3 miles the river narrows then curves right, and more rocks rise forth. These are no ordinary river rocks but surprisingly large, exposed boulders. Be on the watch for a swirling current here. Also watch for feeder branches cutting narrow, sandy ravines as they enter the riverbed. Bluffs continue to be present on one side of the river or another. Sometimes these bluffs have been undermined during high water. Subsequently, bluff-top trees have fallen into the Flint, giving the area a generally ragged appearance, especially as the disturbed bluff becomes covered with brushy vegetation.

Beyond the big boulders, sandbars continue to be common; the sharper the curve, the higher they grow. Town Creek comes in on your right at 8.4 miles. The Flint enters a wide slower stretch as it passes under a power line at 8.6 miles. In some places snags extend nearly all the way across the river. From afar it looks as though you might not be able to make passage, but passages can be found. The water consistently swiftens amid these snags.

The Flint bisects an old bend at 9.3 miles. The river is riddled with ever-changing shallows as floods shift the sands of the riverbed. The waterway curves to the left at 10.4 miles and splits around an island. During lower water the left channel becomes dry. At this point Whitewater Creek comes in on your right. You'll notice its clear nature. This confluence is subject to change following high water, but Whitewater Creek always enters on the right-hand side of the river.

Below the confluence with Whitewater Creek, the bluffs are especially high on the right-hand bank and are topped with dense pines. This whole area is worth exploring by water or foot. The left bank is part of the Montezuma Bluffs Natural Area. The now faster river soon cuts through another old bend, creating an oxbow. Drift over to the left-hand bank. Soon the waters take you to the boat ramp on your left and the takeout at 11.7 miles.

MONTEZUMA AND THE RIVER The Flint River has played an important role in this stretch of Georgia as it flows through Macon County and the town of Montezuma. Before Georgia was a state, Muskogee Indians roamed the area. The Muskogee claimed to be direct descendants of the Aztecs of Mexico, so European settlers named the town on the east bank of the Flint Montezuma, for the Aztec emperor. Intermarriage merged the Muscogee with the settlers.

The waterway was the preferred travel venue until 1851, when the railroad came through the town of Oglethorpe, which stood on the west bank of the Flint. The two towns were connected by ferry. Despite the railroad, steamboats operated on the Flint, moving goods and people until local agriculture shifted entirely to rail transportation.

In 1902 a bridge was built across the Flint, connecting Montezuma to Oglethorpe and further reducing the river's role. Later a railroad bridge crossed the river as well. But the Flint refused to be forgotten, reminding the two cities of its power with floods in 1925, 1949, and 1994.

A drive through Montezuma as you head toward Montezuma Bluffs Natural Area will showcase its historic homes that stand on the high ground east of the Flint River. Today the waterway's role is as a recreational showcase for Macon County and a destination for the Georgia paddler.

17 Ocmulgee River near Abbeville

The Ocmulgee here is a full-blown Piedmont waterway, flowing yellow-clear at normal flows.

County: Wilcox, Dodge
Start: Phelps Bluff N32° 4' 26.9", W83° 17' 45.8"
End: Half Moon Landing N32° 0' 3.23", W83° 17' 45.09"
Length: 7.2 miles
Float time: 3 hours
Difficulty rating: Easy to moderate
Rapids: Class I
River type: Piedmont river with one rocky shoal
Current: Moderate
River gradient: 3.2 feet per mile
River gauge: Ocmulgee River near Warner Robins; 2.0 feet suggested minimum runnable level. Above 5.0 feet the river can become dangerously swift.

Season: Year-round
Land status: Private
Fees or permits: No fees or permits required
Nearest city/town: Abbeville, Georgia
Maps: USGS: Abbeville North, Abbeville South; DeLorme: *Georgia Atlas and Gazetteer,* page 51
Boats used: Canoes, kayaks, johnboats
Organizations: Altamaha Riverkeeper, Inc., P.O. Box 2642, Darien, GA 31305; (912) 437-8164; www.altamahariverkeeper.org
Contacts/outfitters: Georgia Department of Natural Resources, 2 Martin Luther King Jr. Drive SE, Suite 1252 East Tower, Atlanta, GA 30334; (404) 656-3500; www.gadnr.org

Put-in/takeout information:

To takeout: From exit 101 on Interstate 75, take U.S. Highway 280/Highway 30 east toward Abbeville for 29 miles to Abbeville and Half Moon Road, which is about 200 yards east of the Wilcox County Courthouse. At 0.7 mile reach the Half Moon Boat Landing, adjacent to the Ocmulgee River.

To put-in from takeout: Backtracking on Half Moon Road, return to US 280/Highway 30 and follow it east, away from Abbeville and over the Ocmulgee River, to reach Highway 87 after 3.4 miles. Turn left onto Highway 87 north and follow it for 4.6 miles to Highway 230. Stay left with Highway 230 and follow it 1.6 miles to River Road. Turn left onto River Road and follow it a short distance to a boat ramp on your right. This boat ramp has a shaded picnic area.

Paddle Summary

Quality landings at both ends of the trip enhance this Ocmulgee paddle. Sweeping bends, where sandbars form, alternate with straightaways. Heavy streamside vegetation obscures the civilized world, save for a few houses at the beginning and end of the paddle. Old oxbows and sloughs give the river a swampy appearance in places, despite its mostly swift current. One oxbow shortcut, known as the New River, offers a rocky rapid that will surprise most paddlers. For those wanting a calmer paddle, the rapid can be avoided by keeping with the main river.

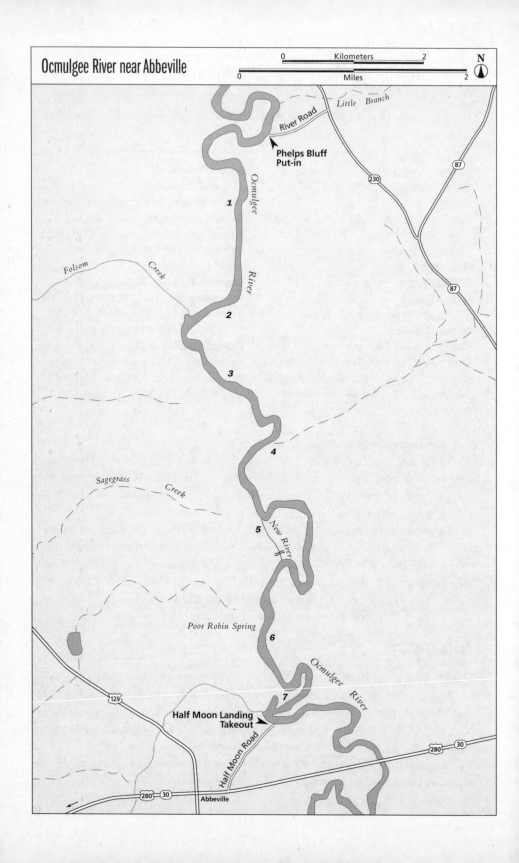

Ocmulgee River near Abbeville

Kilometers
0   2

Miles
0   2

N

River Road

Little Branch

Phelps Bluff
Put-in

87

230

Folsom Creek

Ocmulgee River

1

2

3

4

Sagegrass Creek

New River

5

6

Poor Robin Spring

Ocmulgee River

7

129

Half Moon Landing
Takeout

Half Moon Road

280 30

280 30

Abbeville

River Overview

The Ocmulgee River and its tributaries drain the heart of Georgia. The Ocmulgee is born near Monticello at the confluence of the Yellow and Alcovy Rivers. This river was an important travel corridor before railroads, cars, and airplanes.

Gathering steam south of Atlanta, the Ocmulgee comes together and passes through Macon, continuing its southerly journey before making a hard east turn to meet the Oconee River. Together these two large Piedmont streams form the Altamaha River. The often-silty river offers more than 250 miles of paddling pleasure, most of which you will have to yourself. Though it does pass through Macon as well as through or near a few other towns, the river is often bordered by wildlife management areas, making it even more remote.

The Paddling

After gazing upon the Ocmulgee River at Half Moon Landing, you will be surprised at the river near Phelps Bluff. At Half Moon Landing the Ocmulgee is a swift, deep waterway; at the put-in it is a shallow, sandy stream. This is because much of the river is flowing on the far side of an island.

Leave the boat ramp and float down a shallow waterway. What is left of the river further divides and goes through some rocky, log-choked channels to the left that parallel blufftop houses. A wider channel leading right will connect to the main river. The rocky left channel will also make a connection, but it can be tough at the onset. Either way, you will soon join the primary river.

The vegetation is thick along the Ocmulgee, with cypress and willow trees growing in dense stands along the shoreline. Occasional low bluffs of soil anchor oak stands. At the height of summer the shoreline will be so thickly vegetated as to seem like a jungle. The tan sandbars offer a seemingly barren contrast to this lush greenery. The tan waters flow surprisingly swiftly through this valley. The Ocmulgee resumes its bends at 2.0 miles, and a slough forms where Folsom Creek comes in on the right at 2.3 miles.

From this point forward, the Ocmulgee continues to twist and turn. In many places the river's edge can be a crushing jungle, and sandbars provide the only entry and exit. Some of the outside-bend bluffs have caved in and left fallen trees in the water below. These fallen trees provide harborages for fish but never extend across the river and completely block passage. In the sharpest curves, you will see from one sandbar to the next.

The banks remain low down here as the river widens on straightaways and narrows in curves. At 4.9 miles the river curves to the left and a smaller channel leads right. The smaller channel to the right is locally known as the "New River." It is a swift shortcut that bisects the former main river. This section is more swift and interesting than the other—longer—route.

Shortly after entering the New River, you'll see a dead lake to your right that is often choked with logs, blocking access. Continue down the main channel as it

You can see from one sandbar to the next on sharp bends.

narrows to 40 feet and forms a small but noisy shoal. It has to drop fast and steeply to decline the same distance that the longer channel does. Ahead the gradient sharpens. Jagged limestone rocks and a small island at the bottom of the New River make for a trickier rapid than you'll expect, so be careful going through here. The noise of the rapid is really surprising given the quiet nature the rest of the river.

After the river channels come together, the current speeds down an extended straightaway. At low water you'll see more rock exposed here. Shortly a bluff builds on river-right and has a little civilization atop it. The Ocmulgee slices across another oxbow at 6.6 miles, then curves by a very big sandbar. Houses begin to appear as you make a supersharp bend to the left and enter the city limits of Abbeville. Just after making the sharp left curve, you will see some rock riprap on your right and the Half Moon Landing boat ramp.

THE OCMULGEE AS TRANSPORTATION CORRIDOR Since the Ocmulgee drains the heart of Georgia and reaches all the way to the sea, the final mileage as the Altamaha River, it is only natural that it played a part in the development of early Georgia. As primitive roads began to crisscross the Ocmulgee River Valley, ferries were established to cross the river

at budding communities like Milledgeville and Monticello and communities to be, such as Fort Hawkins, later known as Hawkinsville, which is not far upstream of this paddle.

Travelers not only crossed the Ocmulgee but floated down it as well. Sometimes the river flowed as a brown torrent; sometimes it flowed hardly at all. Farmers and entrepreneurs would build log rafts and load them with farm goods, guiding their craft by pole as they floated to the confluence with the Oconee River, which was also a major artery for transporting agricultural products from the Georgia heartland. Together these two rivers became the Altamaha, which flowed east to the port of Darien.

Upon arriving at Darien, the goods would be sold; the rafts were dismantled and sold for lumber. This was a common practice on rivers throughout the United States in the early 1800s— it simply wasn't feasible to fight the log rafts back upstream. The raftsmen would then return by foot to their Ocmulgee Valley homes. Later this problem was overcome with the advent of steamboats, which began to ply the Ocmulgee both upstream and down. But with its winding course and shifting sand shallows, this river was not friendly to the steamboats, although they did make it all the way to Macon during the spring high waters. River towns and plantations took advantage of this, establishing landings where they could load their goods for somewhat-regular steamboat schedules.

The era of the steamboat was short-lived as railroads began to track throughout the Peach State. By the early 1850s the sight of a steamboat smokestack was rare indeed. The Union Army's destruction of Georgia's infrastructure during the War Between the States included the railroads, so after the war the Ocmulgee once again became an important transportation vein, especially for harvesting the seemingly endless pines that covered the Georgia Coastal Plain. Of course, the pines weren't endless and were harvested to the point where wood products no longer made their way down the river. By the early 1900s, the era of commercial transportation on the Ocmulgee River was just a memory.

18 Ocmulgee River near Bullard

This part of the Ocmulgee flows fast and wild as it winds through a wide valley protected by overflow swamps.

County: Houston, Twiggs
Start: Bullard Landing N32° 37' 31.7", W83° 32' 32.1"
End: Highway 96 N32° 32' 31.9", W83° 32' 18.5"
Length: 10.0 miles
Float time: 5.5 hours
Difficulty rating: Easy to moderate
Rapids: Class I
River type: Piedmont stream
Current: Moderate to swift
River gradient: 2.0 feet per mile
River gauge: Ocmulgee River near Warner Robins; 2.0 feet suggested minimum runnable level. Above 5.0 feet the river can become dangerously swift.

Season: Year-round
Land status: Private
Fees or permits: No fees or permits required
Nearest city/town: Warner Robins, Georgia
Maps: USGS: Warner Robins NE, Warner Robins SE; DeLorme: *Georgia Atlas and Gazetteer*, page 43
Boats used: Canoes, kayaks, occasional johnboat
Organizations: Altamaha Riverkeeper, Inc., P.O. Box 2642, Darien, GA 31305; (912) 437-8164; www.altamahariverkeeper.org
Contacts/outfitters: Georgia Department of Natural Resources, 2 Martin Luther King Jr. Drive SE, Suite 1252 East Tower, Atlanta, GA 30334; (404) 656-3500; www.gadnr.org

Put-in/takeout information:

To takeout: From exit 18 on Interstate 16 southeast of Macon, take Jeffersonville-Bullard Road west for 3.8 miles to U.S. Highway 129 Alternate/U.S. Highway 23/ Highway 87. Turn left onto US 129 Alternate/US 23/Highway 87 and head south for 7.2 miles to Highway 96. Turn right and follow Highway 96 west for 5.8 miles to the bridge over the Ocmulgee River. Turn left once you're past the bridge over the river to the Houston County boat ramp, on the southwest side of the bridge.

To put-in from takeout: Backtrack on Highway 46 east to US 129 Alternate/ US 23/ Highway 87. Turn left onto Highway 87 and travel north for 7.2 miles to River Road (Jeffersonville-Bullard Road is to your right). Turn left and follow River Road for 2.8 miles to dead-end at the Bullard boat ramp.

Paddle Summary

Overflow swamps help keep this section of the Ocmulgee river corridor wild. Numerous fallen trees leave the relatively large Piedmont stream mostly to paddlers. Its tan waters twist and turn, speeding past fallen trees in a setting of solitude. Rich, heavily wooded banks provide a serene frame for the river's often-convoluted course.

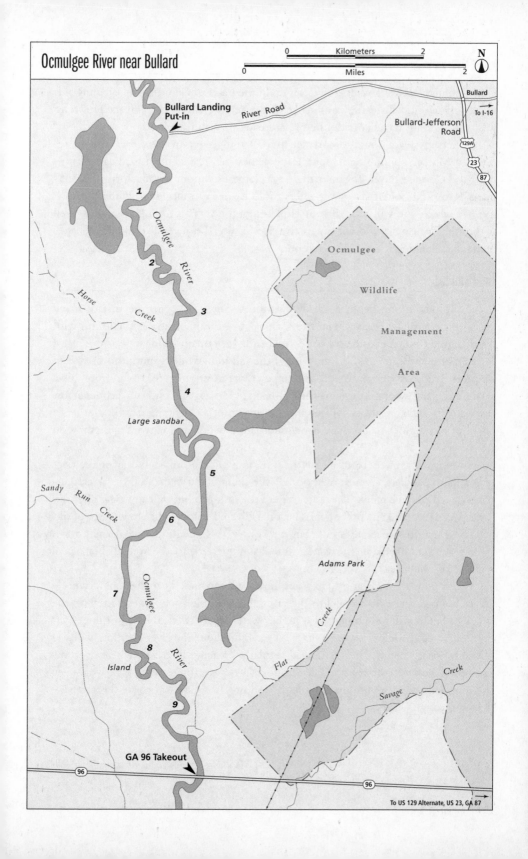

River Overview

The Ocmulgee River and its tributaries drain the heart of Georgia. The Ocmulgee is born near Monticello at the confluence of the Yellow and Alcovy Rivers. This river was an important travel corridor before railroads, cars, and airplanes.

Gathering steam south of Atlanta, the Ocmulgee comes together and passes through Macon, continuing its southerly journey before making a hard east turn to meet the Oconee River. Together these two large Piedmont streams form the Altamaha River. The often-silty river offers more than 250 miles of paddling pleasure, most of which you will have to yourself. Though it does pass through Macon as well as through or near a few other towns, the river is often bordered by wildlife management areas, making it even more remote.

The Paddling

Leave the put-in and begin downriver as the Ocmulgee begins the first of many curves in its initial 2.5 miles. The banks alternate—the high side is steep mud with overhanging trees; the insides of bends are brushy or contain sandbars.

Palmetto and cane grow at the base of the hillsides, while Spanish moss sways in the trees. Trumpet vine shows off its orange colors in summer. Ash trees grow thick. River birch and sycamore occupy their riverside spots as well. Birdsong echoes across the waters, which are about 80 feet wide at this point. Depending on whether it is a curve or a straighter section, the banks alternately widen and narrow, tightening on the curves.

Extensive fallen trees block all but the most intrepid motorboaters, leaving the river primarily to paddlers. Cypress trees occupy the sloughs that branch off the river, remnants of old river channels. The water has a brownish tint but will run clear after dry spells. Trees, logs, and any other debris become covered with a light brown layer of silt.

The river runs generally south, but it takes a very serpentine route. Bright green willow thickets overhang the waters, literally growing into the water. Their smell drifts across the river.

The sounds of civilization are scant; however, you may hear the lonely whistle of the railroad that runs parallel to the river about a mile back. Tan sandbars on the inside of bends will be submerged at higher water levels, when the surprisingly swift current sweeps paddlers into tree snags—be careful then. The river overflow will also cut across sharp bends. The Ocmulgee regularly breaches its banks, where overflow swamps lie between the river and civilization. These overflows swamps are what keep the river wild. Judging from these untamed shores, it is hard to believe this river has flowed through Macon.

Willows provide shade on a small sandbar. ▶

At 3.5 miles Horse Creek flows in on your right. Beyond Horse Creek, the Ocmulgee makes a long straightaway. At 4.5 miles the river has cut across an extreme bend, leaving an oxbow to the right of the present flow. Even so, the river still bends enough here to form a large sandbar suitable for picnicking or camping.

Magnolias begin to appear with more frequency downriver. Another fairly long straightaway ensues beyond the sandbar. The curves resume before Sandy Run Creek comes in without much fanfare on your right at 6.6 miles. Beyond this confluence, river bluffs rise to 20 or more feet. At 8.1 miles the river divides around an island formed by the bisecting of another sharp bend. The main channel spurs around the outside of the island. Old maps show the river simply making a sharp curve here. However, the Ocmulgee has cut through the bend here, creating the island.

Highway 96 begins humming in the distance. But the river is making twists and turns aplenty, so you have more river to float. At 9.5 miles the Ocmulgee forms another island where Flat Creek comes in on your left. Flat Creek's multiple mouths are lost among the brush and overflow swamps at the river's edge. You're just about at the end of your trip here. Pass a power line cut, then reach the Highway 96 bridge and the takeout at 10.0 miles.

THE OCMULGEE MOUNDS Upstream a few miles of this paddle, on the northeast side of the Ocmulgee River in Macon, stand the Ocmulgee Mounds, erected between A.D. 900 and 1400. The mounds lie within the Ocmulgee National Monument—a 702-acre area that preserves more than 12,000 years of cultural history, including not only the mounds but also the Ocmulgee Old Fields, once inhabited by aboriginal Georgians.

In pre-Columbian times, Indians traveled middle Georgia using the Ocmulgee, so the mounds were constructed to be visible from the river. The area was continually inhabited by Indians well into the 1800s, when the Creeks, who controlled the mounds at the time, ceded the territory.

The mounds were damaged as the city of Macon grew, but in 1936 the national monument was established to preserve them. Today you can visit the mounds, hike trails, walk the park boardwalk, and view exhibits. For more information visit www.nps.gov/ocmu.

19 Oconee River

This surprisingly wild and remote section of the Oconee includes a dam portage.

County: Oconee, Greene
Start: Barnett Shoals Road N33° 51' 19.9", W83° 19' 36.4"
End: Oconee Campground on Highway 15 N33° 43' 16.9", W83° 17' 31.6"
Length: 12.8 miles
Float time: 8 hours
Difficulty rating: Easy (one portage)
Rapids: None
River type: Piedmont river with wilderness aura
Current: Moderate to swift
River gradient: 5.1 feet per mile
River gauge: Oconee River near Penfield; minimum runnable level 300 cfs
Season: March to November

Land status: Private; national forest
Fees or permits: No fees or permits required
Nearest city/town: Watkinsville, Georgia
Maps: USGS: Barnett Shoals, Greshamville; DeLorme: *Georgia Atlas and Gazetteer*, page 28; USDA Forest Service: Oconee National Forest
Boats used: Canoes, occasional johnboats
Organizations: Oconee River Land Trust, 380 Meigs Street, Athens, GA 30601; (706) 552-3138; www.orlt.com
Contacts/outfitters: Oconee National Forest, 1199 Madison Road, Eatonton, GA 31024; (706) 485-1776; www.fs.fed.us/conf

Put-in/takeout information:

To takeout: From exit 130 on Interstate 20, take Highway 44 east for 2.5 miles to downtown Greensboro. Turn left on Highway 15 north and follow it 12 miles to the Oconee River National Forest campground, on your right. If you pass over the Oconee River Bridge, you have gone too far. Follow the campground road to the boat launch below the campground.

To put-in from takeout: From Oconee Campground, turn right and head north on Highway 15 for 6.1 miles to Oliver Bridge Road. Turn right onto Oliver Bridge Road and follow it for 3.6 miles to a four-way stop. Keep straight at the four-way stop as Oliver Bridge Road becomes into McRees Mill Road. Follow McRees Mill Road for 1.8 miles to meet Barnett Shoals Road. Turn right onto Barnett Shoals Road and follow it for 0.6 mile to the bridge over the Oconee River. The put-in is on the left before you cross the Oconee, the northwest side. The dirt road to the put-in can be rutted and muddy.

Paddle Summary

This section of the Oconee is surprisingly wild and remote. A dam must be portaged a little less than 2.0 miles in—a carry-around that separates you from the few boaters who float this Piedmont gem. Beyond the dam, surprisingly swift waters travel a thickly wooded, wildlife-rich corridor. Give all day for this trip, or consider camping in the Oconee National Forest, which borders the river downstream.

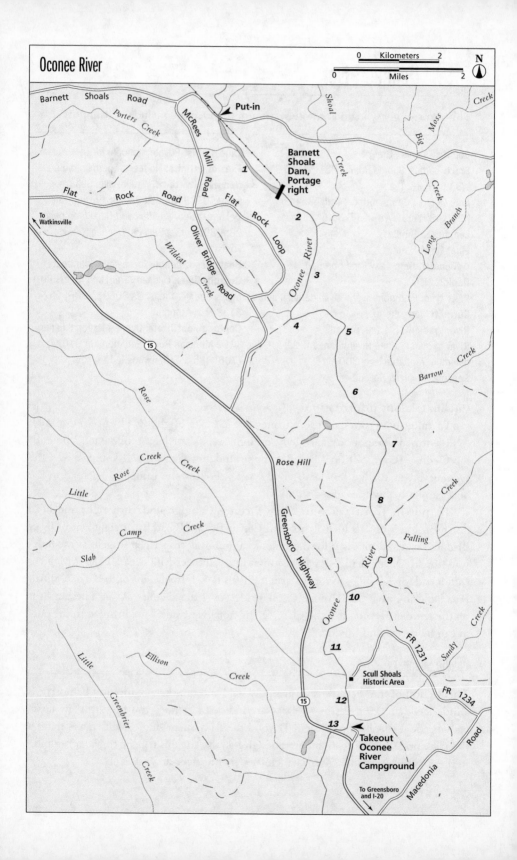

Oconee River

Kilometers
Miles

N

Barnett Shoals Road

Porters Creek

McRees Mill Road

Put-in

Shoal Creek

Big Moss Creek

1

Barnett Shoals Dam, Portage right

2

Flat Rock Road

Flat Rock Loop

Oliver Bridge Road

Oconee River

3

Wildcat Creek

To Watkinsville

15

Long Branch

4

5

Barrow Creek

6

7

Rose Creek

Rose Hill

8

Creek

Little Rose Creek

Rose Creek

Greensboro Highway

9

Falling

Camp Creek

Oconee River

10

Slab

11

Little Greenbrier Creek

Ellison Creek

Scull Shoals Historic Area

FR 1231

Sandy Creek

FR 1234

15

12

13

Takeout Oconee River Campground

Macedonia Road

Creek

To Greensboro and I-20

River Overview

The Oconee is one of Georgia's larger and more powerful rivers. Starting in northeast Georgia, the North Oconee and Middle Oconee join to form the main Oconee River; from there the river heads southeasterly off the fall line. It is detained twice, at Lake Oconee and Lake Sinclair, before continuing south to meet the Ocmulgee River and together form the Altamaha River. All together the Oconee offers more than 160 miles of paddling, most of it in relative solitude.

The Paddling

The Oconee River is born a few miles upstream of the put-in at the confluence of the Middle and the North Oconee Rivers. Leave the put-in and drift below Barnett Shoals Bridge, passing upscale houses that line the river just downstream. The Piedmont river almost always has a stain to it, ranging from tan to yellowish when really full of sediment.

Quickly leave the houses behind, while the Oconee makes a nearly straight track. The current becomes listless as it nears Barnett Shoals Dam. This upper stretch is sometimes used by anglers in johnboats to fish for bass and catfish. With the widening of the river, it becomes increasingly obvious that the Oconee River is being dammed. Then you notice the dam horizon and the huge drop-off of the tree line. Barnett Shoals Dam was built in 1910 and is now part of the greater Georgia Power system.

When approaching the dam, look for an island and a small channel on river-right. Paddle around the right side of this island and to within 30 feet of the dam spillway. Take out here on the right bank. A narrow trail goes around and below the dam. It is challenging but doable. I've done it toting not only a canoe but also a mess of camping gear.

Interestingly, spawning bass and crappie are stopped at the dam and will mass there in spring. Once back on the water, enter rocky shoals that may be hard to get through at low water. Along the banks river birch, sycamore, and ash overhang the river. Fallen trunks conceal largemouth bass, redeye, and bream but provide little obstacle for the paddler. Alligator gar swim just below the river's surface. Herons fly away upon your approach. Low bluffs, occasionally of rock, alternately rise and fall. Sometimes fields are visible beyond the line of trees astride the river.

Oconee National Forest lands border the Oconee on river-left, a little below Barrow Creek, at 6.7 miles. Riverside camping is allowed in the national forest. Upon entering the national forest, the river scenery isn't appreciably different—it has been wild nearly all the way. The banks can be extremely brushy, prohibiting entry and exit from the river and keeping it at once lush and secluded. Sandbars, located inside bends, provide the only river egresses. Wildlife is abundant, including beavers and muskrats.

At 11.9 miles pass Scull Shoals Historic Area. The locale has been inhabited for thousands of years and was the site of Georgia's first paper mill, later a cotton mill and

Paddlers must portage around this dam

even a hospital. The stone pilings of an old covered bridge are visible in the river. Pull over and check out the building remnants from days gone by, left to fade into history until 1959, when the area became part of the national forest. From here the Scull Shoals Trail travels along the left bank to Oconee River Campground. By water it is a little less than a mile before you drift to the campground boat ramp on your left.

SCULL SHOALS VILLAGE

The area on river-left of this paddle, just before the takeout, is known as Scull Shoals. Inhabited by Georgia's Indians for thousands of years, Scull Shoals was occupied by white settlers starting in 1782. The Creeks didn't like it one bit, but they were eventually moved west by treaty in 1802. This event, coupled with Eli Whitney's invention of the cotton gin in 1793, made the Oconee River Valley attractive for cotton growers.

Scull Shoals already had a gristmill and sawmill powered by the Oconee River; a cotton gin followed. The river even powered a paper mill for a while. The community continued to grow as the greater mill area prospered. Scull Shoals found its stride, becoming a mill town centered on processing yarns and cloth from the area's cotton. At one time the mills employed more than 600 people, and businesses of all sorts sprang up to serve these workers.

Just like the rest of Georgia and the South, Scull Shoals suffered after the Civil War, and the mill owners resorted to using convict labor for a time. The untamed Oconee River caused the mill problems as well, alternately flooding the town or not providing enough water to power the mill. The land was being exhausted, too, and much topsoil was lost after a century of poor farming practices. Scull Shoals began to die off, and eventually everyone left. Relics, primarily brick walls of the buildings, remain. Today you can visit the site, which is part of the national forest; interpretive information is available.

20 Ogeechee River

This section of the Ogeechee offers a mix of Piedmont and Coastal Plain characteristics.

County: Screven, Jenkins
Start: Scarboro Landing N32° 42' 40.3", W81° 52' 44.7"
End: Rocky Ford N32° 38' 56.7", W81° 50' 26.7"
Length: 7.5 miles
Float time: 3.5 hours
Difficulty rating: Moderate
Rapids: Class I
River type: Swift coastal plain river bordered by swamps
Current: Moderate to swift
River gradient: 1.1 feet per mile
River gauge: Ogeechee River at Rocky Ford Road; minimum runnable level 160 cfs

Season: Year-round
Land status: Private
Fees or permits: No fees or permits required
Nearest city/town: Rocky Ford, Georgia
Maps: USGS: Four Points, Rocky Ford; DeLorme: *Georgia Atlas and Gazetteer,* page 46
Boats used: Canoes, kayaks, johnboats
Organizations: Ogeechee Canoochee Riverkeeper, P.O. Box 1925, Statesboro, GA 30459; (912) 764-2017; www.ogeecheecanoochee riverkeeper.org
Contacts/outfitters: Georgia Department of Natural Resources, 2 Martin Luther King Jr. Drive SE, Suite 1252 East Tower, Atlanta, GA 30334; (404) 656-3500; www.gadnr.org

Put-in/takeout information:

To takeout: From Millen take Highway 17 south for 13 miles to Rocky Ford and Rocky Ford Road. Turn right onto Rocky Ford Road and follow it 1.8 miles west. Cross the bridge over the Ogeechee then turn left to a ramp, located on the southwest side of the bridge.

To put-in from takeout: Backtrack to Highway 17. Turn left (north) onto Highway 17 toward Millen and follow it for 4.4 miles. Turn left onto Scarborough Landing Road (County Road 205) just after Highway 17 crosses railroad tracks near Scarboro Baptist Church. Follow CR 205 just a short distance to the put-in, which is steep.

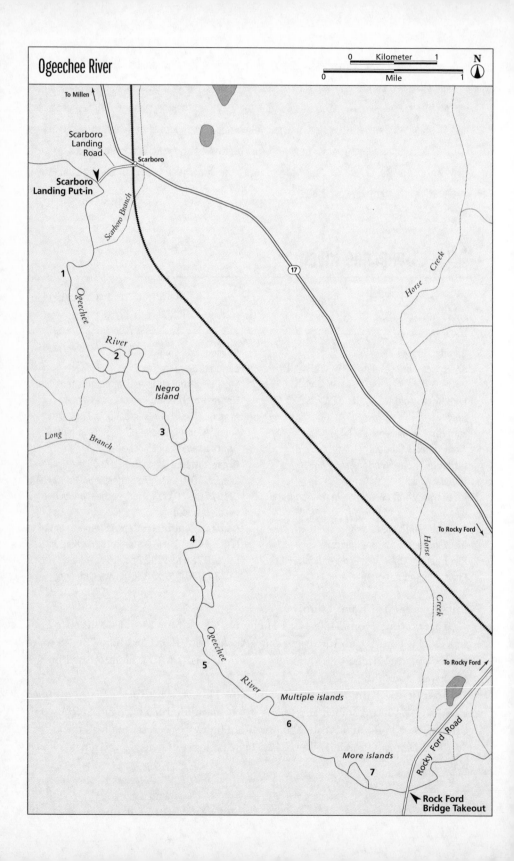

Paddle Summary

The Ogeechee River starts at a bluff and artesian spring, then proceeds to wind through a wide corridor of overflow swamps and amid wooded islands where the main river breaks into smaller, intimate and swift channels. In the warm season, when the bordering vegetation is ultrathick, the Ogeechee resembles a jungle river.

The irregular banks and overflow swamps retard development and create a mostly wild river corridor. Expect to go around fallen trees, maybe under them, and to dodge a few limbs along the way. That is why going during warmer weather is a good option—it's no problem getting in the water to work your boat around a deadfall.

River Overview

The Ogeechee River drains southeast Georgia, west of Savannah. This free-flowing river offers more than 170 miles of paddling before reaching the Atlantic Ocean. It starts near Washington, Georgia, northwest of Augusta.

The river is quite small in the Piedmont, where it finally becomes paddleable near Louisville. Because this upper stretch is dogged with fallen trees, this paddle starts well downstream, and even then it can be troublesome. Farther down in the Coastal Plain, the waterway opens up in excess of 200 feet before meeting salt water.

The Paddling

Take note of the artesian spring at the landing here. The crystal outflow has been corralled with a pipe that leads to other pipes and then sprays upward, creating a noisy artificial waterfall. The river is about 60 feet wide at this point; it has left the Piedmont and is changing to more of a Coastal Plain stream. Coloration ranges from tea to tan, depending on sediment from recent rainfalls. Trees grow tall on the shoreline, creating a tall and graceful wooded corridor.

The Ogeechee makes an immediate curve to the right, leaving the bluff of Scarboro Landing. The alternating characteristics of the riverbanks are visible. The inside bend is a low shore of cypress, ironwood, and willow, with overflow swamps extending beyond view. The outside bend is generally higher ground, with oaks above water-loving vegetation. Sand and some mud form the banks where exposed. The current flows slower on straightaways and faster on bends or where the river divides around islands.

The Ogeechee frequently changes width. Fallen trees are a regular river feature and can be problematic when the river narrows. This is what keeps most paddlers off the river above Scarboro Landing. At 0.8 mile the river narrows and speeds up before slowing down on a long straight section, heading almost due south. Look for massive cypress trees along the shore. Scarborough Bluff Plantation owns the left bank for miles, and the bank remains in a wild state.

At 1.6 miles the river splits around the upper end of Negro Island and makes a big curve. It is in these narrow channels that fallen trees can be a problem. When you enter a channel, look for cut trees where other paddlers have made a passage. Take note that the cleared passage is not always the channel with the most water flowing. And the proper channel, as well as the channels themselves, is subject to change with a meandering river such as this.

Watch for occasional small sandbars for resting or picnicking. Most of the sandbars are partly vegetated with grasses leading to trees higher atop them. The river begins to divide around islands where Long Branch comes in on river-right at 3.2 miles. Downstream, more sloughs spread the water, but the current remains steady. Alligators may lurk in the sloughs. The banks are thickly wooded, almost junglelike in appearance. If trees aren't growing thick themselves, then vines are growing atop and around the trees. Spanish moss hangs from limbs. Waterweeds grow along the river's edge in slack water.

At 5.2 miles a few fishing shacks appear on river-left just beyond the Scarborough Bluff Plantation boundary. Some overhang the river, but it is normally open over the middle. At 5.7 miles the river makes a big bend then splits around numerous islands with numerous channels. Some really large oak trees grow in higher areas above the river. At 6.8 miles the Ogeechee once again splits around islands and makes sharp bends before gathering above the Rocky Ford Bridge. Look for very large cypress trees growing riverside in the last mile above the bridge. The takeout is on river-right just beyond the bridge.

THE OGEECHEE LIME

The Ogeechee lime tree was discovered and named by none other than famed naturalist William Bartram. After its discovery in 1765, Bartram wrote that "no tree exhibits a more desirable appearance than this, in the autumn, when the fruit is ripe."

This swamp tree ranges from the South Carolina border through the Ogeechee River Valley and southwest into the Florida panhandle. It loves wet sites that are frequently inundated—such as the edges of rivers, swamps, and ponds—and grows best when adjacent to moving water. In Georgia, in addition to the Ogeechee River, the tree is found in abundance along the Altamaha River and the upper Suwannee River, shared by Georgia and Florida.

The "lime" is an edible, oblong-shaped fruit a little more an inch long, containing an acid flesh. It matures in July and August but persists until November and December after the leaves have fallen. The fruit is made into preserves and juice—which Bartram found favorable—and is favored by wildlife as well.

◄ *Cypress trees border much of the Ogeechee.*

21 Ohoopee River

More of a creek than a river at this stage, the Ohoopee flows swiftly around bends, past sandbars, and among fallen trees.

County: Toombs, Tattnall
Start: Highway 152 bridge N32° 17' 4.6", W82° 13' 45.8"
End: Jarrells Bridge Road N32° 13' 6.5", W82° 12' 23.0"
Length: 7.4 miles
Float time: 3.5 hours
Difficulty rating: Easy to moderate
Rapids: Class I
River type: Coastal Plain swiftwater creek
Current: Moderate to swift
River gradient: 2.8 feet per mile
River gauge: Ohoopee River near Reidsville; minimum runnable level 120 cfs
Season: Year-round

Land status: Private
Fees or permits: No fees or permits required
Nearest city/town: Cobbtown, Georgia
Maps: USGS: Cobbtown, Ohoopee; DeLorme: *Georgia Atlas and Gazetteer,* page 45
Boats used: Canoes, kayaks, occasional johnboat
Organizations: Altamaha Riverkeeper, Inc., P.O. Box 2642, Darien, GA 31305; (912) 437-8164; www.altamahariverkeeper.org
Contacts/outfitters: Georgia Department of Natural Resources, 2 Martin Luther King Jr. Drive SE, Suite 1252 East Tower, Atlanta, GA 30334 (404) 656-3500; www.gadnr.org

Put-in/takeout information:

To takeout: From exit 98 on Interstate 16 take Highway 57 south for 7 miles to Cobbtown and Highway 152. Turn right onto Highway 152 and travel west for 0.8 mile to Lynntown Road. Turn right onto Lynntown Road and follow it 4.3 miles to Jarrells Bridge Road. Turn right and follow Jarrells Bridge Road for 1.7 miles to dead-end at the ramp.

To put-in from takeout: Backtrack on Jarrells Bridge Road. Turn left onto Lynntown Road and travel north for 2.1 miles to Connors Church Road. Turn left onto Connors Church Road and follow it 2.4 miles to Highway 152. Turn left onto Highway 152 and follow it 3.4 miles to the bridge over the Ohoopee River. The best put-in is after the bridge on the right-hand (northwest) side.

Paddle Summary

The many turns and fallen trees will keep you on your toes the entire paddle. The Ohoopee's red waters course over white sands bordered by cypress trees, giving it a distinctly coastal flair. The length of this paddle is perfect for allowing yourself time to linger on one of the seemingly innumerable sandbars.

River Overview

The Ohoopee River is the northernmost waterway to display the characteristic burgundy waters and wide sandbars for which Coastal Plain rivers are known. Starting in

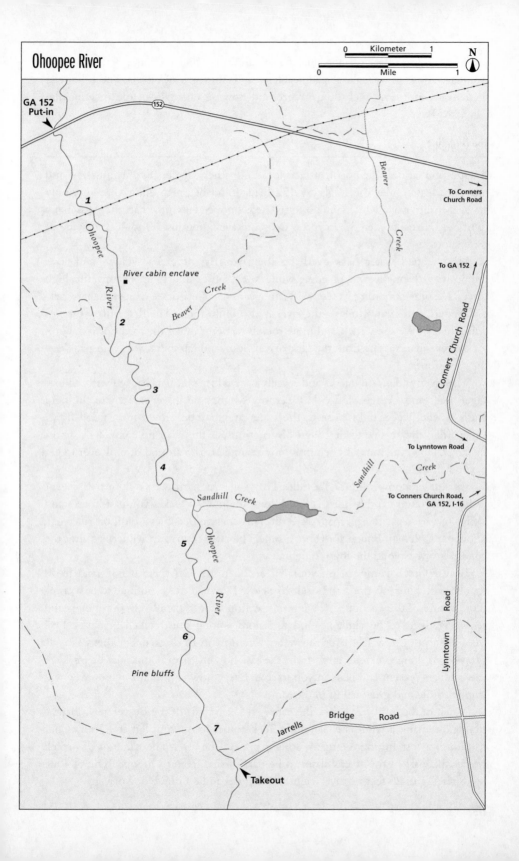

southeast Georgia near Wrightsville, the stream flows quite a distance before enough tributaries flow in to make it paddleable, near I-16 north of Vidalia. The Ohoopee then heads southeast, increasing in size and flowing 60 miles before meeting the Altamaha River.

The Paddling

A large sandbar near the put-in attracts local sunbathers, anglers, and swimmers—and litterbugs. Pass under the Highway 152 bridge and begin to enjoy that burgundy water flowing over a white sand bottom. The Ohoopee falls into character with many twists and turns, bordered by cypress trees and averaging just 30 to 40 feet wide in most spots.

Moss-draped water oaks overhang the river. Bright green willows and river birches rise from the water's edge, while sweet gums and pines occupy the high places. Despite exhibiting its Coastal Plain river characteristics—white sandbars, reddish waters, and cypress trees—the river is also quite rocky. The first riffles you pass will actually have some rock, and more rock is scattered along the river bottom. Look for darker squares rising from the sandy river floor, and tap them with your paddle—they are stone.

The river widens on curves and reveals large white sandbars backed with willow, Ogeechee lime, cypress, and oak. Overflow swamps lie in repose where the sand bluffs recede. Tree trunks close to the water are strained brown from flood flows. Fallen trees may prove to be tough obstructions, as they can lie completely across the river. However, it usually requires only a simple carry-around or pull-over to get beyond them.

Pass under a power line at 1.1 miles. The river may narrow to as little as 10 feet as it shoots through cypress-lined riffles. A long straightaway takes you past houses and cabins in various states of repair/disrepair. This enclave occupies a bluff on river-left, known as Coleman Ridge, for about a mile. The river returns to wilderness after the bends resume beyond the long straightaway.

Beaver Creek comes in on your left at 2.5 miles. On these bends, sand bluffs topped with pines overlook the sandbars below. Downed trees continue to be a common feature of the Ohoopee, leaving this section almost exclusively to paddlers and requiring them to be vigilant—and to slalom among outstretched branches. Live trees hang just a few feet over the water, forcing you to duck under them as well. Occasional sloughs extend away from the fast-flowing river. Continual bends keep the sandbars present and beckon you to stop. Every now and then a cypress tree will gain foothold and grow tall in midstream.

Much of the left bank below the cabin enclave is part of the Beavercreek Plantation and remains a wild state. Sandhill Creek comes in on your left at 4.7 miles, but its mouth is lost among the many sloughs just off the river. The name of this creek reveals this part of the river's claim to be part of the greater Ohoopee Dunes. Pine bluffs rise 15 to 20 feet on river-right at 6.6 miles and continue downriver.

White sandbars beckon a stop.

The fast Ohoopee shortly brings you to Jarrells Bridge, where there is no longer a bridge, just a landing on river-left where locals gather to fish, swim, and commingle.

THE OHOOPEE DUNES
Back 20,000 years ago, give or take a few years, in what is now southeast Georgia, a persistent drought dried the land. The westerly winds kept blowing as this water dearth continued, dropping sand onto the east bank of the Ohoopee River for some 35 river miles and covering over 40,000 acres of land. Before you imagine barren Sahara-like dunes, note that over time an ecosystem unique to Georgia has evolved atop the dunes.

Since the soil is sand based—these are sand dunes after all—vegetation such as oaks and longleaf pines grow stunted in the nutrient-poor soil. One tree just 6 inches in diameter is estimated to be 138 years old. Evergreen shrubs, rare for these parts, namely rosemary and scarlet basil, enhance the landscape with color and aroma, as does flowering woody mint. Lichens and mosses grow in scattered clumps. Despite the poor-soiled landscape, some creatures call it home, including the gopher tortoise, red cockaded woodpecker, and eastern indigo snake.

The Nature Conservancy has purchased a 267-acre parcel of these oval shaped dunes. The state owns 1,809 acres adjacent to the Nature Conservancy tract off Highway 80 west of Swainsboro, upstream of this paddle, and another 742-acre section along the Little Ohoopee River. As far as the rest of the 40,000 acres are concerned, the Nature Conservancy is working with landowners to protect and manage a Georgia treasure that is effectively an island of biodiversity along the Ohoopee River.

22 Savannah River

Don't let the distance of this day paddle scare you. The Savannah is quite swift and will immensely aid your downstream progress under normal conditions.

County: Screven
Start: Stony Bluff Landing N33° 2' 34.6", W81° 33' 23.0"
End: Burtons Ferry Landing on U.S. Highway 301 N32° 56' 11.4", W81° 30' 15.8"
Length: 14.0 miles
Float time: 5 hours
Difficulty rating: Easy
Rapids: Class I
River type: Dam-controlled big river
Current: Moderate to swift
River gradient: 0.8 foot per mile
River gauge: Savannah River at Burtons Ferry Branch near Millhaven, Georgia; no minimum runnable level; maximum runnable level, flood stage

Season: Year-round
Land status: Private; some government land
Fees or permits: No fees or permits required
Nearest city/town: Sylvania, Georgia
Maps: USGS: Millett, Martin, Bull Pond, Burtons Ferry Landing; DeLorme: *Georgia Atlas and Gazetteer,* page 39
Boats used: Powerboats, johnboats, canoes, kayaks
Organizations: Savannah Riverkeepers; www.savannahriverkeepers.org
Contacts/outfitters: Georgia Department of Natural Resources, 2 Martin Luther King Jr. Drive SE, Suite 1252 East Tower, Atlanta, GA 30334; (404) 656-3500; www.gadnr.org

Put-in/takeout information:

To takeout: From Sylvania take US 301/Highway 73 north for 15 miles, passing the Georgia Welcome Center on your left 0.3 mile before reaching the right turn to Burtons Ferry boat landing, before the bridge over the Savannah River. Follow the two-lane road, Old U.S. Highway 301, to the actual landing with a boat ramp.

To put-in from takeout: Return to US 301 toward Sylvania, again passing the Georgia Welcome Center. A short distance beyond the welcome center turn right onto Oglethorpe Trail, and follow it for 7.2 miles to Stony Bluff Landing Road. Turn right onto Stony Bluff Landing Road, and go 0.2 mile to dead-end at a boat ramp.

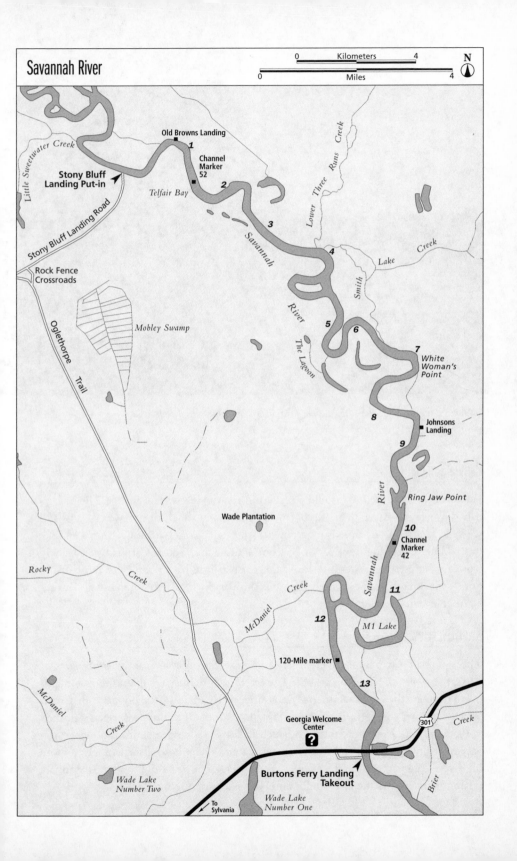

Savannah River

0 — Kilometers — 4
0 — Miles — 4

N

Old Browns Landing
1
Channel Marker 52
2

Stony Bluff Landing Put-in

Little Sweetwater Creek

Telfair Bay

Stony Bluff Landing Road

Rock Fence Crossroads

Mobley Swamp

Oglethorpe Trail

Savannah River

The Lagoon

3

4

Lower Three Runs Creek

Smith Lake Creek

5

6

7
White Woman's Point

8

Johnsons Landing

9

Ring Jaw Point

Wade Plantation

10
Channel Marker 42

11

Rocky Creek

McDaniel Creek

12

M1 Lake

Savannah River

120-Mile marker

13

Georgia Welcome Center
?

McDaniel Creek

301

Brier Creek

Wade Lake Number Two

Burtons Ferry Landing Takeout

To Sylvania

Wade Lake Number One

Wooden wing dams deepen the channel for nonexistent commercial traffic.

Paddle Summary

Have you ever wanted to paddle a really big river? Here's your chance. The Savannah River drains more than 10,000 square miles, and much of this waterway is still wild, despite being dammed upstream of Augusta. Starting at Stony Bluff Landing, this paddle travels the boundary between Georgia and South Carolina past thickly wooded shores that are remote and wild. Expect little to no company most of the time—this stretch of river is used almost exclusively by locals, and then usually during warm, pleasant weather.

River Overview

The Savannah River is one of Georgia's biggest waterways. Born at the confluence of two large rivers, the Tugaloo and the Seneca, which themselves drain the mountains north of them, the Savannah then flows southeasterly, forming the boundary between South Carolina and Georgia its entire distance. Much of the upper river is dammed as Richard B. Russell and Strom Thurman Lakes. Finally released from bondage, the Savannah flows through the town of Augusta and changes to a surprisingly remote big river—the part where this paddle takes place. As it nears the town of Savannah, tidal influence slows the river and it enters the Atlantic Ocean.

The Paddling

At Stony Bluff Landing, the Savannah River is about 200 feet wide, flowing between thickly wooded banks. Just downstream note some channel aids. Wooden berms known as wing dams or weirs extend into the water, deepening the channel for big boats despite the dearth of commercial traffic here. (Barges once went all the way up to Augusta from the coast.) Riprap lies along the banks. You will also notice the channel marker numbers—another legacy of the Army Corps of Engineers, which manages not only the river but also the dams upstream.

Vertical soil bluffs occasionally hover on the outside of bends, but most of the river's edge is thickly vegetated with willow, river birch, and sycamore. The vegetation gives way enough on the inside of bends to create an ever-changing combination of gravel, sand, and soil for landing spots.

The current is fairly swift and tends to boil in places, but there is no threat to the alert paddler—the Savannah is merely exhibiting the characteristics of a large river. The Savannah may have a brownish tint but is actually fairly clear, as the upstream dams keep sediment down.

After passing a few shacks on the right, the river remains wild, despite passing old Browns Landing on the South Carolina side of the river. Sturdy oaks and pines occupy the high bluffs, rising 25 feet or more above the water. Occasional cypress trees are mostly relegated to the back sloughs, which occasionally spur off the main river.

Pass Channel Marker 52 at 1.5 miles. The Savannah widens in excess of 200 feet in places. At 2.7 miles the river begins a long straightaway. You may notice the sign on river-left that states "130." That is River Mile 130 and indicates you are now 130 miles upstream from the Atlantic Ocean. The river mileages are signed every 10 miles.

The left bank is now Department of Energy property, part of the Savannah Nuclear Facility. That shore is off-limits, effectively leaving a wild bank. At 3.8 miles, near Channel Marker 47, Lower Three Runs Creek comes in from the South Carolina side.

The Savannah begins another series of bends. Ahead, the old river curved right and created a big oxbow, but you travel through a cut made by the Army Corps of Engineers when they straightened parts of the river for commercial traffic. You're technically paddling with South Carolina on both shorelines. At 6.4 miles a large slough leads toward the South Carolina side. This is actually Smith Lake Creek. There is an island in midriver. Below the island and slough, the Savannah temporarily widens and you pass a large beach on river-left and Channel Marker 45. The Department of Energy property has ended. There is a boat ramp here, on the South Carolina side at a place known as White Woman's Point.

The river narrows again then curves to reach a boat ramp on the South Carolina side at 8.6 miles. This is Johnson's Landing. Sloughs increase near Ring Jaw Point. Pass some wing dams and Channel Marker 42 at 10.4 miles. Ahead the Savannah River curves right, narrows, and splits around an island. McDaniel Creek comes in on the far side of the island. Pass the marker for River Mile 120 at 12.6 miles.

Downstream, Channel Marker 39 precedes a curve to the right, then the US 301 bridge and your takeout come into view. The old US 301 bridge lies just beyond. The old roundhouse bridge swiveled in the middle to let river traffic pass. Burtons Ferry boat ramp will be on your right.

ELI WHITNEY AND THE COTTON GIN
Eli Whitney is one of America's great inventors. It was on the banks of the Savannah River, downstream of this particular paddle near the city of Savannah, that Eli Whitney invented the cotton gin.

Born in Massachusetts, Whitney graduated from Yale University, then made his way down to Georgia to study law at Mulberry Grove, the plantation home of former Revolutionary War general Nathanael Greene's widow. Cotton was being grown here but wasn't well utilized simply because the seed was so hard to separate from the cotton. Separation had to be done by hand and was extremely slow and so labor intensive as to be prohibitive.

During this time Whitney made some minor but effective changes in ways Mrs. Greene operated her plantation, causing her to believe that he also could solve the vexing problem of separating the seed from the cotton. Before starting to construct the gin, Whitney had to make his own tools and other items.

Unfortunately his invention was caught up in lawsuits—its success brought copiers and outright theft of his idea. Whitney was eventually recognized as the inventor of the cotton gin, but the money he spent on building his invention as well as the lawsuits cut mightily into the profit. However, U.S. cotton exports grew more than forty times their previous level from the early 1790s to the early 1800s.

Whitney was also one of the first to use interchangeable parts in manufacturing. He signed a large contract with the U.S. government to build muskets and made a firearms factory, helping to evolve mass production and the factory concept.

The Mulberry Grove property, the site on the Savannah River where he first made the gin, was burned by Union General Sherman on his brutal march through the Peach State at the end of the Civil War. Today Mulberry Grove, currently owned by the Georgia Ports Authority, is in the middle of a preservation battle.

23 Watson Pond at George L. Smith State Park

This paddle, which doesn't require a shuttle, loops around impounded Watson Pond.

County: Emmanuel
Start: George L. Smith State Park N32° 32' 45.2", W82° 7' 36.3"
End: George L. Smith State Park N32° 32' 45.2", W82° 7' 36.3"
Length: 5.0 miles
Float time: 3.25 hours
Difficulty rating: Moderate
Rapids: None
River type: Impounded millpond grown over with swamp trees
Current: Very little
River gradient: None
River gauge: None; pond level information available at park office
Season: Year-round

Land status: State park
Fees or permits: Georgia Parks Pass entry fee
Nearest city/town: Twin City, Georgia
Maps: USGS : Twin City, Twin City SE; DeLorme: *Georgia Atlas and Gazetteer,* page 45
Boats used: Canoes, kayaks, paddleboats, some johnboats
Organizations: Friends of Georgia State Parks & Historic Sites, 781 Red Top Mountain Road, Cartersville, GA 30121; (770) 975-7533; www .friendsofgastateparks.org
Contacts/outfitters: George L. Smith State Park, 371 George L. Smith State Park Road, Twin City, GA 30471; (478) 763-2759; www .gastateparks.org

Put-in/takeout information:

To put-in/takeout: From exit 104 on Interstate 16 take Highway 23/121 north for 1.5 miles to the Metter town square. Stay with Highway 23 north, and continue for 11.8 miles. Turn right onto George L. Smith State Park Road. Pass the state park office then veer left; the boat ramp is on your right.

Paddle Summary

Watson Pond, also known as Parrish Pond, backs up Fifteen Mile Creek. The dam, a historic mill site, is now part of George L. Smith State Park. Trace a marked water trail that winds north among cypress and Ogeechee lime trees. Be glad the markers are there, for "two turns of a boat can get you lost," as was explained to me.

Reach the north end of the impoundment on the Red Trail, then return via the Blue Trail, which is very narrow and open only to canoes and kayaks, as it works its way in swamp forest along the east bank of the millpond. The paddling is easier at higher pond levels—at lower water the widely buttressed cypress trees become more exposed and narrow the paddle channels. *NOTE:* The park offers paddleboats and canoes for rent.

The Paddling

Spring is a great time to paddle Watson Pond—the water is high and the cypress trees have leafed out. The trails are marked with 2- by 2-inch metal markers nailed to trees.

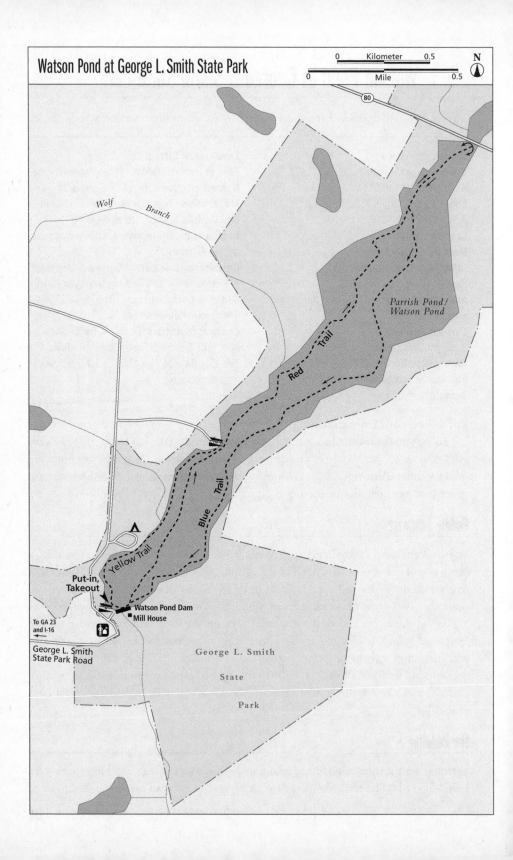

Watson Pond at George L. Smith State Park

As you look out from the ramp, the Yellow Trail leads your left. The Mill House is to the right. The Red Trail leaves from the paddle boat dock, which is off to your right. (If keeping forward from the boat launch, you will soon run into the Red Trail.)

Cypress trees, draped in Spanish moss, thicken on both shorelines. Their tan trunks adorned in bright green leaves and rising forth from coffee-colored waters against a blue sky conspire to make a colorful setting. In the middle of the impoundment, the trees seem randomly dispersed. Pines rise from the camping area to your left, behind the cypresses. Water lilies grow in the stillest of waters.

At 0.7 mile a more clearly defined channel emerges, with cypress and Ogeechee lime trees astride a water trail about 10 to 15 feet wide. The traveled track usually has less waterweeds or other underwater vegetation growing than the swamp areas not traveled by boats. You are going against the current of Fifteen Mile Creek; however, it is all but negligible. Just ahead, look for the other park boat ramp, to your left through the swamp forest.

Cypress trees buttress at the water level. At 1.3 miles the path begins to twist and turn a little bit more and shortly becomes canopied. At 1.5 miles the trail jogs left and enters a very narrow channel barely wide enough for a boat, offering a swamp paddling experience found few other places. Birds twitter in the trees and woodpeckers rattle in the distance.

At 1.8 miles come alongside land on your left. This is one of the few stopping spots available on the Red Trail, so take advantage. Beyond the land, the canopy occasionally opens but is still often shaded. Watch for wood duck boxes here. At 2.0 miles the Blue Trail leaves right. Watch carefully, as this junction is not well marked. The Red Trail keeps forward to emerge at Highway 80 at 2.4 miles. The highway and bridge are decidedly unpleasant compared with deep swamp, so turn around and backtrack to the Blue Trail. The markers on the Blue Trail are set lower on the trees, as this trail is used exclusively by paddlers. Hopefully your swamp paddling skills have been honed on the Red Trail—the Blue Trail requires more precise maneuvering. The channels are often less than 3 feet wide, especially at lower water levels when the exposed tree buttresses make the channels narrower. More waterweeds grow here, sometimes making it difficult to paddle. Expect slow progress, picking your way through this gorgeous swamp forest. The turns come quickly, and you can't get any forward momentum without coming to a major turn.

The Blue Trail works south, eventually coming close enough to land, but is divided between you and a dense growth of some swamp trees. In places along the Blue Trail, expect to paddle over floating logs. At 3.4 miles the trail opens into a clear pondlike area that's open to the sky overhead. This is the first treeless area on the Blue Trail. This exposure to the sun allows water grasses to grow thick in the summertime, and it feels as though you are paddling in stew.

The open area soon ends. Enter an ultra-dense swamp forest where you may be playing "bumper boats" with the trees beside the trail. After this thicket of trees the trail becomes manageable again, nearing land at 3.6 miles. This is a field that rises

directly from the swamp, and you come within sight of a house just outside the state park boundary. Despite being in the swamp forest, the trail stays close to the field, and the light from the adjacent open area provides contrast to where the paddle trail leads. It's easy to tell when you're getting closer to the end as the swamp forest opens at 4.4 miles. The Blue Trail curves left into a little bay, staying along the margin between the cypress trees densely growing your left and the clearing of the pond to your right.

Leaving the bay, reenter swamp forest. Come directly against forested land, then reopen onto open water. This ends the Blue Trail. From here you can see the boat ramp and boat rental area to your south. Backtrack to the boat ramp, or take a spin by the Mill House, which is off to the left, before completing the paddle.

GEORGE L. SMITH STATE PARK PRIMER Your paddle destination came to being in 1880, when Fifteen Mile Creek was dammed, forming the pond. The Mill House was built atop the dam, with floodgates to create waterpower to turn a turbine and then power all kinds of things, including a sawmill to cut timber and a gristmill for grinding corn. It even used waterpower to bail cotton. The whole structure is original except for the floor, and the gristmill is still in working order.

If you are coming this way, why not camp? The park campground is laid out in a loop sloping down toward George L. Smith Lake. Deft paddlers will be able to pull their boats directly to the campsites amid the hundreds of trees growing out of the water. Most of the twenty-six campsites run along the lake and fill every weekend from spring through fall. Reservations are highly recommended.

Anglers can often be seen bank fishing on the stream below the mill dam. Fishing is popular on the lake, too. Largemouth bass can be caught year-round, crappie when it's cooler, and bream when it warms up. You can also get your shoes dirty walking around some of the park's 7.0 miles of land trails. So consider expanding your paddling trip here to include some of the other park activities, such as camping, fishing, and hiking.

◄ *Paddler-eye view of channel in swamp forest*

South Georgia

24 Altamaha River near Baxley

The Altamaha makes for a unique paddling experience. The big, wide river is generally shallower than you might think for such a large body of water and has small riffles that speed the flow of an already moderate current.

County: Appling, Toombs
Start: Grays Landing N31° 57' 59.1", W82° 25' 42.6"
End: U.S. Highway1 N31° 56' 24.0", W82° 21' 21.9
Length: 6.0 miles
Float time: 2.5 hours
Difficulty rating: Easy
Rapids: Class I
River type: Massive, wide coastal plain river
Current: Moderate to swift
River gradient: 1.1 feet per mile
River gauge: Altamaha River near Baxley; no minimum runnable level; runnable year-round, but stay off at flood stage

Season: Year-round
Land status: Private; public
Fees or permits: No fees or permits required
Nearest city/town: Baxley, Georgia
Maps: USGS: Grays Landing, Baxley NE; DeLorme: *Georgia Atlas and Gazetteer,* page 53
Boats used: Pontoon boats, fishing skiffs, johnboats, kayaks, canoes
Organizations: Altamaha Riverkeeper, Inc., P.O. Box 2642, Darien, GA 31305; (912) 437-8164; www.altamahariverkeeper.org
Contacts/outfitters: Georgia Department of Natural Resources, 2 Martin Luther King Jr. Drive SE, Suite 1252 East Tower, Atlanta, GA 30334; (404) 656-3500; www.gadnr.org

Put-in/takeout information:

To takeout: From Baxley take US 1 north for 13 miles to cross the Altamaha on a bridge. At the far end of the bridge, look right for a road heading downhill to the right and back under the bridge to the US 1 boat ramp.

To put-in from takeout: Return to US 1 and follow it north for 2 miles to Cedar Crossing (County Road 364). Turn left onto Cedar Crossing and follow it for 1.5 miles. Turn left onto Old River Road (County Road 336), and travel 3.1 miles. Turn left onto Grays Landing Road, and go 1.4 miles to end at Grays Landing public boat ramp.

Paddle Summary

The Altamaha River is bordered with huge sandbars and bluffs topped with oaks and other deciduous trees. Scenic state-owned wild lands border the south shore of this entire paddle. Houses occupy the banks only at the paddle's beginning and end. The generally shallow river has small riffles that speed the flow of an already moderate current. Bring sunscreen and a hat with you—the wide river provides little in the way of shade.

River Overview

The Altamaha is formed a short distance from the confluence of the Oconee and Ocmulgee Rivers. At this point it is already a huge waterway, but it remains free

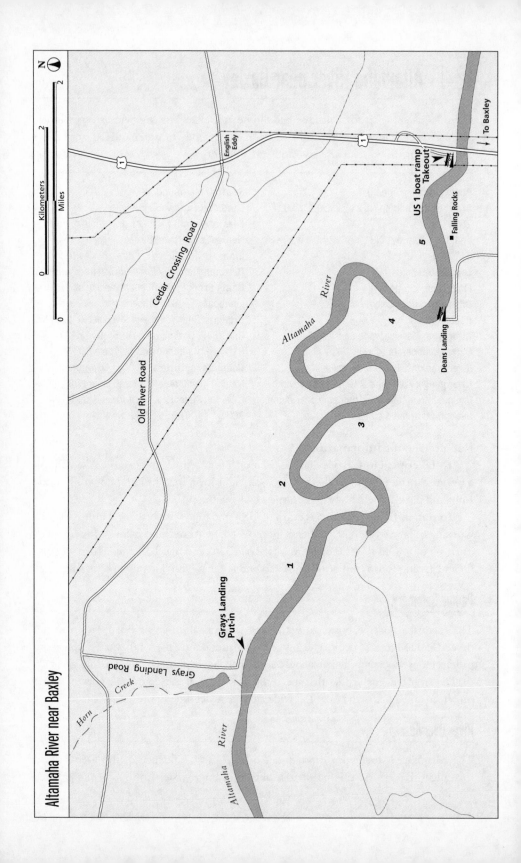

Altamaha River near Baxley

N

Kilometers
0   2

Miles
0   2

Old River Road

Cedar Crossing Road

English Eddy

To Baxley

US 1 boat ramp Takeout

Falling Rocks

Deans Landing

Altamaha River

Grays Landing Put-in

Grays Landing Road

Horn Creek

Altamaha River

1

2

3

4

5

flowing easterly to the Atlantic Ocean for 120 miles. A trip down the Altamaha is one of Georgia's most distinctive paddling experiences no matter where you go. Within its watershed is a treasure trove of flora and fauna. The waterway has a brownish tint but can even look greenish in fall when the water is at its lowest. At high water it will be murky.

The Paddling

Grays Landing has a small park and quality boat ramp. The mighty Altamaha is 300 feet wide plus at this point. Sandbars stretch out in front of you at low water. The water is surprisingly clear for a huge Coastal Plain river that drains two massive Piedmont waterways—the Ocmulgee and the Oconee. The confluence of the Ocmulgee and Oconee, where the Altamaha is born, is just a few miles upstream from Grays Landing, as the South Georgia product flows southeasterly for 137 miles to meet the Atlantic Ocean near the town of Darien.

Pass a few habitations along the left (north) bank. The south bank is part of the Bullard Creek Wildlife Management Area, which offers decently high shores and is completely forested with pine, oak, and sweet gum. The Altamaha riverbed is not all sand. Rocks will be exposed at low water. Note the shells in the sandy shallows, indicators of healthy water. It is in this time of low water that the canoeing is the best. The water will be the clearest, and the frequent shallows dissuade many motorboats. Also, the sandbars are at their biggest, availing campsites galore.

Willow and cypress grow on the margins closest to the water. River birch thrives also. Fallen trees are occasionally interspersed along the shores, but with the river in excess of 300 feet, passages are abundantly clear. The river is so wide that you will do best to choose one side of the waterway or the other. That way stopping is easier and you can also enjoy the riverside scenery.

Soon leave civilization behind. The size of these gigantic, uninhabited sandbars will amaze and make for great canoe camping opportunities. The tan riverside "sand deserts" are occasionally scattered with small willows and driftwood. The riverbed is always shifting, and during times of flood new channels are cut and old channels become sloughs, grassed-over flats, or hilly sandbars. The main current crisscrosses the greater river corridor and changes its exact path with the flow rate of the river.

The first bends come at 1.5 miles. Here the Altamaha has cut across a larger old bend. Huge sandbars form that are the size of multiple football fields. Pastureland encroaches on the left shoreline, but instead of being a detriment, it offers a grassy interlude between forested banks. Here the Altamaha falls into a pattern. On the inside of bends, massive sandbars reveal themselves, backed by a slow-rising shore of mostly willow. On the opposite bank low sand and soil bluffs rise just high enough for oaks and other deciduous trees to grow. However, these bluffs are undermined in high water, causing trees to continually cave into the river. This fallen timber adds more scenic value, but it is along these bluffs where the fastest current flows.

Walking across big sandbar on the Altamaha

Be vigilant if you try to ride this faster current through the partially submerged timber.

At 3.6 miles the Altamaha River bisects yet another old bend of the river. There are numerous snags in this channel. After rejoining the main channel you can see a large slough of the old channel coming in on your left. The exposed sandbars of the old channel are covered with grass in the warm season. Just ahead, curve left and pass around an island. At the lowest of water, the inside passage of this island will be dry. The right bank becomes rocky, and a bluff rises. Just ahead on river-right is Deens Landing public boat ramp. The rock bluff topped with houses just downstream of Deens Landing is known as Falling Rocks, for the propensity of stone to fall into the river here. The bluffs give way and the river curves right, forming one last sandbar. Pass under power lines and the US 1 bridge comes into sight. The landing is on the left just after the bridge.

A RARE FLOWER AND MORE The Altamaha River watershed, which includes two other big Georgia rivers with paddles detailed in this guidebook, the Oconee and the Ocmulgee, has more 120 species of rare and/or endangered plants, by far more than any other watershed in the

state. The Altamaha can also claim to be one of the most biologically diverse watersheds in the East. Of special interest are eleven types of pearly mussels, seven of which are found only on this river. You should see mussel shells along the banks and in shallows on your paddle.

This free flowing, undammed river—crossed only five times by road bridges and twice by rail en route to the ocean—spreads its floodplain up to 5 miles wide in points, making for a wilderness corridor rich with all sorts of plants and animals, from manatees to eagles to centuries-old pines. It is this wide wetland that has kept the Altamaha less disturbed and home to so many rare plants. The estuary of the Altamaha is valuable and relatively undisturbed as well.

Perhaps the watershed's most interesting—at least the rarest—plant is Radford's balm (*Dicerandra radfordiana*), a species of mint first discovered in 1981 and known only to exist in two places, both in McIntosh County, downstream toward the coast. The fall-blooming plant, first discovered by a graduate student, has an aroma resembling cinnamon. Who knows what other undiscovered species exist in the valley of this Georgia treasure?

25 Chesser Prairie at Okefenokee Swamp

This paddle starts at the swamp's east end, near the wildlife refuge visitor center and the Okefenokee Adventures outpost.

County: Charlton, Ware
Start: East Entrance, Suwannee Canal N30° 44' 16.0", W82° 8' 29.2"
End: East Entrance, Suwannee Canal N30° 44' 16.0", W82° 8' 29.2"
Length: 6.5 miles
Float time: 3.5 hours
Difficulty rating: Easy to moderate
Rapids: None
River type: Old canal; open-water prairie
Current: Easy to moderate
River gradient: None
River gauge: None; call refuge for swamp levels
Season: Year-round
Land status: Public—Okefenokee National Wildlife Refuge
Fees or permits: Okefenokee National Wildlife Refuge entrance fee; paddlers must sign in before entering the water and out upon exiting.

Nearest city/town: Folkston, Georgia
Maps: USGS: Chesser Prairie; DeLorme: *Georgia Atlas and Gazetteer,* page 69; Okefenokee National Wildlife Refuge map
Boats used: Canoes, kayaks, johnboats, tour boats
Organizations: Okefenokee National Wildlife Refuge, Route 2, Box 3330, Folkston, GA 31537; (912) 496-7836; www.okefenokee .fws.gov
Contacts/outfitters: Okefenokee Adventures, Route 2, Box 3325, Folkston, GA 31537; (866) 843-7926; www.okefenokeeadventures .com. Located at put-in, they rent boats and are the authorized concessionaire for the refuge.

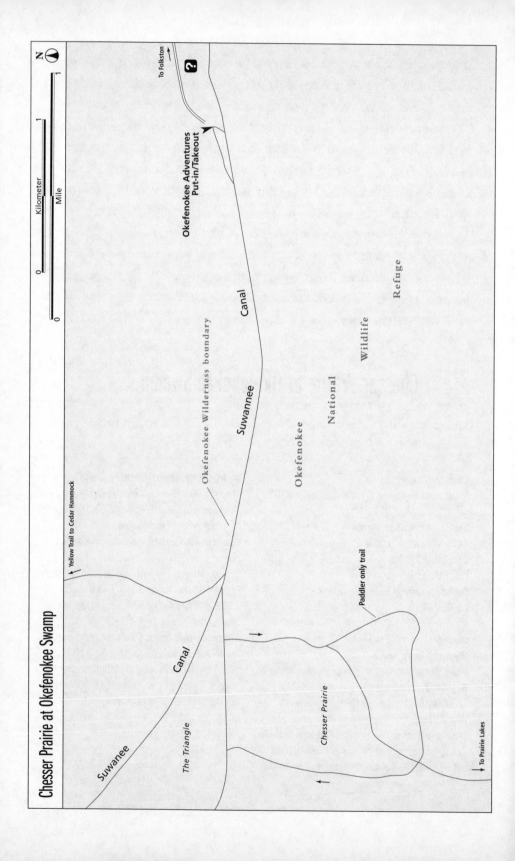

Chesser Prairie at Okefenokee Swamp

N

Kilometer

0   1

Mile

0   1

To Folkston

Okefenokee Adventures
Put-in/Takeout

Yellow Trail to Cedar Hammock

Okefenokee Wilderness boundary

Suwannee
Canal

Suwanee
Canal

The Triangle

Chesser Prairie

Paddler only trail

To Prairie Lakes

Okefenokee   National   Wildlife   Refuge

Put-in/takeout information:

To put-in/takeout: From Folkston take Highway 121/Highway 23 south for 7 miles to Okefenokee Swamp National Wildlife Refuge. Turn right onto Okefenokee Drive to enter the refuge. Go for 4.3 miles and dead-end at the Okefenokee Adventures and the East Entrance to Suwannee Canal. The boat ramp starts on the far side of the building beside Suwannee Canal.

Paddle Summary

NOTE: You must pay a refuge entrance fee and sign in and out at Okefenokee Adventures before leaving on this paddle.

Depart from the boat ramp and head west on either the Suwannee Canal or the parallel canoe trail. Travel west for a little over 2.0 miles, then joined the side trail to Chesser Prairie. Here you can enjoy some open paddling in a wide wetland with scenic tree islands. This part of the paddle hints at the vast nature of the refuge.

Backtrack via the Suwannee Canal or the canoe trail. Be apprised that biting flies and other insects can be unpleasant during summer. The yellow flies also can be incessant and brutal at this time. Spring and fall are popular times to visit. I have paddled here in all four seasons—each offers its own rewards. If you are in doubt about the current insect conditions, call the refuge before planning your paddle.

River Overview

Okefenokee Swamp is a vast wetland in Georgia's southeastern corner. Nearly 400,000 acres, the refuge offers more than 100 miles of paddling waterways and is a nationally renowned paddling destination. Most of the Okefenokee Swamp is within the confines of the Okefenokee National Wildlife Refuge, which is charged with preserving the swamp and its creatures. They do this by maintaining strict rules for entry, exit, fishing, hunting, and camping to maintain the wild and pristine character of this Peach State treasure. If you wish to paddle more in the Okefenokee, please refer to the Suwannee River paddle, and to the Okefenokee refuge Web site listed above.

The Paddling

Leave the boat ramp. The route immediately splits, and outgoing traffic stays right as you pass under a little bridge. The canal here is canopied. Ogeechee lime, oaks, titi, and pines border the leaf- and pine needle–littered canal. The island dividing in-and-out traffic soon ends and you enter the canal proper, which is the Orange Trail. The parallel canoe trail is an alternate way to get to Chesser Prairie. Unfortunately, low water levels and fire had closed the trail as of this writing; therefore, this description travels the Suwannee Canal. However, if you have the opportunity, take the canoe trail. This way you can avoid the motorboat traffic along the canal as well as the motorized tour boat.

View of prairie on a summer day

The canopy over the Suwannee Canal ceases. Cypress knees and grasses grow at the river's edge where the brush isn't overhanging. Alligators lurk all along the canal and will be commonly seen during warmer times. The Suwannee Canal was dug in the 1890s to drain the swamp and develop it as a vast agricultural area. After several years the crew digging the canal realized that the swamp simply wasn't draining—but not before 13 miles of the canal were completed. At 0.5 mile a small channel comes in on the left; just beyond that you can see a small prairie to the right. Watch for other small channels leading left.

The view down the waterway is dominated by majestic pines draped in Spanish moss that flank the canal. At 1.0 mile the canal angles to the right as a small channel closed to the public leads left. Watch for bay trees, also known as swamp magnolia. They will have creamy white blossoms in summer. Continue to gain occasional glimpses into prairies on either side of the canal when the tree corridor breaks. At 1.6 miles a sign indicates the national wildlife refuge wilderness boundary of the Okefenokee. More than 350,000 of the nearly 400,000 acres of the swamp are federally designated wilderness.

Shortly reach a series of signed junctions. First a spur trail leads right to Cedar Hammock. Ahead is a major split. To your right is the way to Chase Prairie. To the left, the route of this paddle, is Grand Prairie and Prairie Lakes. Just ahead, the day-use canoe trail comes in on your left.

At 2.1 miles reach the boat trail leading toward Grand Prairie, as well as Chesser Prairie and Monkey Lakes. Turn left here to enter Chesser Prairie and a very interesting area—islands of cypress rise from the prairie, creating a mosaic of beauty. The trails back here are about 10 to 15 feet wide, maybe 20 feet in places, and bordered with water lilies and other aquatic vegetation. The fire scars of 2007 are visible above the water.

At 2.5 miles the trail splits again. Here a paddler-only trail leads left toward Cooter Lake. This trail is subject to water levels and is not always open. If you can make it, more power to you; otherwise, just stay with the boat trail toward Grand Prairie. The boat trail here bears right. The beautiful prairie continues, although one side or another of the watery path often is wooded. In summer the underwater vegetation grows thick and may tangle with your paddle and impede the path. This prairie area is open to the sun overhead.

At 3.2 miles reach a four-way water trail junction. The Prairie Lakes Trail continues forward. The paddler-only trail traveling by Cooter Lake comes in on the left. You, however, turn right, heading back toward the Suwannee Canal. This trail turns almost due north, cutting through prairies and islands. Watch for fern fields growing beside the trail in addition to the watery vegetation.

The trail widens just before leaving Chesser Prairie to meet a canal. This canal is connected to the Suwannee River Canal on both ends and forms an area known as The Triangle, which you could paddle around if you are still feeling frisky. Head east now and complete the loop portion of the paddle at 4.4 miles. The channel leaving south here is the one you took heading into Chesser Prairie. Keep forward (eastbound) to soon meet the Suwannee River Canal. The rest of the paddle is a backtrack to the East Entrance.

THE SWAMP Like Georgia's national forests in the north, the federal government acquired the Okefenokee Swamp after natural resources—primarily timber—were extracted. Also as with the national forests, many residents were removed from the land when the refuge was established. Between 1909 and 1927, more than 431 million board feet of timber were removed from the swamp. After the harvest, the Okefenokee Preservation Society pushed Congress to purchase the swamp in order to allow it to renew and become what it is today—one of the largest protected wetlands in the Southeast.

The Okefenokee is a huge saucer-shaped depression approximately 100 feet above sea level. Beneath the waters, peat deposits more than 15 feet thick cover the swamp floor, inspiring pre-Colombian Indians holding sway over the area to call it the "Land of the Trembling Earth." By the 1830s the natives had been driven out, casualties of the Seminole Wars. Early Georgia settlers came behind them, settling the islands that exist within the swamp.

The settlers left their names in the Okefenokee at places like Chesser Prairie, through which this paddle passes, Chase Prairie, Floyds Island, Billys Island, and more. They not only lived off the land but also the waters that surrounded them. Prairies such as Chesser Prairie cover about 60,000 total acres within the swamp. These prairies are naturally created in times of drought when fires burn the deep layer of vegetation and peat, leaving water to fill the void.

While early settlers had established their locales, others saw the Okefenokee as a giant fertile agricultural area. Of course it had to be drained first, and that is how another part of this paddle—the Suwannee Canal—came to be.

The draining of the Okefenokee, much like the draining of the Everglades, was a failure that ended up serving public users a century later. Finally the Hebard Lumber Company realized that the way to obtain the riches of the Okefenokee was not to drain the swamp and then grow crops but to clear existing resources in the form of the old-growth forests ranging throughout the swamp. Today paddlers will take note that in the decades that have passed since this harvest, the management of the U.S. Fish and Wildlife Service has resulted in a comeback not only of the timber but also of the swamp's wildlife.

26 Flint River below Albany

Quality landings on both ends of the paddle, as well as an outfitter, make this trip user-friendly.

County: Dougherty, Mitchell
Start: Radium Landing N31° 32' 26.9", W84° 8' 23.4"
End: Flint River Park N31° 26' 18.8", W84° 8' 31.2"
Length: 9.0 miles
Float time: 4 hours
Difficulty rating: Easy to moderate
Rapids: Class I
River type: Coastal Plain river with bluffs
Current: Moderate
River gradient: 0.5 foot per mile
River gauge: Flint River at Newton; no minimum runnable level; maximum runnable, level flood stage
Season: Year-round

Land status: Private
Fees or permits: No fees or permits required
Nearest city/town: Abbeville, Georgia
Maps: USGS: Albany West, Baconton North; DeLorme: *Georgia Atlas and Gazetteer,* page 57
Boats used: Canoes, kayaks, johnboats
Organizations: Georgia River Network, 126 South Milledge Avenue, Suite E3, Athens, Georgia 30605; (706) 549-4508; www.garivers.org
Contacts/outfitters: Flint River Outpost, 11151 Old Georgia Highway 3, Albany, GA 31705; (229) 787-3004 or (888) 572-6697; www.mitchellcountyga.net/html/river_park. They rent canoes and kayaks; also provide shuttle for this very trip.

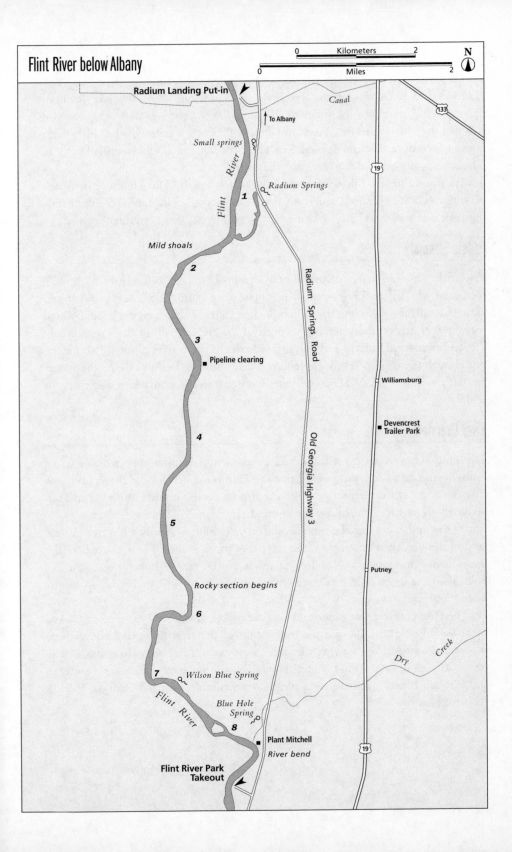

Flint River below Albany

Radium Landing Put-in

Canal

To Albany

Small springs

Flint River

Radium Springs

Flint River

1

Mild shoals

2

3

Pipeline clearing

Williamsburg

4

Devencrest
Trailer Park

Radium Springs Road

Old Georgia Highway 3

5

Putney

Rocky section begins

6

Dry Creek

7

Wilson Blue Spring

Flint River

Blue Hole Spring

8

Plant Mitchell

River bend

Flint River Park
Takeout

0   Kilometers   2

0   Miles   2

N

Put-in/takeout information:

To takeout: From the intersection of Highway 234 (Oakridge Drive) and U.S. Highway 133 (Radium Springs Road) on the south side of Albany, take Radium Springs Road south for 8.2 miles to the Flint River Outpost. Along the way you will pass the put-in turn into Radium Landing Park at 0.8 mile, which is just after a convenience store. Radium Springs Road becomes known as Old Georgia Highway 3 before reaching the takeout on your right.

To put-in from takeout: Head north back up the Old Highway 3, which becomes Radium Springs Road. Travel for 7.4 miles; the left turn into Radium Landing Park is just after you cross Marine Ditch and just before a convenience store.

Paddle Summary

The dark yet clear waters of the Flint River flow strongly below Albany, down a scenically wooded corridor with surprisingly steep bluffs. Small, rocky shoals and clear-blue springs, including the famed Radium Springs, enhance the paddle. Watch for wading birds on more remote sections of the river. Much of the banks, where shaded, are covered in ferns and lush groundcover. Cypress trees regally reach for the sky. Though the trip is 9.0 miles in length, it can easily be done in a day, as the waters are fairly fast moving. *NOTE:* The wide nature of the river makes it a fairway for winds.

River Overview

The Flint River rivals the Chattahoochee as Georgia's most important big river. From beginning to end, many argue that the Flint is the best for paddlers among the two. Born in a culvert beneath the Atlanta airport, the Flint flows south beyond this inauspicious start to form county-line boundaries.

By the time it reaches the Pine Mountains, the Flint is already a big river. While cutting through these mountains, the river is at its most scenic. It is also where the most challenging rapids are located, namely Class III Yellow Jackets Shoals. At this point the river drops off the fall line before settling down and continuing its southbound journey.

The Flint continues to widen and become more convoluted before being backed up at Lake Blackshear. Beyond the impoundment the river flows to Albany, where it is stalled again before flowing through the town and beyond, where this paddle occurs. By this point the Flint is a full-blown, massive waterway as it makes its way to and through Bainbridge before reaching Lake Seminole, near the Georgia, Florida, Alabama borders.

Looking downstream from the put-in ▶

The Paddling

The noise you hear after leaving the boat ramp is not a rapid; it's the outflow from the Albany water treatment plant. You will immediately notice the river's scenic banks, which are composed of limestone with ferns growing from them. The land rises beyond the limestone bluffs and is heavily wooded. Moss-draped cypress trees overhang the river. Sycamores grow a little higher, and oaks crown the shoreline. At normal flow the river will be plenty clear, especially since it is flowing from the Georgia Power Dam just a few miles upstream.

Pass a few houses on river-left and leave civilization behind for the most part. Less than 0.5 mile into the trip, a small spring bubbles from the left bank and will reveal itself at low water. A keen eye will spot yet another spring just below the first one. When the water is high and murky, these small springs will likely be lost altogether.

In the shallows note the plethora of mussels, displaying the health of the river. The Flint is on an extended straightaway, stretching 180 to 200 feet wide, but flows surprisingly swift. At 1.5 miles look left for the outflow of the old Radium Springs area. The large brick structure resembles a bridge here. The actual springs are a ways back from the river.

Below Radium Springs the Flint constricts, speeds up, and offers some shoals. These rapids are not a navigational challenge. However, you do have to deal with potentially troublesome limestone rocks. The wooded corridor continues to rise on both sides of the river, more than you would imagine would go on in South Georgia. In places the sloped banks will not be wooded to the shoreline but instead will have brush or exposed sand. These open shorelines are more gently sloping and will be more available for boat landings.

At 3.2 miles a pipeline clearing extends across the river. Just downstream, a culvert borders the river at a rocky shoal. When paddling close to shore, check out the cypress trees—their bases can be 8 feet across with huge knees alongside them. At 5.8 miles the Flint narrows, curves to the right, and becomes rockier, featuring some surprisingly sizable limestone boulders. The waterway speeds up as the rocks become more prevalent.

Sandbars increase in size and number as well and will be larger at low water. Look downstream for the stack of Plant Mitchell, a Georgia Power facility. It's just above your destination, so you know you're getting near the end when you see it. Look for the inflow of Wilson Blue Spring on river-right just after 7.0 miles. At 7.8 miles the river splits around islands. The primary channel, canopied by tall trees, goes around the left side. The current speeds up. Watch for exposed rocks here.

The Flint curves into a rocky swift section closely bordered by sycamore and cypress. Plant Mitchell is visible ahead. You can see the water outflow from the power plant. The current speeds up as it passes the structure then flows under some power lines. One last speedy shoal leads you to Flint River Park and the steep boat ramp on river-left.

RADIUM SPRINGS RESORT

Before Georgia was a state, there was Radium Springs—the largest upwelling along the banks of the Flint River. Noted for its scenic beauty, the spring emits consistently 68-degree water in a large, crystalline-blue bowl contained within a limestone frame—a flow that can exceed 70,000,000 gallons per day.

Passersby from pre-Columbian Indians to American tourists of a century ago came to the springs for its purported health benefits. Radium Springs lies within the Upper Floridan Aquifer, part of a complex plumbing network that cave divers have explored and mapped.

Radium Springs put Albany on the map for many tourists heading Florida way. Barron Collier, the same man who developed much of southwest Florida, came upon Radium Springs and saw its potential. He bought the place and had the waters chemically analyzed. The springs contained trace amounts of radium, thus the name of both the upwelling and the resort Collier constructed around it. This resort was anchored by a casino, hotel, spa, and other facilities to serve the tourists.

Over the next several decades Radium Springs became not only a stopover for tourists but also a gathering spot for Albany residents, who held events such as weddings there. However, the 500-year flood of 1994 followed by the 100-year flood of 1998 so severely damaged the resort that despite attempts to repair and manage it, the resort was ultimately torn down in 2003. Plans are afoot to reopen the springs to the public, perhaps as a botanical garden. Stay tuned.

27 Ichawaynochaway Creek

This sandy Coastal Plain stream winds southeasterly under a partial tree canopy and over, under, and around fallen logs.

County: Calhoun, Baker
Start: Highway 62 bridge N31° 28' 9.2", W84° 34' 14.6"
End: Highway 216 bridge at Milford N31° 22' 57.7", W84° 32' 47.4"
Length: 10.7 miles
Float time: 5 hours
Difficulty rating: Easy
Rapids: Class I
River type: Coastal Plain creek that wants to be a river
Current: Moderate
River gradient: 1.0 foot per mile
River gauge: Ichawaynochaway Creek at Milford; minimum runnable level 120 cfs

Season: Year-round
Land status: Private
Fees or permits: No fees or permits required
Nearest city/town: Newton, Georgia
Maps: USGS: Leary; DeLorme: *Georgia Atlas and Gazetteer*, page 57
Boats used: Canoes, kayaks, johnboats
Organizations: Georgia River Network, 126 South Milledge Avenue, Suite E3, Athens, GA 30605; (706) 549-4508; www.garivers.org
Contacts/outfitters: Georgia Department of Natural Resources, 2 Martin Luther King Jr. Drive SE, Suite 1252 East Tower, Atlanta, GA 30334; (404) 656-3500; www.gadnr.org

Put-in/takeout information:

To takeout: From Newton take Highway 37 north for 8 miles to Highway 216. Turn left and follow Highway 216 west for 4 miles to Milford. Keep west on Highway 216 a short distance to cross the bridge over Ichawaynochaway Creek, then turn left onto a dirt road that cuts back to the creek and ends under the Highway 216 bridge, on the southwest side of the stream.

To put-in from takeout: Backtrack east on Highway 216 for 0.3 mile. Turn left onto Milford Church Road, and travel 5 miles to Highway 37. Turn left onto Highway 37. After 0.3 mile enter Calhoun County. Continue a total of 4.5 miles to intersect Highway 62 in the town of Leary. Stay left on Highway 62 west through Leary, following it 3.5 miles to cross the bridge over Ichawaynochaway Creek. Turn right and return to the stream on a dirt track, on the northwest side of the bridge.

Paddle Summary

Ichawaynochaway Creek is as wild as its name sounds. The stream constantly changes its ways—from narrow, log-choked creek to wide, slow swamp waterway to rocky stream with rapids. The clear waters offer varying tints of brown, depending on their depth. Fallen logs are visible throughout, whether they are in the water, under the water, or around the water. Expect to navigate under, over, and around deadfalls in the course of a paddle, especially the first few miles. Wildlife is abundant on the stream. A quiet paddler will see numerous turtles and fish in the water—alligators, too.

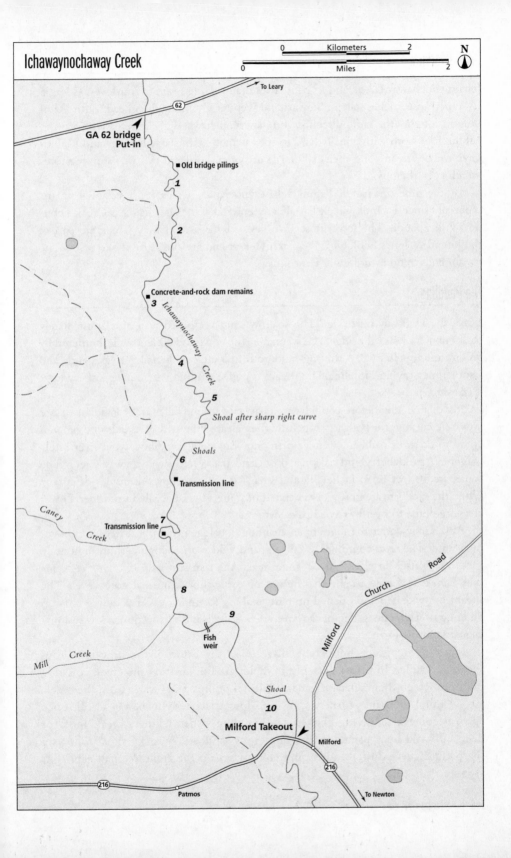

Ichawaynochaway Creek

0 — Kilometers — 2

0 — Miles — 2

N

To Leary

62

GA 62 bridge Put-in

■ Old bridge pilings

1

2

■ Concrete-and-rock dam remains

3

Ichawaynochaway Creek

4

5

Shoal after sharp right curve

Shoals

6

■ Transmission line

Caney

Creek

Transmission line ■ *7*

8

9

Fish weir

Mill Creek

Shoal

10

Milford Takeout

Milford

Church Road

Milford

216

216

Patmos

To Newton

River Overview

Ichawaynochaway Creek and its tributaries drain a large swath of southwest Georgia. Its uppermost reaches start in Stewart and Webster Counties, then head south. Running in roughly the same direction as Ichawaynochaway Creek are its two primary tributaries—both with equally hard to spell names—Chickasawhatchee and Pachitla Creeks. The streams and their tributaries are often bordered by low, swampy shores, which keep them wild.

By the time this paddle begins, Ichawaynochaway Creek is a substantial stream, especially since Pachitla Creek has already entered. Chickasawhatchee Creek enters below this paddle. The lowermost 15 miles of Ichawaynochaway Creek are part of the Joseph W. Jones Ecological Research Center and are closed to public access. The stream ends upon meeting the Flint River.

The Paddling

Leave the Highway 62 bridge. The shallow, sand-bottomed waterway immediately passes under a railroad bridge. The wannabe river is a good 40 feet wide, bordered by willow and tupelo trees. A shifting-sand bottom is affected by fallen trees, bends, and a sometimes-caving shoreline. The stream is coffee colored where deep; otherwise it is translucent.

It won't be long before you'll have to navigate around fallen trees. Paddlers before you have cut logs for passage. Hopefully, they cleared the passage the day before you come to do your paddle. Consider bringing your own saw. Above you, river birch, magnolia, sparkleberry, and oaks reach out and shade Ichawaynochaway Creek. The banks are 10 feet or so in height, and small sandbars occupy the insides of curves. Often the sandbars are grassy or vegetated in some way, especially in summer. Lower areas are home to overflow swamps of cypress.

At 0.8 mile concrete pilings of an abandoned bridge now collect trees in times of high water. The river continues its curving and wild ways. Along the shore, limestone rock reveals itself in places. At 2.9 miles reach the remains of an old concrete-and-rock dam that is now a rapid that be can be easily shot at normal water levels. The stream has widened and opened up here, making for much easier paddling as far as dodging obstacles goes. The banks have risen as well, and this section is less swampy. Bigger sandbars form.

Limestone appears more frequently and is the cause of the now-numerous shoals and riffles. In places, agricultural fields are not far from the creek corridor, but trees screen them. Occasional agricultural pumps draw water from the creek. At 4.4 miles the banks turn swampy and low as Ichawaynochaway Creek once again becomes narrow, log-choked, and winding. When taking a break, look for deer and wild boar prints on the numerous sandbars. A rocky shoal follows a sharp right curve. Just ahead, a piney bluff rises on the right. A small cabin sits atop it.

Limestone shoal

You begin to notice a pattern. When the banks are higher, the creek winds less and is more open with less deadfall in the water. When the banks are low and swampy, the stream curves more and has more water hazards. A high bluff topped with pine stays on the left bank some distance, as the creek is experiencing a relatively straight stretch. At 5.7 miles limestone shoals bordered with cypress trees make for a fun paddle and scenic sight. Several small shoals follow as the flow speeds. Occasional cabins are scattered on the river now. Pass under a transmission line at 6.2 miles. The banks are generally higher here, and cedar trees find their place along with live oaks and pines. Together they provide ample year-round greenery.

Pass under a second transmission line at 7.1 miles. Caney and Mill Creeks come in on your right downstream. The current is slower here, and sandbars become smaller and more wooded. The open, white shells of mussels clearly reveal themselves when the exposed limestone river bottom flows over shallow and swift waters. At 8.7 miles negotiate a limestone rock rapid and possibly an old Indian fish weir. Below this rapid the current slackens considerably and widens to 70 feet. Reach another shoal at 9.9 miles. The creek curves around an island just before reaching the Highway 216 bridge. A few final rocky shoals accompany you to the span. The takeout is on your right.

RESEARCH ON ICHAWAYNOCHAWAY

The lowermost 15 miles of Ichawaynochaway Creek are blocked to public access. This is where the Joseph W. Jones Ecological Research Center is located. This 29,000-acre outdoor laboratory started out as a quail-hunting plantation established in the 1920s by Robert W. Woodruff, the famed chairman of Coca-Cola. In 1991 this plantation was converted into the research center that it is today and named for one of Woodruff's Coca-Cola compadres. The reason for closing Ichawaynochaway Creek to public access is ostensibly to maintain the integrity of the research going on within the confines of the center.

The center is divided into two management zones—one studying the effects of sustainable forestry and the other conservation of the natural ecosystem located within the boundaries of this outdoor laboratory. The area includes not only the lower part of Ichawaynochaway Creek but also 13 miles of river frontage on the lower Flint River. The protected communities are primarily longleaf–wire grass woodlands and wetlands along the creek. The Flint River segment includes cypress sloughs, hardwood hammocks and riverine environments related to the limestone bed of the Flint, along with the springs along the river.

The forestry research is centered on longleaf pine woods and how such woods respond to various management strategies. The research center also undertakes wildlife research and management. While gathering this information, the center disseminates its findings with visiting university students and professors. The center also works with private landowners to help them manage their plots. For more information please visit www.jonesctr.org.

28 Kinchafoonee Creek

Kinchafoonee Creek flows in tortured convolutions and presents many beautiful sights: dripping sheer bluffs draped in ferns, translucent blue springs, waterfalls tumbling over limestone walls, cypress knees and roots intertwined among the waterworn limestone.

County: Lee
Start: Highway 32 bridge N31° 43' 9.6", W84° 11' 8.7"
End: Creekside Drive N31° 39' 44.5", W84° 10' 56.8"
Length: 6.0 miles
Float time: 3.5 hours
Difficulty rating: Easy
Rapids: Class I
River type: Coastal Plain creek bordered with bluffs aplenty
Current: Moderate to swift in spots
River gradient: 1.2 feet per mile
River gauge: Kinchafoonee Creek near Dawson; minimum runnable level 85 cfs

Season: Year-round
Land status: Private
Fees or permits: Launch fee at Creekside Drive takeout
Nearest city/town: Leesburg, Georgia
Maps: USGS: Leesburg; DeLorme: *Georgia Atlas and Gazetteer*, page 49
Boats used: Canoes, kayaks
Organizations: Georgia River Network, 126 South Milledge Avenue, Suite E3, Athens, GA 30605; (706) 549-4508; www.garivers.org
Contacts/outfitters: Georgia Department of Natural Resources, 2 Martin Luther King Jr. Drive SE, Suite 1252 East Tower, Atlanta, GA 30334; (404) 656-3500; www.gadnr.org

Put-in/takeout information:

To takeout: From the Albany Bypass (U.S. Highway 19/Highway 82) take exit 6A US 19 north, Slappey Boulevard). Follow US 19 north for 3.5 miles to Creekside Drive. Turn left onto Creekside Drive to enter a residential area and follow it for 0.6 mile. Look for Alicia's Shear Place, turning right into the driveway for 219 Creekside Drive, and head down the driveway to a backyard launch. Look for a sign saying WELCOME BOAT LAUNCH. There is a fee for this launch.

To put-in from takeout: Backtrack to US 19 and turn left, heading north on US 19 for 3.7 miles to the US 19 Bypass on the south end of Leesburg. Turn left onto the US 19 Bypass and travel for 0.2 mile; turn left, staying with Highway 32 west. Follow Highway 32 west for 0.5 mile, crossing the bridge over Kinchafoonee Creek. Turn left onto a gravel road that curves back to the waterway.

Paddle Summary

The natural mosaic of Kinchafoonee Creek took a long time to create. Sandbars occur at nearly every bend and call you to pull over. Limestone rocks offer contrast along the shifting sand stream bottom. You'll be surprised at the contrast between deep and shallow water here. Fallen trees are prevalent nearly the entire distance. The creek is often completely canopied and usually partly canopied. Morning glory, among other

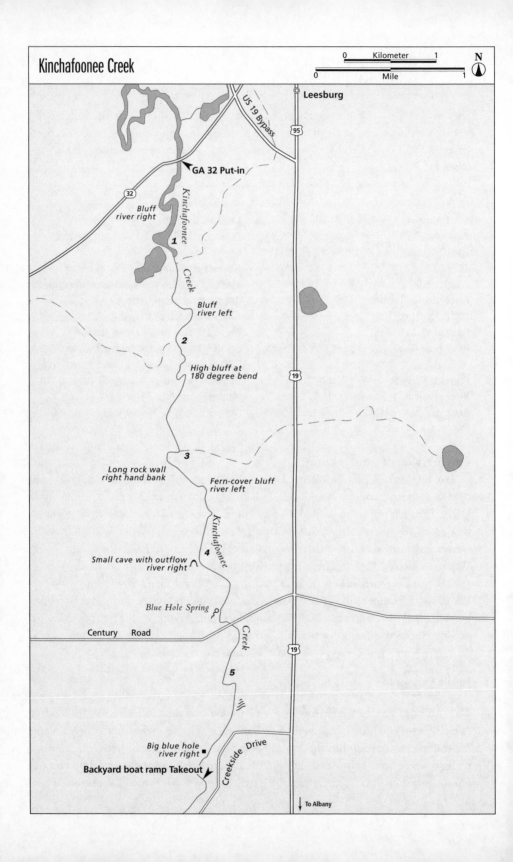

vines, drapes itself over anything not moving in this lush valley. The distance allows for ample time to relax and enjoy all the streamside features.

River Overview

Kinchafoonee Creek is a major tributary of the lower Flint River. Its headwaters start east of Fort Benning, in Middle Georgia. A series of south-flowing streams in Marion, Chattahoochee, and Stuart Counties come together to form Kinchafoonee Creek, which flows through the heart of Webster County and beside the town of Preston. Here more tributaries drain a large area, including Bear Creek.

Kinchafoonee Creek forms the county boundary line between Sumter and Terrell Counties as it continues southeast in an extremely winding fashion. This circuitous course makes the stream hard to navigate—especially at low water—until it fully enters Lee County. The numerous curves and convolutions form many oxbows. By the time Kinchafoonee Creek reaches Highway 32, it is a swift, sand-bottomed stream cutting through gorgeous limestone walls and undercut bluffs draped in ferns. Springs show themselves here and add scenic value to the paddle.

Downstream of this paddle, Kinchafoonee Creek continues to meet Muckalee Creek in the backwaters of Lake Chehaw. The closer you get to the lake, the more houses are on the stream, but it is paddleable all the way to Lake Chehaw.

The Paddling

Kinchafoonee Creek is about 40 feet wide at the put-in point and offers a good sandbar for loading. Live oak and cypress trees overhang the shallow, clear waterway. River birch and sycamore are common as well. The translucent water reveals the sandy stream bottom and all that lies upon it, including embedded trees.

Immediately reach a large sandbar on a sharp right turn. Sandbars are common on the inside of all bends on this creek. The sandy bottom often shifts; therefore, currents and channels will change with the pattern of fallen trees. The depths of the stream can range from 2 inches to 8 feet, depending on flow and strata below the water. On straightaways the waterway can become very wide and shallow.

At 0.4 mile a high bluff rises as the river curves left. These first bluffs will have rocks mixed in them. The creek corridor will be very heavily vegetated in summer, from both brush and dense trees. Cypress trees will grow in mid-river between sharp curves.

The sounds of Highway 32 fade. Reach another high bluff on river-left at 1.7 miles. An alluring sandbar stands across from it. Take note of the limestone outcrops that are intermingled with the varied shapes of the cypress knees rising amid the limestone. It makes for an interesting waterside landscape. At 2.4 miles Kinchafoonee Creek makes a 180-degree bend and curves right to pass below a high, fern-covered rock bluff rising 40 feet directly from the water. Limestone grottos continue alongside the river in many spots. Other bluffs will be sandy and not vegetated.

Fern lined bluff with collapsed bluff segment downstream

Kinchafoonee Creek continues making sharp convolutions. Some of these sharp bends will have cuts where the river bisects them in times of high water. At 3.2 miles reach a long, gorgeous rock wall on the right-hand bank. At the waters edge, honeycombed grottos rise to form a solid limestone fortification covered in vegetation. At 3.5 miles another spectacular overhanging bluff with ferns rises on river-left. The downstream portion of this bluff collapsed and now narrows the creek. Gorgeous walls continue on one or both sides of the river. At 4.0 miles watch for a small, cave-like crevice on river-right with the water flowing from it.

Streamside houses began to appear with more frequency starting at 4.2 miles. Century Road isn't far away. At 4.5 miles pass a chilly, blue-hole spring coming out on river-right. It emerges from a vent and rises, pushing sand outward, staying 68 degrees year-round. A couple of curves will lead you under the Century Road Bridge. The waterway divides around an island below the bridge and passes through some very mild, rocky shoals. The now-slower waterway continues to partition around islands.

At 5.4 miles come upon a sheer bluff, with lots of water dropping off in various places forming noisy, chilly waterfalls. Paddlers going under these waterfalls will certainly cool down on a hot South Georgia summer day. You'll hear the echoes of these falls long before you see them. The ferns are especially thick here. The aquatic features aren't over yet, as you come to a big spring on river-right at 5.7 miles. The spring is 10- by 10-feet wide and 8 feet deep, emerging from a dark vent. The slow current eventually takes you to the backyard boat ramp on river-left at 6.0 miles.

MORE TO LOVE THAN JUST GEORGIA PEACHES
As you drive through southwest Georgia, maybe en route to your paddle, you will undoubtedly see some pecan groves. The lower Flint River Valley is the heart of Georgia's pecan industry, and Georgia is the nation's leading producer of pecans, making this area the American epicenter of pecan production.

Interestingly, pecans are not native to Georgia. This member of the hickory family naturally grow from Illinois to the Gulf of Mexico in the lower Mississippi River Valley and west into Texas. In fact, the name given to pecans by early Americans was "Illinois nuts." Indians often used pecans after boiling them and pounding them into a paste.

Settlers took a page from the Indians' diet in using this nut, first popularized as a food by none other than Thomas Jefferson, who had pecan trees imported from Louisiana to his home at Monticello. Jefferson gave some pecan trees to George Washington, and now they are the oldest trees at Mount Vernon, Washington's plantation.

Over time the Indian name "pecan" became used for this large tree that was planted in groves throughout the Southeast, including Georgia. However, it wasn't until the early 1900s that southwest Georgia became a major player in the pecan industry. Real estate investors planted pecan trees by the thousands as an enticement to sell land around Albany. An industry was born, and by 1920 Georgia produced more than 2.5 million pounds of pecans. By the 1950s Georgia had established itself as the number-one producer of pecans in the United States and remains so to this day, averaging 88,000,000 pounds of pecans each year! A managed acre of pecan trees will produce about 1,000 pounds of pecans on an average year.

Pecan trees are not only prized for their fruit but also for their valuable lumber, which is used to make furniture, flooring, and paneling. Wood from Georgia pecan trees was used for the torches of the 1996 Olympic Games held in Atlanta.

29 Muckalee Creek

Muckalee Creek is an incredibly winding and scenic stream. Large plantations border much of the upper stream banks and effectively keep it wild.

County: Lee	**Land status:** Private
Start: Highway 32 bridge N31° 43' 53.9", W84° 7' 29.6"	**Fees or permits:** Entrance fee if leaving vehicle at the Parks at Chehaw
End: Forrester Parkway N31° 39' 27.37", W84° 6' 21.72"	**Nearest city/town:** Leesburg, Georgia
Length: 8.2 miles	**Maps:** USGS: Albany Northeast, Albany West, Leesburg; DeLorme: *Georgia Atlas and Gazetteer,* pages 49, 50
Float time: 4 hours	
Difficulty rating: Easy to moderate	**Boats used:** Canoes, kayaks
Rapids: Class I	**Organizations:** Georgia River Network, 126 South Milledge Avenue, Suite E3, Athens, GA 30605; (706) 549-4508; www.garivers.org
River type: Coastal Plain swamp creek punctuated with rocky rapids	
Current: Moderate to swift in spots	**Contacts/outfitters:** Georgia Department of Natural Resources, 2 Martin Luther King Jr. Drive SE, Suite 1252 East Tower; Atlanta, GA 30334; (404) 656-3500; www.gadnr.org
River gradient: 3.2 feet per mile	
River gauge: Muckalee Creek at Highway 195, near Leesburg; minimum runnable level 80 cfs	
Season: Year-round	

Put-in/takeout information:

To takeout: From the Jefferson Street exit on the Albany Bypass (U.S. Highways 19/82) on the north side of town, take Jefferson Street (Highway 133) north a short distance to Philema Road (Highway 91 north). Turn right onto Philema Road and follow it for 4.8 miles to Graves Springs Road. Head north on Graves Springs Road for 0.5 mile to a four-way stop and Forrester Parkway. Turn left onto Forrester Parkway and follow it 0.6 mile to the bridge over Muckalee Creek. Beyond the bridge, a rough sand road heads down to the creek. I recommend leaving your car on Forrester Parkway and carrying your boat from the creek to the road after your paddle.

To put-in from takeout: From Forrester Parkway, backtrack to Graves Springs Road. Turn left and head north up Graves Springs Road for 5.3 miles to Highway 32. Turn left onto Highway 32 and follow it 1 mile to a left turn just before the bridge over Muckalee Creek. Follow the road down to the creek.

Alternate takeout/put-in: For the takeout follow Philema Road for 1.2 miles, then turn left into The Parks at Chehaw. Take the first left past the guard station and follow the road to dead-end at the picnic area and dock on Lake Chehaw. To reach the put-in from The Parks at Chehaw go for 3.6 miles and turn left on Graves Springs Road and continue with put-in directions above.

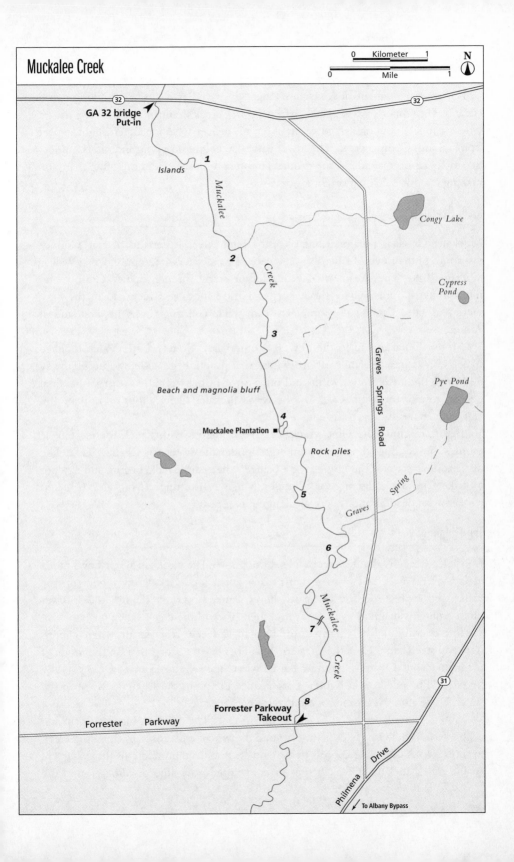

Muckalee Creek

GA 32 bridge
Put-in

Islands

1

Muckalee

32

32

Congy Lake

2

Creek

Cypress
Pond

3

Pye Pond

Beach and magnolia bluff

Graves Springs Road

4

Muckalee Plantation ■

Rock piles

5

Graves Spring

6

Muckalee

7

Creek

31

8

Forrester Parkway
Takeout

Forrester   Parkway

Philmena Drive

To Albany Bypass

0   Kilometer   1

0   Mile   1

N

Paddle Summary

This particular segment of Muckalee Creek gives you two distinct paddling experiences. The upper part is characterized by the creek's convoluted curving nature where a mix of low bluffs and swampy terrain deliver what a paddler might expect from a South Georgia creek. The lower part then begins dropping and offers numerous rocky rapids that add to the paddle. The stream is canopied more often than not, making it a good destination for a hot day.

River Overview

Muckalee Creek is a major tributary of the Flint River. It starts in Marion County, just south of the town of Buena Vista, where its headwaters are impounded as Walker Williams Lake. The stream then heads southeasterly through Schley County and into Sumter County, where the waters of Little Muckalee Creek add to the flow. Here Muckalee Creek is a swampier stream while coursing along the west side of Americus.

More tributaries add to the flow as it enters Lee County. Little Muckaloochee Creek comes in a few miles above where this paddle begins. Below the Highway 32 bridge the creek flows swiftly and offers several rocky rapids as it makes its final descent toward the Flint River. By the way, Muckalee Creek drops more than 400 feet from its headwaters to its end.

Before reaching the Flint Muckalee Creek merges with Kinchafoonee Creek, though this confluence is now submerged under the waters of Chehaw Lake. The best paddling starts at the Highway 32 bridge, where this paddle begins, and extends to Lake Chehaw, a distance of 13 miles. Much of the upper Muckalee Creek is choked with deadfall and is very challenging in a boat.

The Paddling

Muckalee Creek is about 35 feet wide at the put-in. The clear, tan water flows moderately over a rock bed overlain with many fallen logs. Oaks grow higher on the banks, and cypress trees overhang its shores, flanked by their strange knees. River birch, palmetto, magnolia, and cedar find their place in the creek valley.

The river immediately narrows to less than 15 feet as it speeds up where cypress trees and steep banks close the corridor. Small beige sand bars gather on the inside of the many bends. Overflow swamps extend where the riverbanks are low. Logs, left by floods, will be piled up in tighter spots. Notice the stains on the trees closest to the water. These also reveal times of high water on Muckalee Creek.

Limestone rock borders the creek's edge in spots. The overhanging rocks drip and echo as you paddle by. Fields lie just beyond the wooded line of trees along the creek in spots. Occasional lone cypress trees stand sentinel in the middle of the waterway. At 0.8 mile Muckalee Creek begins its convoluted ways after dividing around the first of many islands. Feeder branches will sometimes create small falls, especially following rains.

At 1.1 miles the creek straightens out, deepens, and continues almost due south. At 1.6 miles pass a clearing and the farm access on river-right. The river turns southeast here. At 2.0 miles the stream convolutions resume. These sharp turns often undercut the banks, and trees fall into the river, creating obstacles for the paddler. Expect to go around or pull over some of these blowdowns.

The river continues to wind and is canopied more often than not. At 3.7 miles come along a high bluff on the right bank. Notice the beech and magnolia trees along this steep east-facing hillside, indicating a moist site. The bluff soon fades away. At 4.1 miles the right-hand bank is cleared and you pass a large house set well back from the shoreline. This is Muckalee Plantation.

At 4.5 miles notice the piled limestone rocks crossing the river. They may have been part of an old bridge, but their reason for being is now lost to time. Channels flow between the pilings. More rock pilings are located in the general vicinity, which speed up the water. A few houses begin to appear in the Graves Spring area, at 5.4 miles. At 7.0 miles the current has slackened, but this is actually where the rapids begin to appear. Pines grow with more frequency down here. Many rapids follow as the creek continues to divide and come together. These rapids usually consist of a creek constriction complemented by rock extending across the waterway. This section of rapids continues for nearly a mile.

Just when things calm down, the Forrester Parkway Bridge appears through the woods to your left. Pass under the bridge and reach a steep, sandy takeout on river-right at 8.2 miles.

Option: If you are up for a longer paddle, you can continue to The Parks at Chehaw, but it is 5.0 miles distant from Forrester Parkway. Allow for plenty of time if you choose to do the entire paddle to Lake Chehaw. Beyond Forrester Parkway, pass one more rapid. The stream continues to be narrow and tree lined. Bluffs rise higher here below the bridge, and the vegetation is junglesque. Nice houses overlook the creek, which remains very beautiful itself. The current becomes nonexistent as the stream is backed up by the lake. Pass under a transmission line at 10.6 miles. Larger boats will be seen tooling around this arm of the lake. Upon entering the main body of Lake Chehaw, you will see the traffic of Philema Road. The paddle ends at the dock of The Parks at Chehaw at 13.5 miles.

THE PARKS AT CHEHAW The Parks at Chehaw, opened in 1977, is the alternate takeout for this paddle. Situated on the banks of Muckalee Creek, this Albany treasure is worth a visit. Originally laid out by Georgia native and famed naturalist Jim Fowler—former costar of the TV show *Wild Kingdom*—this park offers, among other things, wild animals in a natural setting.

Here you can stroll among creatures native to Africa as well as the United States, from cheetahs to eagles. Kids will enjoy the children's farm with its pigs, goats, and miniature horses. But this park is more than a zoo. It offers a campground set beneath pines with separate loops for RV campers and tent campers. The RV campers have hookups, and each loop has its own bathhouse. I enjoyed my overnight stay here. Picnic pavilions and the Creekside Nature Center are available for gatherings. Numerous education programs take place at the nature center, too.

Hiking trails course through the park. Kids have a large playground through which to roam. Bicyclists enjoy the BMX track. The Wiregrass Express is a miniature train for people of all ages. Special events are held throughout the year, and kids camps are run in the summertime. For more information visit www.parksatchehaw.org.

30 Saint Marys River

Once under federal consideration for Wild and Scenic status, many consider this part of the St. Marys River to be its best.

County: Charlton
Start: Tompkins Landing N30° 42' 41.4", W82° 2' 10.1"
End: Traders Hill N30° 46' 56.6", W82° 1' 28.6"
Length: 8.7 miles
Float time: 5 hours
Difficulty rating: Easy
Rapids: None
River type: Blackwater
Current: Slow to moderate
River gradient: 0.2 foot per mile
River gauge: St. Marys River near MacClenny, Florida; minimum runnable level 100 cfs

Season: Year-round
Land status: Private
Fees or permits: No fees or permits required
Nearest city/town: Folkston, Georgia
Maps: USGS: Toledo, Folkston; DeLorme: *Georgia Atlas and Gazetteer,* page 70
Boats used: Canoes, kayaks, johnboats
Organizations: Saint Marys River Management Committee, P.O. Box 251, Folkston, GA 31537; www.saintmarysriver.org
Contacts/outfitters: Canoe Country Outpost, 2818 Lake Hampton Road, Hilliard, FL 32046; (866) 845-4443; www.canoecountryoutpost.com

Put-in/takeout information:

To takeout: From the junction of US 301 and Main Street in downtown Folkston, take Main Street west for 0.5mile to reach Okefenokee Parkway (Highway 121/Highway 23). Turn left and follow the parkway south for 3 miles. Turn left onto Traders Hill Road and follow it for 1.3 miles. Turn left onto Tracys Ferry Road and go 0.5 mile to dead-end at the boat ramp.

To put-in from takeout: From Folkston take U.S. Highway 301/U.S. Highway 1 south for 4.5 miles, crossing the bridge over the St. Marys into Florida. Shortly

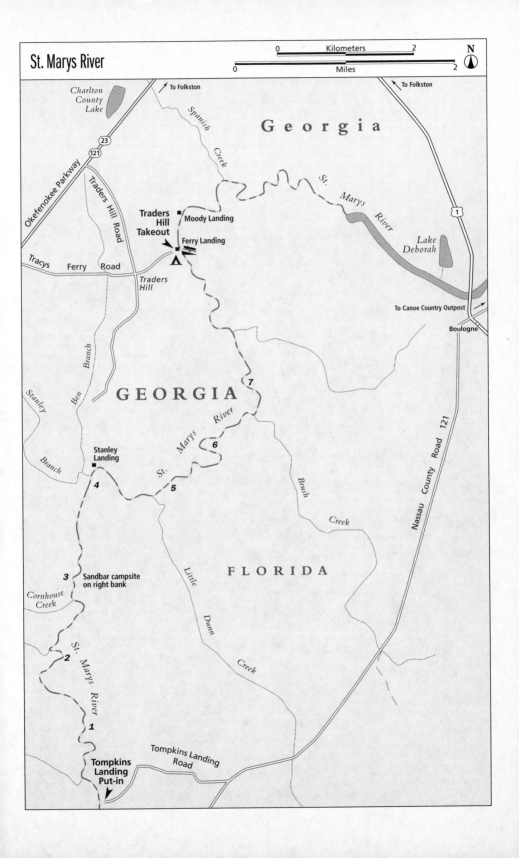

beyond the bridge, turn right onto Nassau County Road 121. Go for 5.2 miles and turn right onto Tompkins Landing Road. Follow Tompkins Landing Road to dead-end at a boat ramp.

Paddle Summary

Starting at Tompkins Landing, the St. Marys River winds through a gorgeous wooded corridor broken by white sandbars, which contrast with the dark waters as the river heads north. Straighter sections have fewer sandbars but more overhanging trees. As you near Traders Hill, the St. Marys becomes tidally influenced, backing the river up or hastening its current, depending on the tides, although salt water never reaches this far inland. An outfitter (see listing above) is available for this exact run, eliminating the need for two cars.

River Overview

The St. Marys River is the border between Georgia and Florida east of the Okefeno-kee Swamp. At 130 miles long, the St. Marys flows into the Atlantic near Fernandina Beach. For its first 40 miles the St. Marys forms a horseshoe before finally heading east to the coast. The part flowing out of the Okefenokee Swamp is known as the North Prong.

After the confluence with the Middle Prong, the river becomes wider and is characterized by bluffs, swamps, and snow-white sandbars. Development along the St. Marys banks is scattered and infrequent, making it an ideal paddling destination. The nearly 80 miles from Moniac to Folkston is the best section for paddlers and makes for a memorable multinight trip.

The Paddling

Leave Tompkins Landing. Georgia is on your left and Florida is on your right the entire paddle; beyond is the sea. The river stretches about 60 feet wide here, with white sandbars below higher bluffs with overhanging oaks. Pine trees grow in the highest margins, above palmetto brush. Closer to the water, willow, tupelo, and cypress trees hold sway. The coffee-colored waters flow silently toward the ocean. The bluffs rise 20 to 30 feet on the high sides.

The river can be quite deep, but it also has many shallows that gradually rise to sand banks. In still other places the drop-offs are quite abrupt. Occasional fish camps, with just a shed or other primitive shelter, dot the banks, especially on the Georgia side. Trees often overhang the St. Marys but rarely form a complete canopy. Fallen logs lie along the water's edge but never pose a hazard or block passage as they do upriver, where the St. Marys leaves the Okefenokee Swamp.

◀ *Close-up view of cypress knees on shoreline*

Small side creeks—often the return flow from overflow swamps that get filled at high water but sometimes simply tributaries—spill loudly back into the St. Marys while cutting through the sand bluffs. On sheer north-facing banks, moss and ferns form green carpets. In other places rock is exposed alongside the river.

At 2.0 miles the river makes a pair of sharp bends as a branch of Cornhouse Creek comes in on the left. At 3.1 miles, on a right-hand curve on the Florida side, pass a fine sandbar that rises up to a level, shaded spot and makes for a good campsite. Beyond here the river makes an almost due-north straight track with steep banks on both sides, forming a green corridor. At 4.1 miles the straightaway ends on a right-hand curve as Stanley Branch comes in on river-left. The high ground beyond the confluence is the old Stanley Landing.

The river now aims northeasterly, but it keeps twisting enough to have sandbars. It has broadened to 100 or more feet and has deepened as well. Though some land is posted, there are plenty of places to stop, picnic, or camp. Beyond the confluence with Brush Creek at 7.0 miles the river keeps meandering but now has a mostly northward track. Large sandbars are fewer, although smaller stopping points of sand hang on the inside of bends. The river narrows a little bit and curves left before the big metal dock of Traders Hill Landing comes into view on river-left.

TRADERS HILL Traders Hill is a sloping bluff on the St. Marys and the takeout for this paddle. Traders Hill was established in 1755 as the highest point of navigation on the St. Marys, approximately 45 miles from the coast. Its success as a trading post gave the place its name, and the hill was the local gathering spot for all goings-on. This was not only a point of trade for ships but also for those bringing crops from land. Since it was on the border with Florida, just across the river, ne'er-do-wells and runaways from the law drifted back and forth across the river, especially when Florida was in the hands of Spain.

When Charlton County was established in 1854, Traders Hill was the natural choice for county seat. Despite its river location, business patterns changed with the arrival of the railroad. The boats full of wares stopped coming, the people moved away, and the county seat was moved to Folkston. Today the locale is a recreation destination complete with a campground, boat ramp, and swim area—and more than 250 years of history.

31 Satilla River

The Satilla demonstrates its propensity for curves as it passes through forested terrain.

County: Brantley, Pierce
Start: Herrin Lake Landing N31° 16' 30.2", W82° 0' 51.3"
End: U.S. Highway 301 N31° 17' 32.1", W81° 57' 27.1"
Length: 9.0 miles
Float time: 5 hours
Difficulty rating: Easy
Rapids: None
River type: Winding blackwater stream
Current: Slow to moderate
River gradient: 0.8 foot per mile
River gauge: Satilla River at Atkinson; minimum runnable level 200 cfs

Season: Year-round
Land status: Private
Fees or permits: No fees or permits required
Nearest city/town: Nahunta, Georgia
Maps: USGS: Patterson SE, Hortense; DeLorme: *Georgia Atlas and Gazetteer,* page 62
Boats used: Canoes, kayaks, johnboats
Organizations: Satilla Riverkeeper, P.O. Box 159, Waynesville, GA 31566; (912) 778-3126; www.satillariverkeeper.org
Contacts/outfitters: Georgia Department of Natural Resources, 2 Martin Luther King Jr. Drive SE, Suite 1252 East Tower, Atlanta, GA 30334; (404) 656-3500; www.gadnr.org

Put-in/takeout information:

To takeout: From Nahunta take US 301 north for 7 miles to a boat ramp on the right (southeast) side of the US 301 bridge over the Satilla River.

To put-in from takeout: Return to US 301 and follow it back south toward Nahunta for 2.1 miles to Raybon Road West (County Road 224). Turn right onto CR 224 and follow it for 3.2 miles. Turn right onto Herrin Lake Road and arrive at the river and boat ramp in 0.4 mile.

Paddle Summary

The Satilla's curves along this stretch create both the white sandbars for which the river is known and the oxbow sloughs as it cuts new channels. Next to no development currently exists on this part of the river. Though the land is private, little of it is posted, and the numerous sandbars make for great picnicking or camping spots.

The paddling distance of 9.0 miles makes this an all-day trip, especially if the water is low, when you may pull over deadfall. But the scenery will reward your efforts, and wildlife is abundant. If you are in the mood and the water is up, the many sloughs will beckon exploration.

River Overview

The Satilla is the most renowned blackwater river that flows entirely in Georgia. It offers more than 160 miles of paddleable waterway, depending on water levels.

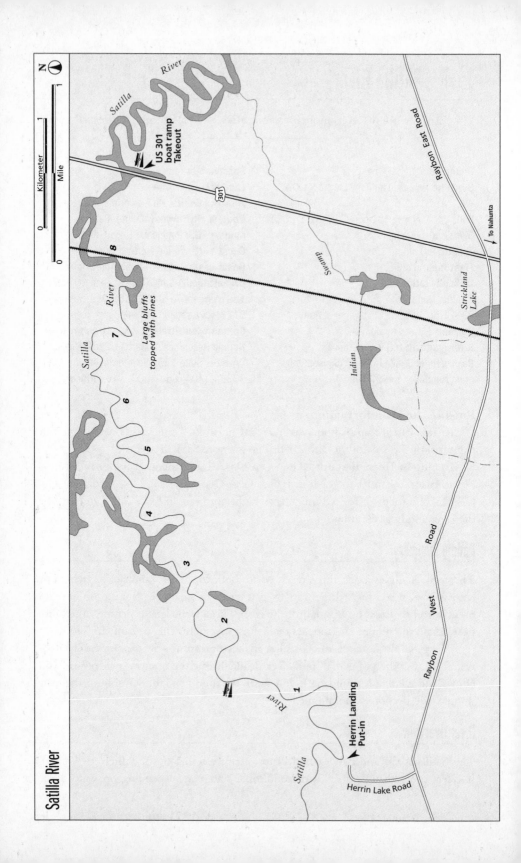

Satilla River

Flowing easterly through the Coastal Plain and through the town of Waycross, the shallow, sinuous stream picks up tributaries as it continually curves its way toward the Atlantic Ocean.

The waterway deepens before merging with the salt water at St. Andrews Sound, between Cumberland and Jekyll Islands—altogether draining more than 4,000 square miles of the Peach State.

The Paddling

Leave the landing to immediately pass a lone cabin. The coffee-colored water runs between banks about 50 feet apart. The river curves nearly constantly. The outer sides of the curve usually have small bluffs of oak, sweet gum, and pine with a palmetto understory. Willows favor the lower areas, along with tupelo and cypress. River birch has a presence as well.

White sandbars immediately commence, unless submerged by high water—when you should not be on the river anyway. Despite the narrowness of the river, the middle is still mostly open to the sun and, because of the sandbars, only partly canopied. Only on the infrequent straightaways does the tree canopy stretch over the Satilla. The textured-sand bottomed varies in appearance, depending on the depth of the water above it. The quiet sloughs extending back from the river are lined with cypress and gum. These trees will also form mini-islands of their own in the middle of the river.

At 1.5 miles a private boat ramp is on river-left, up a slough. Downstream the sandbars decrease in frequency. The right side of the river, beyond the wooded river corridor, has been timbered, making the whole river scenario brighter. The Satilla narrows in places and becomes canopied, forming "squirrel bridges," as a local explained to me. Expect to work around occasional deadfalls, but you'll often find a route has been sawn through by previous river users.

At 4.6 miles the river's windings become extreme, even for the Satilla. Alluring sandbars result from such convolutions. It is in these bends where the river exhibits its wildest aura, where deer tracks cover the sandbars, where owls hoot in the night as you sit before a campfire. At 5.9 miles the river splits around an island. Watch as the river depths continually change—flat sand riffles of reddish water abruptly drop off into deeper black holes.

Fishing can be good on the Satilla. Redbreast sunfish are the most sought for fish here and reach surprising proportions. Largemouth bass can also be caught. At 7.6 miles paddle alongside the largest bluffs on this river section. They are topped with pines overlooking a low forest of willow and river birch, which rises from a sloped sand bank, covering the sand in leaf litter. Come alongside railroad tracks at 8.0 miles. The Satilla widens here as it passes under the railroad bridge and pilings of other, long-forgotten bridges.

The watercourse alternately shallows and deepens beyond the railroad bridge. Some final big sandbars border the water. Soon the US 301 bridge comes into sight.

Morning sun filters the Satilla River Valley.

It is a popular bank-fishing spot. The takeout is on river-right just downstream of the bridge.

UPS AND DOWNS ON THE SATILLA RIVER

The Satilla River, like other waterways in Georgia, has variable flow rates. The U.S. Geological Survey (USGS) gauge used to consider the paddleability of this section of the Satilla River is at Atkinson. Here the river flows under the U.S. Highway 82 bridge east of Nahunta, in Brantley County. This gauge, measuring discharge in cubic feet per second (cfs), has been in operation since March 21, 1930.

The minimum flow rate has historically been in the fall, during November, when summer rains drop off and the river has been lowering since spring. The highest flow rate has been in late winter, specifically the month of March, when the cold-season rains have saturated the land and summer growth hasn't yet arrived to absorb part of the moisture. March average flow is 4,690 cfs, whereas the November flow is only 894 cfs, less than one-fifth of the average March flow. This displays the natural variability of flow rates on the Satilla.

When engaging in a paddle of the river, you must take into account what time of year you will be paddling so that you will know what type of flows you will encounter. Always check the gauge before paddling; that way there will be no surprises. On a paddle trip during March, the Satilla will likely be flowing fast with few sandbars on which to stop. A fall paddle, on the other hand, will have a sluggish current, a plethora of sandbars upon which to stop, and a few fallen trees over which to pull. As you can see from above, the river rarely goes below the minimum runnable level of 200 cfs.

The extremes will surprise. In November 1954 the Satilla averaged only 24 cfs, barely enough to float a Popsicle stick. In April 1948 the Satilla averaged 17,000 cfs, more than 700 times the lowest average monthly rate! The all-time-high daily flow recorded was 68,100 cfs on April 6, 1948. I am sure no one got on the river that day!

32 Suwannee River

This paddle mixes a calm "wide spot" on the river with swift-running narrows; there's gorgeous scenery all along the way.

County: Clinch
Start: Stephen C. Foster State Park N30° 49' 43.1", W82° 21' 39.2"
End: Griffis Camp N30° 47' 2.4", W82° 26' 47.9"
Length: 7.0 miles
Float time: 4 hours
Difficulty rating: Moderate
Rapids: None
River type: Narrow blackwater stream
Current: Moderate to swift in places
River gradient: 0.8 foot per mile
River gauge: Suwannee River at U.S. Highway 441 at Fargo; minimum runnable level 140 cfs
Season: Year-round
Land status: Okefenokee National Wildlife Refuge; private

Fees or permits: Free permit to cross Suwannee River Sill can be obtained at Stephen C. Foster State Park office. Landing fee required at Griffis Camp takeout.
Nearest city/town: Fargo, Georgia
Maps: USGS: Billys Island, The Pocket; DeLorme: *Georgia Atlas and Gazetteer,* page 69
Boats used: Canoes, kayaks, and a few johnboats
Organizations: Stephen C. Foster State Park, 17515 Highway 177, Fargo, GA 31631; (912) 637-5274; www.gastateparks.org
Contacts/outfitters: Okefenokee National Wildlife Refuge, Route 2, Box 3330, Folkston, GA 31537; (912) 496-7836; www.okefenokee .fws.gov

Put-in/takeout information:

To takeout: From Fargo take US 441 south just a short distance to Highway 177. Turn left and head east on Highway 177 for 11 miles to Griffis Camp, a private campground and landing to the left of the road. A landing fee required.

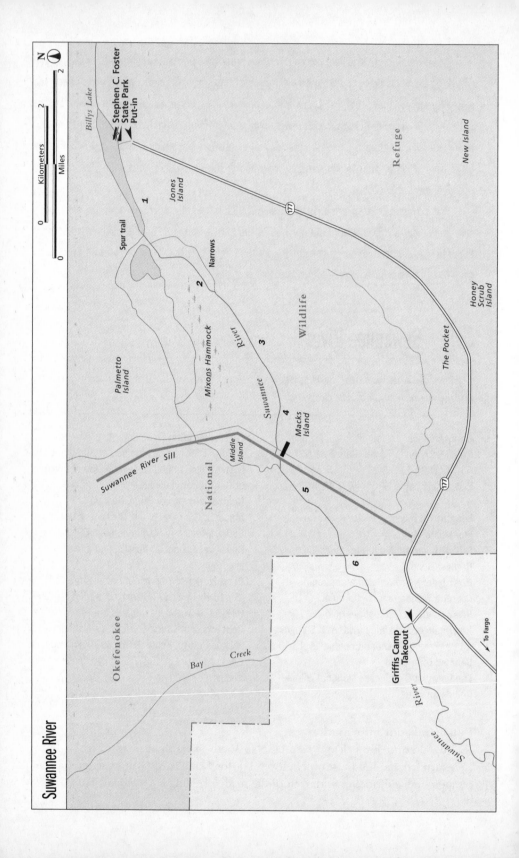

Suwannee River

Stephen C. Foster
State Park
Put-in

Billys Lake

Jones Island

Spur trail

Narrows

Palmetto
Island

Mixons Hammock

Suwannee

River

Macks
Island

Middle
Island

Suwannee River Sill

National

Okefenokee

Bay

Creek

Wildlife

Refuge

New Island

Honey
Scrub
Island

The Pocket

Griffis Camp
Takeout

Suwannee

River

To Fargo

1
2
3
4
5
6

177
177

N

Kilometers
0   2

Miles
0   2

To put-in from takeout: Continue east on Highway 177 to enter Okefenokee National Wildlife Refuge to dead end at Stephen C. Foster State Park boat landing.

Paddle Summary

This paddle enters Billys Lake, a gorgeous "wide spot" on the Suwannee inside the Okefenokee Swamp National Wildlife Refuge. From there the paddle enters the Narrows, where fast-moving water shoots past cypress trees stationed in mid-river. Beyond the Narrows the river keeps a southwesterly track before reaching the Suwannee River Sill, a levee. After the dam the freed river winds past superlative riverside scenery, despite leaving the refuge to reach Griffis Camp, a private launch with campground.

River Overview

Georgia gets little to no credit for being the birthplace of the famed Suwannee River. Emerging from the Okefenokee Swamp, the Suwannee travels southwest 29 miles through the Peach State to enter Florida, which then makes an ironclad grip on the ultimate blackwater river. Made famous by Stephen Foster's classic song "Old Folks at Home" ("Way Down Upon the Suwannee River"), the river flows some 235 miles before emptying into the Gulf of Mexico. It is one of the finest paddle-touring rivers in the country. While exploring the South in 1774, William Bartram described the Suwannee as "the cleanest river I have ever seen, almost as transparent as the air we breathe."

The Paddling

Make sure and get your free permit to cross the Suwannee River Sill from the state park office. Also remember that no camping is allowed between the put-in and the refuge boundary, shortly beyond the Suwannee River Sill.

The paddle begins in the heart of the Okefenokee Swamp. Take the 0.3-mile canal to Billys Lake, where blackwater, naturally darkened from swamp tannins, reflects tall cypresses towering above bright-green lily pads on the water's edge, where alligators lie on the shore in surprising size and numbers. Evergreen bay trees give color in the winter.

Keep west as a spur paddling trail leads right at 1.7 miles, toward Hickory Hammock. Billys Lake soon ends. Enter the Suwannee River Narrows, where the river is often less than 10 feet wide. Pass the dock to Mixons Hammock. (*NOTE:* A permit is required to access the hammock.) The current speeds here between ancient cypress and gum standing guard in midriver. Slalom your way through this tree-crowded and gorgeous piece of Georgia. Look for stumps and living trees growing atop the old stumps.

The river opens to a burned area where you can see black scars at the bases of huge trunks. Forgotten bridge abutments cross the river from past uses. At 4.3 miles

Frank Carroll sea kayaks Billys Lake.

the river seemingly ends at the Suwannee River Sill, a levee. Take the channel leading left, which then curves right to a dam with gates. Be careful here and scout the sill. At very low water you can shoot through, but if the water is high, be prepared to portage. Stay well away from the dam while making your decision.

Soon leave Okefenokee National Wildlife Refuge. Cypress monoliths with massive buttresses stand sentinel. Thin, weak-looking limbs emanate from the squat Ogeechee lime trees, a result of periodic pruning from floods. Pine-oak groves occupy the higher ground, along with their ever-present companion palmetto. The scenery remains wild and superlative as the Suwannee begins to twist and curve and form small sandbars along its 20- to 30-foot width.

In the past, mile markers were nailed to trees indicating distance to Fargo. At 6.2 miles Bay Creek comes in on your right, but you may not even notice it, as sloughs have begun to appear below the sill. Start looking for the clearing of Griffis Camp. It is located on the left as the Suwannee curves to the right near Mile 14 (if the mile marker signs are still there). There may be a sign or a trashcan at the Griffis Camp sandbar. It is best to scout this landing before embarking on your trip.

STEPHEN C. FOSTER

Stephen C. Foster, namesake of the state park where this paddle begins, never saw the Suwannee River—he had only visited the South once, on a steamboat trip to New Orleans. Yet he penned not only the song that made the Suwannee River famous but also many other songs, including the state song of the Bluegrass State, "My Old Kentucky Home." The Suwannee River song, "Old Folks at Home," is Florida's state song.

Born in Pennsylvania in 1826, Foster showed an early propensity for music. Legend has it that he came upon a flute in a store and could play it well before he left, next mastering the piano. He was soon composing music and wrote a nationally popular song when he was but nineteen, "Old Uncle Ned," followed by "Oh Susanna."

Foster began his career as a composer in earnest, but he was a poor businessman and didn't capitalize on his fame. Copyright laws were weak then, exacerbating his troubles. As with most composers, not every song was a hit, and Foster had set the bar high early in life. He didn't take the lesser successes well and began drinking heavily, especially after his wife left him. Riddled with fever, Foster collapsed and fell into a washbasin, which gouged his throat. He died in New York City in 1864 at age thirty-eight, an ignoble end to the most famed composer of the mid-1800s.

Coastal Georgia

33 Altamaha Delta

Starting at Altamaha Park and exploring the Altamaha River Delta, this paddle is one of the best in Georgia.

County: Glynn, McIntosh
Start: Altamaha Park N31° 25' 36.1", W81° 36' 20.8"
End: Darien N31° 22' 5.0", W81° 26' 13.9"
Length: 13.2 miles
Float time: 7 hours
Difficulty rating: Moderate to difficult
Rapids: None
River type: Huge river, tidal creeks and rivers, slave canal
Current: Moderate to swift
River gradient: Tidal
River gauge: Nearest tidal prediction area—Darien, Darien River. Subtract four hours from given tides for starting point at Altamaha Park.
Season: Year-round

Land status: Public—Altamaha State Waterfowl Management Area
Fees or permits: No fees or permits required
Nearest city/town: Darien, Georgia
Maps: USGS: Cox, Ridgeville, Darien; DeLorme: *Georgia Atlas and Gazetteer*, page 63
Boats used: Kayaks, canoes, johnboats
Organizations: Altamaha Riverkeeper, Inc., P.O. Box 2642, Darien, GA 31305; (912) 437-8164; www.altamahariverkeeper.org
Contacts/outfitters: Altamaha Coastal Tours, 229 Fort King George Road, Darien, GA 31305; (912) 437-6010; www.altamaha.com. Rents boats, provides shuttles and guides for Altamaha Delta and the surrounding coast.

Put-in/takeout information:

To takeout: From exit 49 on Interstate 95, take Highway 251 south for 1.1 miles to U.S. Highway17. Turn right onto US 17 and follow it for 1.3 miles into downtown Darien. Turn right onto Broad Street just before the US 17 bridge over the Darien River. Follow Broad Street for 1 block, then turn left and go downhill to the public boat ramp.

To put-in from takeout: Return to US 17 and head south across the Darien River for 4.7 miles to Highway 99. Turn right onto Highway 99 and follow it for 6.9 miles to Highway 341/U.S. Highway 25/U.S. Highway 27. Turn right onto Highway 341/US 25/US 27, and travel 10 miles to the hamlet of Everett, watching for the sign for Altamaha Regional Park. Turn right onto Altamaha Park Road and go 3 miles to dead-end at the park and a boat ramp, which is near the park store.

Paddle Summary

Follow the Altamaha toward the ocean before splitting off into Stud Horse Creek, one of the best waterway names in the Peach State. Stud Horse Creek is a rich, junglesque waterway where alligators congregate in large numbers and birds of all types can be seen.

Soon join Lewis Creek, which forms the northern border of the Lewis Island Tract, which contains some ancient cypress trees and a campsite from which to access

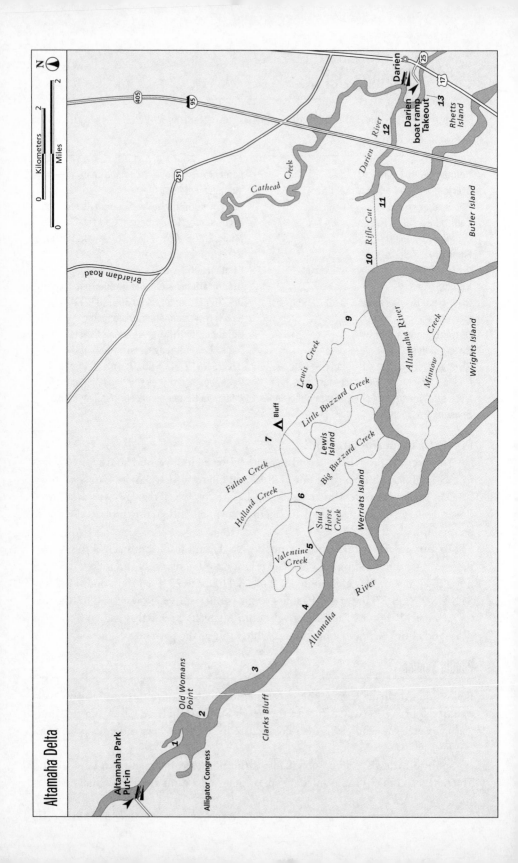

Altamaha Delta

the trees by foot. Next pass a riverside bluff suitable for camping before rejoining the Altamaha River. Next comes the trip down the narrow, canopied Rifle Cut—a slave-built canal that joins the Darien River, your final waterway leading to the takeout.

The shoreline for the entire trip is wild and primitive public land. Numerous side creeks and Lewis Island offer opportunities to explore beyond this paddle. However, these numerous side creeks and other waterways also make navigation challenging—a map-loaded GPS or a topographic map and compass will make your trip much more pleasant. An outfitter serves this paddle, making shuttles much easier.

River Overview

The Altamaha River basin is the second largest on the East Coast. Formed at the confluence of the Ocmulgee and Oconee Rivers, it drains much of Georgia. This lowermost part of the Altamaha is ecologically important as an estuary not only for wildlife but also for the seafood industry.

Here the Altamaha Delta is not merely one river but a series of channels both big and small, including man-made canals that date back to the slave days. These water-ways were important for transporting lumber, which also had a heyday on the coast following the rice cultivation.

This paddle travels not only the mighty Altamaha but also some of these smaller creeks and rivers and a canal known as the Rifle Cut, which was dug as a shortcut for transporting products down the Altamaha to the Darien River and the town of Darien. Beyond this paddle, the Altamaha flows into the Atlantic via Altamaha Sound.

The Paddling

Leave the boat ramp, immediately passing an old railroad bridge of an abandoned line. The first waterway of your trip, the Altamaha River, is a couple hundred feet wide at this point. Spanish moss–draped cypress, willow, Ogeechee lime, and river birch grow along the river margins, while sweet gum and oaks occupy the higher ground. The banks are low, less than 10 feet high.

Shortly pass several houses on the right bank, the only private property between the put-in and Darien. All sorts of concrete and junk are used to shore up the shore-line here. Beyond the houses, the shoreline lowers on both sides, with overflow swamp buffering the river corridor. This uppermost river is tidally influenced; however, salt water doesn't come this high, it simply alters the current speed.

At 1.1 miles the Altamaha River divides around an island. The main river curves left, passing a slough and around Old Woman's Point, which offers a fine sandbar for stopping. If you go around the right side of the island, you will come to another, smaller island and an area known as Alligator Congress, so named because it's a gathering area for the reptiles. If you have any navigational doubts, follow the current.

Beyond Old Woman's Point, the Alligator Congress channel comes in on your right. At 2.2 miles another slough leaves left. The river resumes its southeasterly track

Morning light illuminates fog on Rifle Cut.

and becomes very wide again and is very straight. Wax myrtle, vines, ferns, and palmetto thicken already-thick woodlands.

At 4.4 miles the river begins to bend left. Move over to the left-hand bank. Ahead, at 4.9 miles, two creeks converge nearly together onto the Altamaha River. The first stream, Valentine Creek, is not your choice. This stream starts out about 40 feet wide but quickly closes to about 15 feet wide within sight of the Altamaha and heads northwest. The correct stream, Stud Horse Creek, is about 100 yards downriver and much wider, maybe 110 feet wide at its mouth, and closes to 80 feet wide.

Stud Horse Creek heads north then east away from the Altamaha River. Stud Horse seems much more intimate compared with the wide-open Altamaha. The tides are exerting more influence now; although you're inching closer to the ocean and are in a tidal system, this area is still entirely fresh water. Stay with the main, biggest channel here. At 5.7 miles Big Buzzard Creek leaves south. Follow Stud Horse Creek, which turns north as a wider channel to meet even wider Lewis Creek at 6.0 miles.

Stay right on Lewis Creek as you work around Lewis Island. At this point, begin to count creeks coming into the north bank. Drift over to the south bank. First comes Holland Creek, then Fulton Creek at 6.7 miles. When you see Fulton Creek, about 20 to 25 feet wide, look for an opening on the heavily wooded south side of Lewis Creek bank indicating a campsite and your jumping-off point to explore Lewis Island by foot. The campsite is on a low bluff here and is your ticket for accessing the big trees of the Lewis Tract. There is no trail to the trees, and you will have to swamp-slog 1,500 feet to get there. Take a 230-degree compass bearing to the southwest from the campsite to reach the trees. On your return, take a 50-degree bearing to the northeast. Winter is the best time to do this. In summer the growth is incredibly thick. Good luck.

Continuing east down Lewis Creek, you won't miss the next attraction—the high sand bluff on river-left. This makes for a good campsite and from above offers a good sweep of Lewis Creek. Notice the discarded shells embedded in the sand bluff. This is an old Indian campsite. Curve to the southeast. Sloughs begin to form on the edges of the bank, opening the wooded corridor somewhat. The creek continues to widen, with many sloughs forming. Depending on the wind, you may begin to hear the drone of I-95.

Return to the mighty Altamaha River at 9.4 miles. It is upwards of 400 feet across the river here, purportedly its widest point. Stay with the left bank and downstream (easterly). A keen eye will spot the Rifle Cut. The left bank curves south; when you're about going full south and have a full southerly look downriver, watch left for the canal that is the Rifle Cut. The canal heads due east and on an outgoing tide will be fairly humming. The canal is 30 to 40 feet wide and 1 mile long and is mostly cano-pied but sometimes open. Freshwater trees are still hanging on. Reach the end of the canal at 11.1 miles.

You are now joining the upper Darien River heading southeast. The natural bends of this river are much more noticeable after going down the arrow-straight canal. The cars of I-95 come into view. When you see I-95, bear left, staying with the Darien River to soon pass under the interstate. Here the river perceptibly widens and is continuing its transition to pure tidal stream as spartina grass begins to dominate the shoreline and mudflats expose themselves at lower tides.

Shortly a little civilization comes into view. It looks as though you should head forward toward the buildings, but that is Cathead Creek. Stay right here, curving to the south with the tide. The confluence of Cathead Creek and Darien River can cre-ate some boiling currents. The US 17 bridge comes into view. Pass several docks; the boat ramp is on the left before the bridge.

EVER-ADAPTING DARIEN Darien is a coastal town at the crossroads—a place with a long past and a future that points toward the exponential growth being experienced in other parts of the Georgia coast. The bluff overlooking the Altamaha River Delta was first chosen as a defensive outpost by South Carolinians in 1721. Known as Fort King George, this lonely outpost was erected to protect the south side of the colony. The fort was occupied for only six years by a full garrison of soldiers and was later manned by a skeleton crew of two before being entirely abandoned. Today you can visit the fort site, which is now Fort King George State Historic Park.

In the 1730s Georgia colonist James Oglethorpe recruited Scottish highlanders and their families to establish a settlement on the hilltop, then known as Barnwell's Bluff. The community known as Darien was born, and its favorable position near the mouth of the Altamaha allowed it to become an important trading center. The town exported products from Georgia's interior, which were floated down the river's primary tributaries—the Oconee and Ocmulgee—then from Darien to cities up north or over to Europe. You can still see the tabby building ruins from this trading heyday near the takeout for this paddle.

Later, rice cultivation became an important part of the local economy until the Civil War, when Darien was ruthlessly burned to the ground. The vast pine-and-cypress forests were the basis for the timber boom of the post–Civil War era, which lasted for about fifty years. When the timber ran out, Darien once again adapted and has become an important shrimping center. To this day, you can see the shrimping fleet along Darien's historic waterfront, which has seen changes throughout its history and is sure to see more in the future.

34 Cathead Creek and Rice Canals

Starting on McCullough Creek, this paddle winds southward through a wooded corridor to Cathead Creek and on to canals used for rice cultivation.

County: McIntosh
Start: Cox Road N31° 25' 37.3", W81° 29' 48.0"
End: Darien N31° 22' 5.0", W81° 26' 13.9"
Length: 7.6 miles
Float time: 3.5 hours
Difficulty rating: Easy to moderate
Rapids: None
River type: Creek evolving from fresh water to tidal
Current: Moderate
River gradient: Tidal
River gauge: Nearest tidal prediction area—Darien, Darien River
Season: Year-round

Land status: Public—Altamaha State Wildlife Management Area; some private land on north bank
Fees or permits: No fees or permits required
Nearest city/town: Darien, Georgia
Maps: USGS: Ridgeville, Darien; DeLorme: *Georgia Atlas and Gazetteer,* page 63
Boats used: Kayaks, canoes, johnboats
Organizations: Altamaha Riverkeeper, Inc., P.O. Box 2642, Darien, GA 31305; (912) 437-8164; www.altamahariverkeeper.org
Contacts/outfitters: Altamaha Coastal Tours, 229 Fort King George Road, Darien, GA 31305; (912) 437-6010; www.altamaha.com. Rents boats, provides shuttles and guides on Cathead Creek and surrounding coast.

Put-in/takeout information:

To takeout: From exit 49 on Internet 95, take Highway 251 south for 1.3 miles to U.S. Highway 17. Turn right onto US 17 and follow it 1.2 miles to Darien. Once

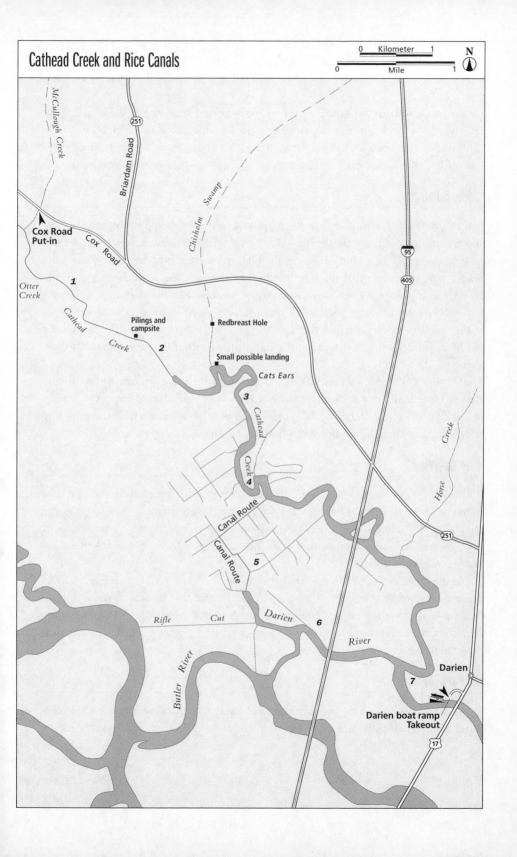

Cathead Creek and Rice Canals

0   Kilometer   1

0   Mile   1

N

McCullough Creek

251

Briardam Road

Chisholm Swamp

Cox Road Put-in

Cox Road

95

405

Otter Creek

1

Cathead Creek

Pilings and campsite

2

Redbreast Hole

Small possible landing

Cats Ears

3

Cathead Creek

4

Creek

Horse

251

Canal Route

Canal Route

5

Rifle   Cut

Darien

6

River

Butler River

Darien

7

Darien boat ramp Takeout

17

in Darien turn right onto Broad Street, just before the US 17 bridge over the Darien River. Go 1 block on Broad Street, then turn left and go downhill to reach the public boat ramp.

To put-in from takeout: Return to US 17 and head north, backtracking to Highway 251, heading north this time to cross I-95 for a total of 4.2 miles from US 17. Reach Cox Road, and travel forward on Cox Road for 0.9 mile to the bridge across McCullough Creek. The put-in is on the left (south) side of Cox Road.

Paddle Summary

From Cathead Creek paddlers can head upstream for a little exploration toward Buffalo Swamp or continue downriver where this tidally influenced waterway begins passing many old rice cultivation canals. The creek then hits the ears of the Cathead, a pair of oxbows that the river has broken through. Keep southeasterly on the ever-widening waterway to pass more old rice canals. Pass another oxbow, leaving Cathead Creek to begin a journey through slave-created canals overhung with vegetation. The tides can run fast through these canals, which adds to the fun of the paddle. Eventually the canals end at the uppermost Darien River, which you follow to the paddle's end.

If you're uncomfortable with the canal part of this paddle, you can always follow Cathead Creek all the way to its confluence with the Darien River. Expect to see lots of wildlife, including alligators and birds. Try to time your paddle with the outgoing tide, putting in three hours after high tide in Darien.

River Overview

Cathead Creek is formed out of the Buffalo Swamp, which it helps drain. The tidal watercourse heads southeasterly toward the Georgia coast, where its two major feeder branches, McCullough and Otter Creeks, join. The wooded watercourse works its way southeasterly in a section that was once cultivated for rice and therefore has many canals cut into it.

As the creek continues, the shores begin to be bordered with grasses, especially in the section starting below the "Cats Ears"—the feature that gives it its name. It then passes a second section of rice cultivation canals before coming near Darien, where occasional docks border the stream near higher ground. Finally, Cathead Creek meets the Darien River and ends.

The Paddling

Put in at the landing on the southwest side of the bridge. McCullough Creek is fresh water but is tidally influenced. The stream is about 30 to 35 feet wide and is bordered

with pines, sweet gum, wax myrtle, and cypress. Spanish moss hangs from the trees. Old rice fields are visible just beyond the wooded river corridor. Keep forward, leaving south from the put-in. Soon enter Cathead Creek. Here go upstream if you feel like exploring more, which is to the right. This trip however heads left, downstream. Just as you enter the stream, to your left an old rice canal meets Cathead Creek. If you don't feel like exploring yet, you will be paddling through some canals later in your trip. Cathead Creek is about 60 to 70 feet wide here and offers fine scenery as it meanders south before turning southeasterly.

The south bank of the land is part of the Altamaha State Waterfowl Management Area. Otter Creek comes in on the right at 0.6 mile and is worth exploring itself. Cathead Creek widens here, and the rice canals continue. After just a little while you'll be adept at pointing them out yourself. In a few places the tree corridor is broken, which allows longer reaching looks into the old rice fields on either side of the creek. In other places cypress trees grow in strands beyond the stream's edge.

At 1.8 miles pass a string of old pilings crossing Cathead Creek. A piney campsite is located on the right-hand bank just below the pilings. The wooded riverside scenery continues to be gorgeous, though grasses are becoming more common. Islands in the distance harbor pines and other trees, creating a mosaic of beauty. Reach the ears of Cathead Creek at 2.8 miles. These will take place in the form of two isles, bordered by old oxbows. This is a fun place to explore if you are inclined. Also there is a small landing on the north end of the west "ear" of Cathead. A small stream, Redbreast Hole, flows in here as well.

The main stream turns southeasterly here. Old rice canals, hand-dug by slaves in the 1800s, become more common. You will be taking one of them soon. Began to slip over to the right-hand bank, and stay with it. At 4.1 miles reach the next grassy oxbow-formed island. Ahead you can see a billboard from I-95. Curve to the right just beyond this island and reach the canal that is your destination. Cathead Creek continues southeasterly and is much wider than the canal.

The GPS coordinates for the entry to the canal are N31° 23' 31.16", W81° 27' 50.23". The canal runs arrow straight southwest. If you have been following the tides out along Cathead Creek, the tide in this canal will be going against you here. There may be trees fallen in this canal, which is about 40 feet wide. Begin to count canals entering on your left. The first canal is choked up, as is the second. The third canal is a little bit wider than the first two. (It actually looks like two canals side by side with a little island in the middle, but count it as one canal.)

Next reach a four-way water intersection. Ahead, the canal you've been following continues forward but is draped in moss-covered cypress trees. A small channel is to your right. To your left is your route on a canal that is just 10 to 15 feet wide. This canal travels due southeast, and the tide can run quickly through here. The way you can distinguish the correct canal on an outgoing tide is that you will now be going with the tide. Upon entering the grass-bordered waterway, pass a lone cypress tree on your right. This channel is barely wide enough for a boat, so don't be alarmed and think you're going down the wrong channel, especially since it is tightly bordered by tall grasses. The GPS coordinates for this canal are N31° 23' 15.32", W81° 28' 14.30". In places the stream is completely canopied and overgrown. It soon turns left, due northeast, before turning back to the southeast. Other canals that once were a part of the system have filled in, so there's little danger of getting lost.

At 5.1 miles reach an intersection. You can see a canal going left that is overgrown. The correct canal goes to your right and angles south-southwest. This canal is a little wider, maybe 15 to 20 feet, and is canopied in places as well.

The canal adventure soon ends. Open onto the upper reaches of the Darien River. Continue following the tide left (southeast) on a mostly wooded corridor. At 5.6 miles the Darien River suddenly widens as the Rifle Cut canal comes in from the Altamaha River on your right. The Altamaha Delta paddle follows Rifle Cut.

The cars of I-95 come into view. When you see the interstate, bear left, staying with the Darien River to pass under the I-95 bridge at 6.3 miles. Here the river perceptibly widens and continues its transition to pure tidal stream, as spartina grass borders the waterway.

Ahead, Cathead Creek meets the Darien River. If you choose not to follow the canals, this is where you will come out. Stay south here with the tide. The confluence of Cathead Creek and the Darien River can create some boiling currents. The US 17 bridge comes into view. Pass several docks; the boat ramp is on the left before the bridge.

RICE CULTIVATION ON THE GEORGIA COAST The cypress swamps along Cathead Creek made for good rice-growing areas. Cathead Creek was strategically located for rice production. These coastal rice plantations had to be in fresh water but also close enough to where this freshwater flow pulsed with the tides. This way rice fields could be flooded, which eliminated the need for hoeing the fields. During the early to mid-1800s, when rice growing in the area reached its zenith, it was done using slave labor. Here is the recipe for developing a rice plantation during that time:

Rice Plantation
1. Clear swamp of all trees by hand.
2. Dig ditches and build banks with hand tools.
3. Build wooden floodgates to control drainage and water flow to rice fields
4. Cultivate rice by hand using mules wearing special rawhide boots to keep them from sinking in the mud.

5. Perform the above tasks in extreme heat and humidity and periods of heavy rain, thick clouds of mosquitoes, and possibly with swamp fever, aka malaria.

In plantation days the canals you see were managed using wooden dams with boards laid vertically and added or removed as necessary to change water levels. The success of rice production here may have propelled further rice production. The bulk of Georgia's rice production came from right here in McIntosh County. These rice fields averaged 300 to 600 acres in size. A total of 2,800 slaves were employed in the rice business here. Yields of more than one million pounds per planter were not unheard of at the time.

Rice production fell off during the Civil War, and after the war the plantations couldn't function efficiently without slave labor. Before the Civil War, imagine slaves clearing the land and building levees and digging canals. As you lightly toil on your paddle, consider the heavy toils that have taken place here in a place now reverted to the back of beyond—where time and the healing hand of nature, with a little help from man, have turned a level, sun-scorched field laced with dikes to a wooded wetland where nature's beasts, from alligator to warblers, now thrive.

35 Cockspur Lighthouse

This is a relatively short, relatively easy paddle to a scenic destination—the Cockspur Lighthouse, which is part of Fort Pulaski National Monument.

County: Chatham
Start: Lazaretto Creek N32° 0' 56.3", W80° 53' 28.6"
End: Lazaretto Creek N32° 0' 56.3", W80° 53' 28.6"
Length: 3.8 miles out and back
Float time: 2.5 hours
Difficulty rating: Easy to moderate
Rapids: None
River type: Tidal creek leading to the Atlantic Ocean
Current: Moderate
River gradient: Tidal
River gauge: Nearest tidal station—Savannah River Entrance
Season: Year-round

Land status: Public—Fort Pulaski National Monument; private
Fees or permits: No fees or permits required
Nearest city/town: Tybee Island, Georgia
Maps: USGS: Fort Pulaski; DeLorme: *Georgia Atlas and Gazetteer*, page 39
Boats used: Kayaks
Organizations: Fort Pulaski National Monument, P.O. Box 30757, Highway 80 East, Savannah, GA 31410-0757; (912) 786-5787; www.nps.gov/fopu
Contacts/outfitters: Dewey's Dockside, 1 Old Tybee Road, Lazaretto Creek, Tybee Island, GA 31328; (912) 786-5727; www.deweys-restaurant.com. Rents kayaks.

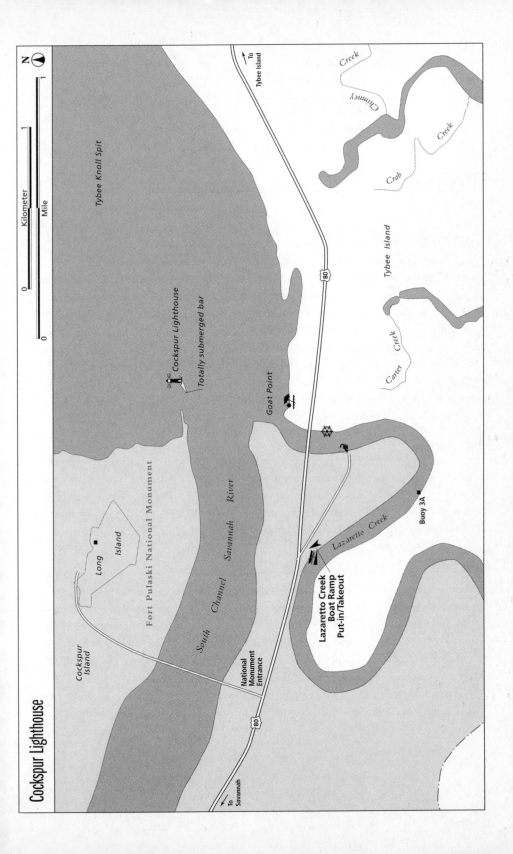

Cockspur Lighthouse

N

0   Kilometer   1

0   Mile   1

Cockspur Island

Long Island

Fort Pulaski National Monument

National Monument Entrance

To Savannah

80

South Channel Savannah River

Cockspur Lighthouse

Totally submerged bar

Tybee Knoll Spit

Goat Point

Lazaretto Creek

Lazaretto Creek Boat Ramp Put-in/Takeout

Buoy 3A

80

To Tybee Island

Carter Creek

Tybee Island

Crab Creek

Chimney Creek

Creek

Put-in/takeout information:

To put-in/takeout: From exit 102 on Interstate 95, take U.S. Highway 80 east for 15 miles, winding through the town of Savannah. Watch for directions to Tybee Island. Once east of Savannah, US 80 east begins crossing islands. Look for the left-hand turn into Fort Pulaski National Monument. Set your odometer. The Lazaretto Creek boat ramp is 0.4 mile beyond the national monument entrance on the right.

Paddle Summary

Starting at the boat ramp on Lazaretto Creek, a tidal waterway, the paddle leads through a grassy estuary before opening onto the Atlantic Ocean at the mouth of South Channel Savannah River, where the fort is located.

Cockspur Lighthouse sits on a rocky island that is submerged twice daily by the tides. Therefore you must time your paddle to reach the lighthouse on the falling tide or a low rising tide. This way you can land at the lighthouse and get out of your boat to climb the structure and enjoy a 360-degree view from atop its heights.

Ideally, begin your paddle at the end of a falling tide, riding it out to the lighthouse. Then you'll have time to explore before riding the tide back up Lazaretto Creek. The tide can be paddled against when leaving the boat ramp, but the problem with going to the lighthouse on a high tide is that there won't be any land upon which to beach your boat. You'll be stuck with merely paddling around the lighthouse and not be able to access it.

River Overview

Lazaretto Creek is part of the greater marsh creek complex between Tybee Island and the town of Savannah in the easternmost corner of the Peach State. This completely tide-influenced waterway connects Tybee Creek with the South Channel Savannah River among other waterways. Marsh grasses border nearly its entire course.

The Paddling

The boat ramp has both a dock and a conventional boat ramp, allowing two means of entering the water. Leave the landing and head left on Lazaretto Creek, which is about 150 feet wide here and bordered by spartina grass. The low-slung shore reveals a big sky. Mud will be exposed between the creek and the grass on a falling tide, which is when you should be paddling here. It's just creek, grass, and sky. Pass Buoy Marker 3A. A line of trees appears as the creek curves back to the north.

Come alongside a small fishing pier on river-left and a marina on the right. Just ahead is the US 80 bridge. Once beyond the bridge, a panorama opens wide before

Cockspur Lighthouse ▶

you. The South Channel Savannah River is coming in on your left. The low-slung brick structure of Fort Pulaski spans the river. The Atlantic Ocean opens wide. Distant lands to the north are in the state of South Carolina. Greater Tybee Island is to the east. Dead ahead is the prize: Cockspur Lighthouse. The tidal current will be much stronger out here. If you wish to stop before the lighthouse, Goat Point is to your left. Watch for the jagged edges of oyster bars along the shoreline however. Reach Navigation Marker 2, a lighted buoy, at the mouth of the river. Look to your right for a small beach, which you can visit on your return trip.

Head toward the white lighthouse. The tidal currents will be pushing all around the bar upon which the lighthouse sits. Go ahead and cruise around the lighthouse before stopping. Notice the plethora of jagged oysters close to the lighthouse. This is not a good place to land your boat. Your best bet for landing is a shell bar on the southwest side, toward the fort. Make sure to securely land your craft before walking to the lighthouse. During your walk you will undoubtedly notice all the old bricks left over from the lighthouse keeper's quarters.

Climb the narrow steps around the outside of this cylindrical structure, then enter it. The first few steps can be quite slippery, as they are submerged often and are covered with ocean vegetation. Enter the lighthouse, and notice the elaborate brickwork inside. The very steep and narrow inner steps lead up to a ladder that heads all the way to the actual light and the outside platform that goes completely around the uppermost part of the lighthouse. Gain a superlative view of the surroundings, including the lighthouse on Tybee Island. Don't be surprised if you see some massive container ships on the North Channel Savannah River, heading to the ocean. These container ships will dwarf your boat.

In 2006 Cockspur Lighthouse was lit for the first time in nearly one hundred years. It is now powered by a solar charger, which can be seen if you climb to the very tiptop of the lighthouse. Note that the original lighthouse cupola is inside Fort Pulaski, which you can easily see to your west; a visit should be made part of your paddle adventure. A hiking trail leads from near the South Channel Savannah River 0.75 mile to the fort. However, most paddlers simply do this paddle then drive over to the fort. Some small shell beaches avail fort landings, but the oyster bars can be vicious.

On your way back, stop by the beach near US 80. This is a small yet steep beach with gnarled cedars, sea oats, grasses, and skeletons of fallen trees. You can stand on the beach as the tide is rising and watch the lighthouse be engulfed by the rising waters.

THE HISTORY OF A LIGHTHOUSE Technically known as the Cockspur Beacon, the destination for this paddle has undergone many changes, the latest of which was its 2006 relighting. Its next evolution is the restoration of the original metal cupola. The current cupola is made of wood and is temporary.

What became the Cockspur Beacon was first built as an unlit brick tower in the late 1830s. In the 1840s the beacon was completed as a full-blown lighthouse, with fixed lamps able to be seen from 9 miles distant. A lantern keeper's house was built as well. The structure was short-lived—a hurricane destroyed it in 1854. The next year the lighthouse was rebuilt bigger and better.

The lighthouse was darkened through the Civil War but was spared during the April 1862 battle at Fort Pulaski. By the way, roughly near the U.S. Highway 80 bridge (under which you pass on this paddle) was the location of the Union forces that bombarded Ford Pulaski, causing the Confederate withdrawal. After the War Between the States, the beacon continued to shine on the sleepy coast. In 1881 a hurricane destroyed the lighthouse keeper's house, forcing the family to reside at nearby Fort Pulaski. An 1893 hurricane inundated the lower part of the lighthouse.

The South Channel Savannah River fell out of favor as a shipping lane for the deeper North Channel Savannah River, rendering the lighthouse unnecessary. The lighthouse was extinguished, became part of the Fort Pulaski National Monument, and was transferred to the National Park Service. Today, despite the erosion of the land upon which it sits, the beacon continues to shine a light on the past of Georgia's coast.

36 Postell Creek on St. Simons Island

One of the beauties of this trip is its variability. You can do this paddle either as a one-way or an out-and-back trip.

County: Glynn
Start: 12th Street beach access N31° 9' 7.0", W81° 21' 56.2"
End: East Beach Causeway N31° 8' 48.1", W81° 22' 31.8"
Length: 2.8 miles one-way
Float time: 2 hours
Difficulty rating: Easy to moderate
Rapids: None
River type: Beach breakers on coastal inlet; small tidal creek
Current: Moderate to swift
River gradient: Tidal
River gauge: Nearest tidal station—Hampton River Entrance
Season: Year-round

Land status: Public beach; private
Fees or permits: No fees or permits required
Nearest city/town: St. Simons Island, Georgia
Maps: USGS: Sea Island, Brunswick East; DeLorme: *Georgia Atlas and Gazetteer,* page 63
Boats used: Kayaks
Organizations: Georgia Department of Natural Resources, Commissioner's Office, 2 Martin Luther King Jr. Drive SE, Suite 1252 East Tower, Atlanta, GA 30334; (404) 656-350; www.gadnr.org
Contacts/outfitters: Southeast Adventure, 313 Mallery Street, St. Simons Island, GA 31522; (912) 638-6732; www.SouthEast Adventure.com. Leads guided tours on Postell Creek and other area waterways.

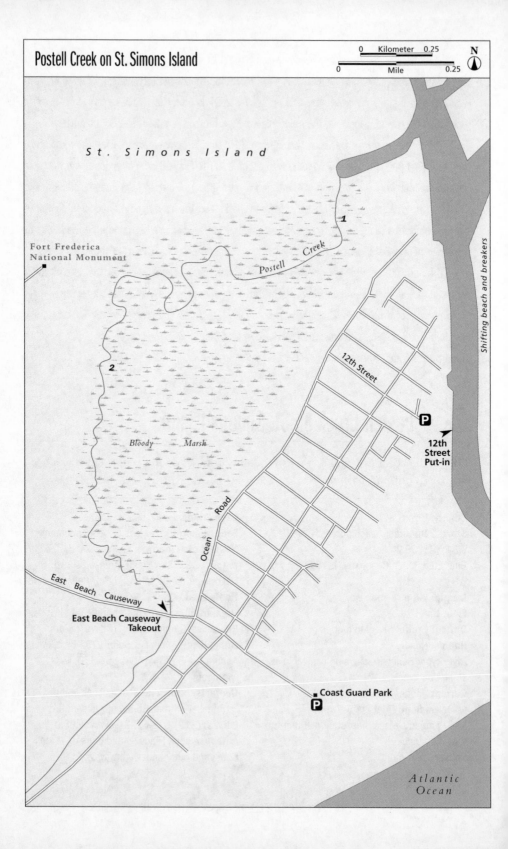

Postell Creek on St. Simons Island

St. Simons Island

Fort Frederica
National Monument

Postell Creek

1

2

Bloody Marsh

12th Street

Ocean Road

P

12th Street Put-in

Shifting beach and breakers

East Beach Causeway

East Beach Causeway
Takeout

Coast Guard Park

P

Atlantic Ocean

0 Kilometer 0.25

0 Mile 0.25

N

Put-in/takeout information:

To takeout: From exit 38 on Interstate 95 take the Highway 25 spur south for 4.2 miles to U.S. Highway 17. Turn right and follow US 17 south for 1.6 miles to Torras Causeway. Turn left onto the causeway and travel 4.5 miles before veering right onto Kings Way. Stay with Kings Way for 2.1 miles, entering the heart of Saint Simons Island and a traffic light at Mallery Street. Keep forward, now on Ocean Boulevard, and following Ocean Boulevard for 1.7 miles to East Beach Causeway. The takeout is just after you turn left on East Beach Causeway, on the far side of the bridge over Postell Creek.

WARNING: There is no parking allowed here. For parking follow East Beach Causeway toward the ocean, where it becomes First Street. Just ahead is Coast Guard Park, which has parking and a beach access, as well as a maritime museum.

To put-in from takeout: Continue north on Ocean Road, which is the continuation of Ocean Boulevard, for 0.7 mile to 12th Street. Turn right onto 12th Street and follow it east for 0.3 mile to dead-end at a public beach access with three parking spots. You must pull your boat over the dunes to access the water.

Paddle Summary

Depending upon where you start, this could be a source-to-sea paddle or a sea-to-source paddle. For summary and description purposes, we will start at the sea. After pulling your boat over the dunes, the wide bar and breakers of the Atlantic Ocean and waterway connecting the Backbone River and Postell Creek open before you. This area, rich with birdlife, offers a chance to walk the beach and paddle/surf the waters around it. Once you are done fooling around here, turn north, following the waterway into Goulds Inlet to reach Postell Creek. Here this paddle turns left and begins tracing the ever-narrowing southerly reaches of this grass-lined waterway as it twists and turns through Bloody Marsh—a large, grassy estuary bordered by land on both sides.

The uppermost part of the creek is so narrow and shallow, especially at low tide, you'll hardly believe it can be paddled. Be apprised that civilization is never far away, but the paddle does afford an opportunity to experience two very different types of water in one paddle. By the way, a shuttle is not necessary for a one-way paddle. Simply leave your boat and walk the 1 mile between the put-in and takeout.

River Overview

Postell Creek extends north and south through Bloody Marsh. It is a completely tidal-dependent waterway that drains Bloody Marsh, the wetland dividing the seaward and landward parts of Saint Simons Island. The creek is just a few miles in length and is connected to the ocean by Backbone River at Goulds Inlet.

Paddling from the ocean, you need to start at low tide or with an incoming tide. Start your trip dragging your boat over the dunes—it's not that far. The roar of the ocean is audible and immense. Start your paddling at Goulds Inlet. This area of wide tidal beach and breakers makes for great exploration and beachcombing. A channel runs between two beach areas. The beach north of here running toward Sea Island offers more foot exploration. Consider combining some beachcombing with your adventure while waiting for Postell Creek to fill. Paddlers can challenge the breakers and surf. To your left, away from the Atlantic, is your route. You'll see birds by the hundreds at times.

After leaving the intertidal zone, head north up the channel. Houses and condominiums stand to your left beyond a rock jetty. You should feel the tide pushing you upstream. If you're not, you need to be starting at the other end. If you do start at the uppermost part of Postell Creek, you need to leave at absolute high tide then ride it out—Postell Creek may be too low toward the end of a falling tide.

The houses on your left soon end. Just past here, on the right, is the Backbone River. A large grassy isle centers the area. If you want to extend your paddle, circle that island and explore Backbone River. Paddling away from the ocean, take the first creek leading left, which is Postell Creek. Note that Postell Creek also keeps forward here. This left turn is before the power lines, which you will see ahead.

Pass under the power lines shortly after the left turn. Note that the tide pushing in here is somewhat gentle. Smaller creeks split off Postell Creek, but the main track is evident. Docks of houses extend to the water's edge. The creek continues twisting and turning past houses. It leaves the docks and the east side of Bloody Marsh and then straightens. If you have any doubts about which way to go, just stay with the biggest channel.

The meanderings soon resume. The creek twists so much that at points it seems you are going around in circles. The creek meanders over to the west side of Bloody Marsh and nears Fort Frederica National Monument, which can be seen over the spartina grass on a higher tide. Pass a few more docks from houses over there. The stream is slowly but surely narrowing, becoming hardly wider than a kayak is long. As you twist and turn, the American flag of the Maritime Museum and old Coast Guard station becomes visible, but it's still a little ways before you get to the bridge. You know the paddle is about to end when you can barely get a double-bladed paddle into the water without hitting either bank. The takeout is on the right just before the East Beach Causeway Bridge, which is just a low span.

COLONIST BY ACCIDENT OR BY FATE? James Oglethorpe may never have made it to what became Georgia if it wasn't for his political achievements in England. Across the water, the English had a problem with debtors' prisons, where a large number of citizens were

languishing in filthy conditions. Many of these debtors were good people caught in a financial depression.

A friend of Oglethorpe's had been sent to such a prison, and as a member of Parliament, Oglethorpe led the charge to pass the Debtors Act, which protected the rights of those in financial trouble. Oglethorpe was hailed across the country and thus became a candidate to establish a new colony in America. This new colony, known as Georgia, would be a place where poor Englanders could make a new start. In 1732 Oglethorpe and a select group of settlers landed in Charleston, South Carolina, before moving south to found the town of Savannah.

The Spanish, who were entrenched in what is now Florida, had eyes on this area as well. Thus the stage was set for the Battle of the Bloody Marsh, through which Postell Creek, part of this paddle, flows. Oglethorpe constructed a fort on St. Simons Island as part of a greater community called Frederica, bolstering England's claim on this part of the Georgia coast. England declared war on Spain, which carried over to the New World. In 1742 the Spanish came to claim St. Simons Island as theirs.

Oglethorpe was faced with bad circumstances—he was outnumbered and out equipped—but in the end England won the Battle of Bloody Marsh when Oglethorpe tricked the Spaniards into thinking he had reinforcements coming. What is now Bloody Marsh allegedly ran red with the blood of Spaniards, which was likely an exaggeration. Nevertheless, Spain never again claimed Georgia or threatened the colonies again.

Having successfully founded and defended the Colony of Georgia, James Oglethorpe returned to England. He lived to see Georgia become one of the original thirteen states of the fledging United States of America. While out here on your paddle, you can visit Ford Frederica National Monument.

37 Redbird Creek

A relatively short out-and-back trip up a tidal waterway, protected on all sides by state park property.

County: Bryan
Start: Fort McAllister State Park campground boat ramp N31° 52' 48.9", W81° 10' 42.4"
End: Fort McAllister State Park campground boat ramp N31° 52' 48.9", W81° 10' 42.4"
Length: 4.0 miles round-trip
Float time: 2 hours
Difficulty rating: Easy to moderate
Rapids: None
River type: Tidal creek
Current: Moderate
River gradient: Tidal
River gauge: Nearest tidal station—Fort McAllister, Ogeechee River
Season: Year-round

Land status: Public—Fort McAllister State Park
Fees or permits: Parking permit for Fort McAllister State Park
Nearest city/town: Richmond Hill, Georgia
Maps: USGS: Burroughs, Oak Level; DeLorme: *Georgia Atlas and Gazetteer,* page 55
Boats used: Kayaks, canoes
Organizations: Ogeechee Canoochee Riverkeeper, P.O. Box 1925, Statesboro, GA 30459; (912) 764-2017; www.ogeecheecanoochee riverkeeper.org
Contacts/outfitters: Fort McAllister State Park, 3894 Fort McAllister Road, Richmond Hill, GA 31324; (912) 727-2339; www .gastateparks.org

Put-in/takeout information:

To put in/takeout: From exit 90 on Interstate 95, take Highway 144 east for 6.6 miles to the Highway 144 spur. Turn left onto the Highway 144 spur and follow it 4 miles to dead-end in the state park. Continue past the park visitor center toward the campground. Upon entering the campground, follow the loop road right and then turn right at the sign for visitor parking/boat ramp. This ramp is reserved for hand-carried craft and campground users only.

Paddle Summary

You'll most likely be enjoying this paddle all by yourself. This part of the Georgia coast is growing rapidly, making the acreage protected by Fort McAllister State Park all the more important.

Leave the boat ramp on Savage Island, and begin to wind your way westerly up a large tidal stream bordered with spartina grass. Expect to see avian life and maybe some watery critters too, even a manatee or dolphin. As you paddle west, Redbird Creek continues to get smaller until it divides into waterways of seemingly equal size. Here you can turn around or paddle until reaching the point where either branch can no longer be paddled.

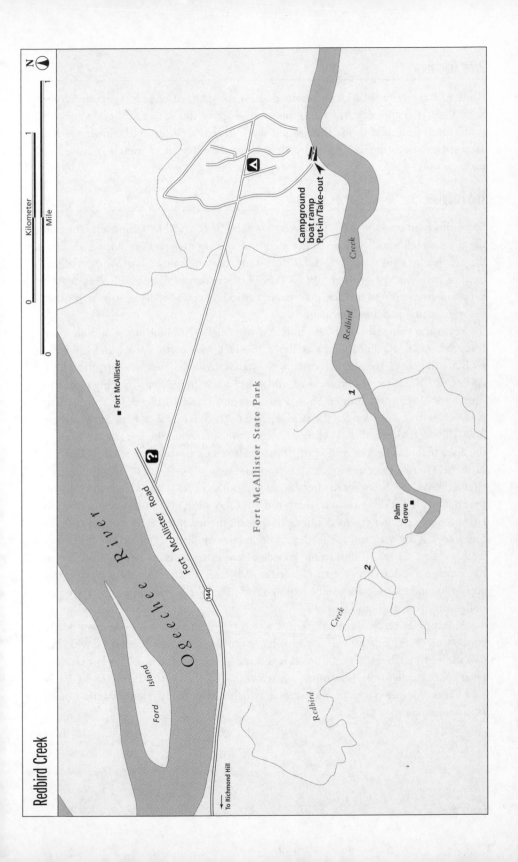

Redbird Creek

River Overview

Redbird Creek is a tidal creek originating on the western edge of Fort McAllister State Park. It cruises easterly along the south edge of the state park before curving southeast to join the Florida Passage and the Intracoastal Waterway. Its lower reaches are used by motoring anglers and paddlers, but the uppermost stretch is visited by paddlers only.

The Paddling

Since this is an out-and-back paddle, you will be best served by taking advantage of the tides, which means following the incoming tide up the creek, exploring the area, then returning with the falling tide. That means you will want to start your paddle an hour or two hours before low tide. *NOTE:* The tides on this uppermost creek are not very strong, so going with the tides is not critical to your paddle as it is with other Georgia coastal paddling destinations.

Leave the campground boat ramp and turn right, heading upstream and away from the ocean. Redbird Creek is about 150 feet wide at this point and bordered with marsh grasses. Beyond this marsh grass stands a forest of pines, cedars, and palms. At low tide, mudflats will be exposed, and you're likely to see many wading birds and shorebirds looking for dinner. Soon a small stream leaves to the right (north). This is the creek that flows under the road leading to Savage Island. Stay with the bigger body of water. Ahead, the woods reach close to the water on the left (south) bank of the river before it becomes all spartina grass. The creek is now narrowed to 100 feet or so. At 1.0 mile the creek splits both right and left.

Redbird Creek narrows further. Ahead you can see a palm grove. (It is just beyond vision if you're paddling close to the right-hand shoreline.) Redbird Creek begins to curve more as smaller creeks continue to spur off the main track. It's as though Redbird Creek is the vein and the feeder creeks are the capillaries. The primary course is easily evident. Curve around to the far side of the aforementioned palm grove. From this vantage a paddler can see that live oaks and other trees grow here as well. In this area, at low tide some bars will be exposed that are gravelly enough to get out without getting your feet muddy.

At 2.0 miles reach a point where Redbird Creek and a feeder stream of nearly equal size come together. It is hard to figure out which one is Redbird Creek, but it is the right channel. A small island is formed at this confluence. The left channel peters out after 0.4 mile, becoming so narrow that it's difficult to turn around. Redbird Creek does the same after a distance, which is why many paddlers turn around at the confluence.

Looking upstream on Redbird Creek ▶

If you are feeling adventurous, try to follow Redbird Creek as far as it will go. Baitfish will skitter away as your boat comes their way. It is very unlikely you will see other paddlers up here. Most certainly you will not see motorboaters, which is one of the beauties of this paddle.

FORT McALLISTER AND SAVAGE ISLAND The put-in for this paddle is on Savage Island, one of the sea islands sprinkled along the coast of Georgia. Here the Ogeechee River nears the ocean, and during the Civil War its bluffs became a place of importance for the Confederacy to defend nearby Savannah from attack by the Union. Times were mostly quiet on the banks of the Ogeechee. However, Fort McAllister was the last stop during Sherman's March to the Sea, which essentially ended the Civil War. Later Henry Ford bought the land and preserved the fort's earthworks, which in turn led to its evolution as a historical site, a great place to camp, and now part of the Georgia state park system.

Fort McAllister was the most southerly of Savannah's defenses. At the Civil War's outset, Robert E. Lee, then in charge of the lower coast area, came to Fort McAllister and recommended improvements to the fort. His ideas proved helpful when Union ironclad boats and other ships bombed the fort. Rather than crumbling under pressure as brick forts were doing, Fort McAllister's sandy walls absorbed the impact of newer, heavy artillery shells and could be rebuilt overnight. However, because battles were few and far between, the men of the garrison mostly battled boredom. Officers kept strict discipline and kept the soldiers busy as possible.

Fort McAllister dueled with the ironclad *Montauk* on several occasions, mostly to a draw. Finally Sherman decided to attack the fort by land, as it stood between him and the capture of Savannah. It wasn't long before the 230 Union troops stormed the moat and earthworks of Fort McAllister and took over. The Rebels then withdrew from Savannah and Sherman had his prize.

Before or after your paddle, make sure to tour Fort McAllister and the adjacent museum. The views from the fort are inspiring. So is the setting, beneath the live oaks that grow on the earthworks. Times were different back when soldiers manned this lonely outpost. Take note of how the soldiers used the material on hand for what then were state-of-the-art fortifications, namely sand. Check out the gun emplacements and massive earthworks and underground quarters, called "bombproofs."

If you are going to paddle Redbird Creek and tour the museum and fort, why not camp here? The campground is laid out in a grand loop cut by crossroads. Savage Island, on which the camping area of Fort McAllister stands, is attached to the mainland by a dead-end causeway traversing the salt marsh and creeks that encircle the island. The causeway cuts down on traffic, making this island getaway a peaceful and serene camping experience and a veritable oasis for campers.

Overhead are wide-reaching live oaks, sweet magnolias, sturdy laurel oaks, pines, and palms. Spanish moss clings to the trees and sways in the summer breeze. A walk on the hiking trail system here, located near Redbird Creek, will complete your recreational grand slam at Fort McAllister State Park.

38 Wassaw Island via Wilmington River

This potentially tough yet rewarding paddle requires making use of the tides.

County: Chatham
Start: Priest Landing N31° 57' 48.5", W81° 0' 51.1"
End: Priest Landing N31° 57' 48.5", W81° 0' 51.1"
Length: 12.6 miles round-trip
Float time: 8 hours
Difficulty rating: Moderate to difficult
Rapids: Tidal
River type: Large tidal river leading to barrier island
Current: Moderate to swift
River gradient: Tidal
River gauge: Nearest tidal station—Wilmington River, North Entrance
Season: Year-round

Land status: Public—Wassaw Island National Wildlife Refuge, private
Fees or permits: No fees or permits required
Nearest city/town: Savannah, Georgia
Maps: USGS: Isle of Hope, Wassaw Sound; DeLorme: *Georgia Atlas and Gazetteer,* page 39
Boats used: Kayaks
Organizations: Wassaw Island National Wildlife Refuge, Parkway Business Center Drive, Suite 10, 1000 Business Center Drive, Savannah, GA 31405; (912) 652-4415; www.fws.gov/southeast/wassaw
Contacts/outfitters: Savannah Canoe and Kayak, P.O. Box 5405, Savannah, GA 31414; (912) 341-9502; www.savannahcanoeand kayak.com. Guides trips to Wausau Island.

Put-in/takeout information:

To put in/takeout: From exit 94 on Interstate 95, take Highway 204 east for 10.5 miles, then turn right onto the Highway 204 spur. Stay with the Highway 204 spur for 7.5 miles. At a four-way stop, turn left onto McWhorter Street, 0.4 mile past the turn into Skidaway Island State Park. After 1.9 miles continue forward on O.S.C.A. Road as McWhorter Road bears left. After 1.0 mile dead-end at Priest Landing. A restricted road continues to the right. Walk your boat down to the Wilmington River. There is no boat ramp here; it is a launch for hand-carried craft only.

Wassaw Island via Wilmington River

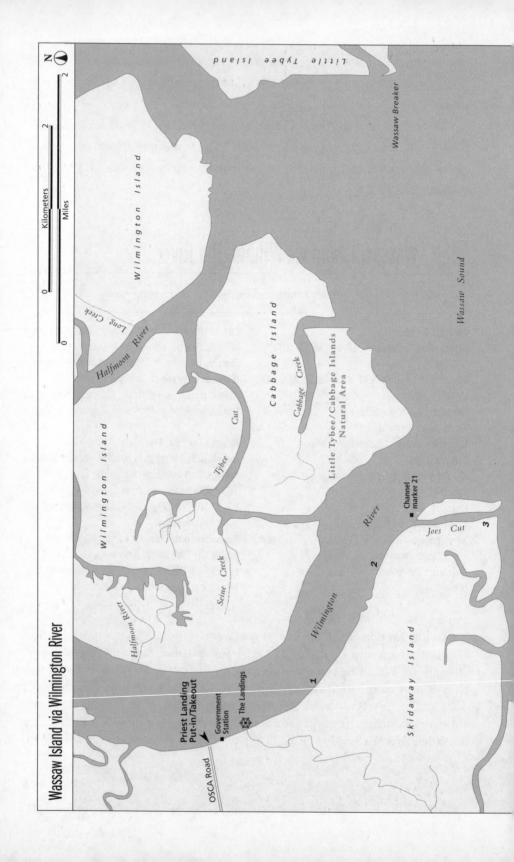

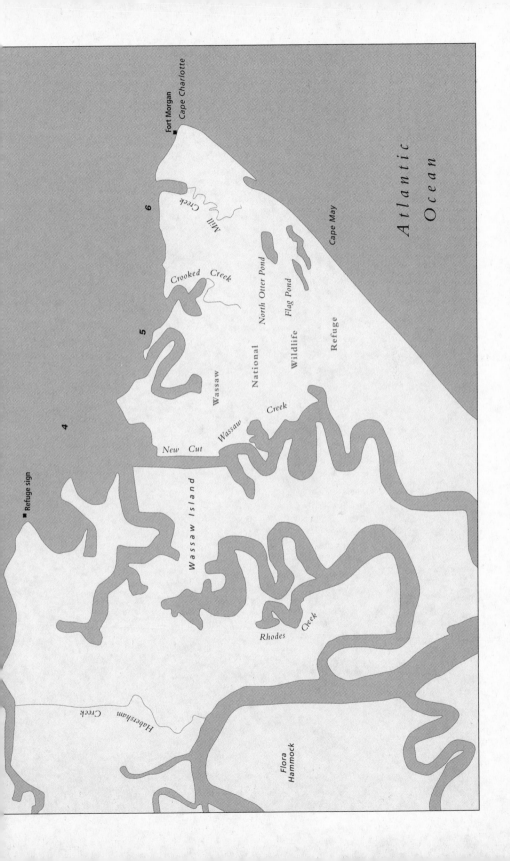

Paddle Summary

Before we discuss this paddle, you must understand the necessity of using the tides to make this paddle doable. Ideally, you need to catch the outgoing tide on the Wilmington River, arriving at Wassaw Island before or at low tide. Give yourself three hours to arrive at Wassaw Island; therefore, leave any time from high tide to about three hours before low tide. Then you can explore the island and take the incoming tide back up the river. Also factor in the winds.

If you go with the right tides and a favorable wind situation, this can be a good paddle. However, if you go during unfavorable conditions, this paddle can turn into a nightmare.

Warnings given, the paddle leaves Priest Landing and heads down the wide Wilmington River, with Wilmington and Cabbage Islands across from it. Follow the south shore of the Wilmington River, entering Joes Cut. Beyond Joes Cut the trip continues along the south side of Wassaw Sound, curving past several tidal creeks of the Wassaw National Wildlife Refuge. Finally arrive near Cape Charlotte, where you can beach your craft in the safety of the sound, then explore old Fort Morgan and the barrier beach that faces out into the Atlantic Ocean. Remember to factor in sufficient time for your return paddle.

River Overview

The Wilmington River is a large tidal river beginning at the eastern end of Savannah. It flows southeasterly, dividing several of the islands on the immediate coast, including Skidaway Island. Once near the ocean, the Wilmington River opens into Wassaw Sound, which in turn opens into the Atlantic Ocean.

The Paddling

Houses, grasses, and shell bars of Wilmington Island are visible across the river from the put-in. Enter the grassy area in the water and turn right, immediately passing under the bridge of a government station. Just ahead to your right is "The Landings" Marina. As you continue down the Wilmington River, a few houses are visible off to your right. Hug the right shoreline, which is alternately shell bar and sea grasses. Shorebirds will be flitting on the shell bars; wading birds will be seen as well. Civilization begins to fade behind you, and ahead lies nothing but water, grass, and islands in a wide-open landscape.

At 2.5 miles reach green Channel Marker 21. In the past there was a wrecked sailboat here. Also note the shell bar, which encourages a stop. Here a creek known as Joes Cut heads almost due south, allowing you to avoid entering Wassaw Sound.

◀ View of remains of old fort along shore of Wassaw Island

Paddle through this grass-lined creek of about 80 feet in width and open into a larger waterway coming in on your right. Another shell bar stands at this confluence. Continue south, crossing the mouth of the waterway. Wassaw Sound is open to your left. A sign indicating the Wassaw Island National Wildlife Refuge is on a point to your right. Turn southwest, crossing this waterway and staying with the shoreline.

Come alongside Dead Man's Hammock, lined with palms and cedar. Wassaw Island and the sandy point of Cape Charlotte are visible to the south. On a calm day you could cut across the sound, but why bother? The shoreline scenery and tidal creeks are much more interesting. Grass, land, and water commingle along this south edge of Wassaw Sound. As you come closer, the individual trees of Wassaw Island distinguish themselves.

If the seas out on the Atlantic are rough, I recommend pulling into Mill Creek at 6.3 miles, just before the mouth of the sound. Conversely, if the water is calm you could paddle around Cape Charlotte and land on the Atlantic side of Wassaw island. Make your own judgment. The safest route is to land before Cape Charlotte, pulling your boat well away from the water. Then stretch your legs and explore the wooded island by foot. While walking along Cape Charlotte, you will undoubtedly notice the strange concrete structure in the water. This is the remains of Fort Morgan, the only fort built specifically for the Spanish American War in the late 1890s.

Allow yourself plenty of time to paddle back to Priest Landing. There is no camping allowed on Wassaw Island; however, Little Tybee Island lies across the north end of Wassaw Sound. It is owned by the Georgia Department of Natural Resources, and camping is allowed there.

SKIDAWAY ISLAND STATE PARK
Skidaway Island State Park is located very near the put-in for this paddle. If you want to combine the paddle with camping out and exploring Savannah, consider staying at Skidaway Island State Park. The camping area is large and attractive and is a destination in its own right. The park itself is a compact 553 acres and is nearly surrounded by civilization, but its location is ideal.

Campers who are history buffs like to visit Savannah, which has one of the largest historic preservation districts in the country. Colonial and Civil War history converge in this coastal town that played a critical role in Georgia's past. The town is well aware of its history, and the Savannah area is a treat to see.

This campground is a great spring/fall destination. It is set in a very pretty forest of fern-covered live oaks, tall pines, and palms draped in Spanish moss. Yaupon, wax myrtle, and palmetto form brush borders between many campsites. The eighty-eight campsites are spread over a wide area, so much so that you may get lost driving on the winding roads.

The campground fills on holiday weekends from St. Patrick's Day through Thanksgiving. Make reservations well in advance if you are coming then. Otherwise, sites are generally available. Although busiest, spring and fall are the best times to visit.

Have you ever seen a 20-foot-tall ground sloth? Well, at this park stands a replica of one—the tallest land mammal that ever lived. More than 10,000 years ago, ground sloths fed on tree vegetation of the coastal plain of what became Georgia. In 1823 slaves of an area planter named Stark alerted him to some odd and large bones. These bones and Skidaway Island became known as the place of the giant sloth. Today you can see a replica of this skeleton and learn about life in the day of the giant sloth among other interesting things at the interpretive museum.

Birding is popular here, and the interpretive museum offers an introduction to birding. Hikers can take off on the 5.0 miles of trails at the park and do a little birding of their own. The Sandpiper Trail travels through several ecosystems. Smaller birds will be out along Avian Way. Larger shorebirds may be out by the Skidaway Narrows. Check out the Confederate Earthworks, set up to defend the waterways during the Civil War. Short on defenses, the South may have used what is known as a "Quaker cannons" to deter the Union. Soldiers would cut down palm trees and paint them black to make them look like cannons, providing a mirage of increased defense! An observation tower allows more views of the salt marsh.

The Big Ferry Interpretive Trail is longer and departs from near the campground. See the moonshine still from prohibition days and Confederate earthworks. Travel a boardwalk over a freshwater marsh, and consider what life was like back when the Old Ferry Road led to a landing where locals would boat to Savannah to trade.

Paddling Index

About the Author

Johnny Molloy is an outdoor writer based in Johnson City, Tennessee. A native Tennessean, he was born in Memphis and moved to Knoxville in 1980 to attend the University of Tennessee. In Knoxville he developed his love of the natural world that has since become the primary focus of his life.

It all started on a backpacking foray into Great Smoky Mountains National Park. That first trip, though a disaster, unleashed an innate love of the outdoors that has led to his spending more than one hundred nights in the wild per year over the past twenty-five years, backpacking and canoe camping throughout our country. Over the last ten years he has upped the ante, averaging 150 nights out per year.

After graduating from the University of Tennessee with a degree in Economics, Johnny continued to spend an ever-increasing time in the natural places, becoming more skilled in a variety of environments. Friends enjoyed his adventure stories; one even suggested he write a book. He pursued his friend's idea and soon had parlayed his love of the outdoors into an occupation.

The results of his efforts are more than thirty books, including hiking, camping, and paddling guidebooks; comprehensive guidebooks about a specific area such as *A FalconGuide® to Mammoth Cave National Park;* and true outdoor adventure books, many about the state of Georgia. Johnny has also written articles for numerous magazines and for Web sites. He continues to write and travel extensively to all four corners of the United States, endeavoring in a variety of outdoor pursuits.

For the latest on Johnny, visit www.johnnymolloy.com.